The English Medieval Minstrel

The
English Medieval Minstrel

JOHN SOUTHWORTH

THE BOYDELL PRESS

First published 1989 by The Boydell Press

The Boydell Press is an imprint of Boydell & Brewer Ltd
PO Box 9, Woodbridge, Suffolk IP12 3DF
and of Boydell & Brewer Inc.
Wolfeboro, New Hampshire 03894–2069, USA

ISBN 0 85115 536 7

British Library Cataloguing in Publication Data
Southworth, John
   The English medieval minstrel.
   1. England. Minstrels, 1272–1327, history.
   I. Title
   780′.942
   ISBN 0–85115–536–7

Library of Congress Cataloging-in-Publication Data
Southworth, John, 1929–
   The English medieval minstrel / John Southworth.
      p.   cm.
   Bibliography: p.
   Includes index.
   ISBN 0–85115–536–7
   1. Minstrels – England – History.   2. Performing arts – England –
History.   3. England – Civilization – Medieval period, 1066–1485.
I. Title.
PN1969.M5S68   1989
791′.0942′–dc20   89–34402
                                                                          CIP

The paper used in this publication meets the minimum requirements of American Standard for Information Sciences – Permanence of Paper for Printed Library Materials, ANSI Z39.48–1984.

Printed and bound in Great Britain by The Camelot Press PLC, Southampton

Contents

Preface

It would be ungracious of anyone writing about minstrels not to acknowledge a debt to Sir Edmund Chambers, whose chapters of his *Mediaeval Stage* on the Minstrel Life and Repertory have been, for me, a constant mine of reliable reference.

The present work owes its inception to two people: Dr Constance Bullock-Davies, whose study of minstrels appearing at the Pentecost feast of 1306, *Menestrellorum Multitudo*, provided both a necessary nucleus of biographical information on the climactic period of minstrel history and a potent stimulus to further research; and Dr Richard Barber, who invited me to extend some chapters of my own of a similarly detailed kind, based on an Ipswich feast of 1297, into this wider, historical survey. For the rest of my debt to earlier writers, I can only refer the reader to my 'List of Books' as an inadequate but sincere acknowledgement to the work of many fine scholars, on which I have drawn.

My own approach to the minstrels is determined to some extent by my background as a professional theatre performer and director; I see them quite simply – not as objects of antiquarian interest – but as former colleagues. As I explain in my final chapter, though minstrelsy in its full and proper meaning belongs wholly and uniquely to the middle ages, the minstrels themselves did not suddenly die or disappear from the scene as the middle ages crumbled away around them in the sixteenth century; they took divergent paths and different names, but continued to keep the flag of the performing arts flying, against much opposition, through the difficult days ahead. I believe there is still a little bit of their independent spirit and anarchic gaiety in everyone of us who gets up on stage or concert platform – or, for that matter, in club, cabaret, in the street, or in front of a television camera – to entertain the public in return for a reward. We are all in their debt.

I have one or two more personal debts to acknowledge. Professor Fahy of Bedford College and Professor Bent of Nottingham took time to guide my early, faltering steps in the right direction; Mr Roy Walker and Mr Geoffrey Hines have, as usual, been constant in their interest and encouragement; and Dr Bullock-Davies was good enough to read and comment on my initial study of the Ipswich feast, comprising mainly chapters two and six of the present book. Responsibility for what follows – especially its mistakes – remains, of course, entirely mine.

I want to say a word of appreciation to the many librarians who have aided my research – without whose efficient and friendly service any such project as this, undertaken in a non-academic situation, would be a lost cause from the start: to the staff of Manchester Central Library (Social Sciences) where I did most of my basic research, and to all my friends at Ipswich Library, especially Miss Lynne Doy and others involved in the Inter-Library Scheme.

A final word of thanks to Rosemary and my family for putting up with my table-talk about minstrels for so long and so patiently, and to my son William for reading my text in its final stages and for his many helpful suggestions.

J.S.
Ipswich, 1988.

Illustrations

Acknowledgements

The author and publishers would like to thank Michael Alexander and Penguin Books Ltd. for their kind permission to quote from Professor Alexander's fine translations of Anglo-Saxon verse in *The Earliest English Poems*, Harmondsworth, 2nd edn., 1977.

The illustrations are reproduced by kind permission of the following, who hold the copyright:

Bibliothèque Nationale, Paris 10
Bibliothèque Royale Albert 1er, Brussels 66
Bodleian Library, Oxford 11, 13, 16, 18, 21, 136, 140
British Library 12, 26, 27, 63, 71, 72, 74, 86, 87, 133, 152
The Independent 55
Master & Fellows of Pembroke College, Cambridge 7
Musée Municipal, Saint Germain-en-Laye 15
National Monuments Record 41

1

Who Were The Minstrels?

The presence of minstrels at every level of society and on all kinds of occasion is an undoubted fact of English life throughout that whole period of some six hundred years – let us say, from Alfred the Great to Henry VIII – that we call the middle ages.

But who were these people, and what precisely did they do? The romantic image of a male figure in colourful costume, standing beneath the battlements of a towering castle as he strums on his lute, is deeply entrenched in the popular imagination. He sings ballads, makes jokes, and (like Blondel) is fiercely loyal to his liege-lord whom he will follow, if necessary, to the ends of the earth. No 'medieval banquet' would be complete without him.

The historian will have some reservations to make. He may point out that in the great age of chivalry, the twelfth century, the lute was still unknown in England, that then and for many years to come, the small harp was the undisputed national instrument; that the costume our minstrel is wearing is probably French, not English, in style; that the profession was never exclusively male, but included a small but significant proportion of women and young girls. Worst of all, that the faithful Blondel may never have existed outside of a minstrel lay.

But all is not lost. As so often the case, the popular image, however inaccurate in detail, contains a kernel of truth which, in the final analysis, may prove more important than scholarly quibbles. Minstrels *did* invariably play an instrument – whatever other skills they might possess – and could often sing and joke; though never uniform, their appearance was distinctive. For the most part, and so far as we can judge, those minstrels fortunate enough to be retained by particular lords (a varying but always sizeable proportion of the whole) *were* loyal to their patrons – they had good reason to be. And if the romantic hue with which we now tend to surround their profession is contradicted by the obloquy heaped upon it by a large part of their contemporaries and by the harshness of the lives that many of them led, it may also reflect something real about the way they liked to see and portray themselves in their songs and stories; as sharing a vision of freedom perhaps, of untrammelled celebration of the joys of life – of life itself – which appealed as much to idealists and artists like Francis of Assisi as to the wayward and irresponsible. There *was* an

1

attraction about the minstrel life – a defiance of the rigidly-imposed hier-archies of medieval society, a disregard of convention and of the feudal ties that held others to their native manor or burgh for the whole of their lives – that aroused in its time as much envy and admiration as it did suspicion and contempt.

But were the minstrels really like that? To what extent, if any, are we to accept as truth their own highly-coloured and often self-glorifying ac-counts of themselves and their lives? (If the story of Blondel is a fiction – as scholars believe – it was a fiction perpetrated by a minstrel: the Min-strel of Rheims.)

The reader will be able to form his or her own judgement on these questions after reading the chapters that follow. While it is impossible to generalise about the motives of people so far removed from us in time, we may come to feel that there was too high a price to pay for the relative freedom of the minstrel life for it to easily accommodate romantics. It is one thing to set out on a spring morning with no money in your pocket, but with a song in your heart and on your lips; it is another to find yourself, at dusk, cold and hungry in a dark wood, listening to the baying of wolves or chased away by a farmer's dogs from the shelter of a barn. People who set out on such a journey, in such a spirit, have a way of finding themselves, in a matter of weeks or days, back at their starting point – which, as a matter of fact, is exactly what happened to St Francis on that first of his missionary journeys from Assisi in the guise of a jongleur.

Which leads us on to a similar, but more serious misconception about the kind of people that the minstrels were, and the nature of their lives; more serious because it goes beyond the understandable simplifications of the popular imagination to affect even the way scholarly historians deal with the minstrels, and has led, I believe, to a depreciation of the import-ant contributions that minstrels have made to the development of music and literature in the middle ages.

I have come to recognise and define it as 'the myth of the wandering minstrels'. The evidence I have to present will speak for itself more clearly and convincingly than any unsupported assertions I make here; but I would ask my readers to be on their guard from the start against the idea that minstrels were necessarily, even commonly, of this 'wandering' kind, because the chances are that they have already been prejudiced by it – as I was myself when I began my exploration of the sources. We shall meet with many different kinds of minstrels in the course of our survey and notice many changes in their status and activity over six centuries. Throughout that whole period, their mobility is an unchanging feature of their lives that can hardly be exaggerated; many were almost constantly in motion – though naturally, even here, there were exceptions; but we shall encounter surprisingly few 'wanderers' in the sense of rootless people who are travelling aimlessly. Even the popular entertainers de-

2

scribed in the next chapter, journeying in bands and family groups from one local fair to another, may well have arrived at something approximating to a yearly itinerary – as fairground people do today – and, like their modern counterparts, have made use of winter quarters for themselves and their animals. It is indeed quite rare to find a minstrel on the move who is not specified in the record as belonging to a particular place (expressed usually in terms of personal allegiance), or travelling to one.

The origin of the term indicates that the minstrel was associated with a particular court, and by implication with a patron. The Old French word *menestrel* makes its first appearance as applied to an entertainer or musician in a poem by Chrétien de Troyes in about 1164. Its Latin root is *ministrellus*, meaning a minor court official – a 'little servant' or 'minister' of the king; but with the secondary meaning (almost as early) of someone who practised a *mestier* or craft. [1]

The most common Latin terms for them (which reach back to the dawn of the middle ages and beyond) are *mimus*, *histrio* and *joculator*, used almost indiscriminately. One of the complications of medieval research is the use throughout the whole period of three languages: Latin for official records, learned writing and, of course, all church documents; French at court and in the households of the nobility which, as time goes by, is used increasingly also by the emerging bourgeoisie, the merchant and other literate classes; and finally English, virtually disappearing as a written language at the Conquest – though naturally the mass of the population continued to speak it – until its revival in the thirteenth century for devotional books and sermons, and as a verse medium for the 'minstrel' romances. Throughout this whole span of time – and indeed until the close of the middle ages – minstrels are still referred to in Latin documents by the old names. So there can be no question of any break in continuity; from the middle of the thirteenth century, *ministrellus* is simply added to the list of Latin variants.

Starting then from a specialised and limited use in the royal and baronial households, 'minstrel' is gradually adopted in ordinary English speech and writing to designate a host of men and women who live by their wits as entertainers at every level of society; all those professional performers known (in Latin) as *mimi et histriones*, or (in French) as *jugleurs* or *jongleurs*, or (in Old English) *gleemen*, are now embraced by this one word, 'minstrel'.

They included musicians – composers, instrumentalists and singers – oral poets and tellers of tales (often to a musical accompaniment), fools, jugglers, acrobats and dancers; actors, mimes and mimics; conjurors, puppeteers and exhibitors of performing animals – bears, horses, dogs, even snakes. All are described in the records I shall cite as *mimi et histriones*, *joculatores* or, from 1266, most usually as minstrels. (I should add here, perhaps, that our *present*, more restricted understanding of 'minstrel' as meaning simply a musical performer, dates only from the sixteenth century, when the varied skills of the medieval minstrels as general entertainers and 'little servants' had already divided into a number of distinct specialisms: players, jesters, clowns, tumblers and musicians. Their instrumental skills were what they were left with when the others had departed. In a similar way, the old French word *jugleur*, the equivalent of minstrel, has been gradually impoverished in meaning to become our present 'juggler'.)

Joculator is usually translated as 'jester', but this is misleading. It is true, that *joculator* – hence *jongleur* – derives from a Latin verb 'to joke', and that the English 'jester' comes from *gestour*, a teller of *gestes* or stories; but *joculator* is used in a much broader sense by Latin chroniclers throughout the middle ages – along with *histrio* and *mimus* – to mean almost any kind of professional entertainer, including harpers, whereas 'jester' has particular, sixteenth-century associations with the 'artificial' and stage fools familiar to us from Shakespeares's plays. However, the one thing that *joculator* did *not* mean was a fool. As Miss Welsford points out, the only Latin words which can certainly be translated as 'fool' are *stultus, morio, follus* (in French, *fol* or *sot*), *fatuus* and *sannio*.[2]

What then were the original characteristics that held this great variety of performers together as an easily identifiable group which, at the same time, enable us to separate them from their contemporaries in all the succeeding periods and reigns of our survey? What is it also that made them unique to the middle ages so that the words 'minstrel' and 'medieval' belong so inescapably together?

In the first place, the minstrels were *professionals* in the simple sense that they depended for their livelihood – if not exclusively, primarily – on their performing skills. There were always people about in medieval England who could play instruments, compose verse, sing or entertain their fellows in a variety of ways who nevertheless were *not* minstrels. The *troubadours* and *trouvères* – poets and composers of a new type of courtly verse and song originating in Provence in the eleventh century – make an interesting example. Some of them, as we shall discover, were indeed minstrels in the sense that they worked for material rewards; but others who are known to have performed their compositions within their own elite circles were decidedly not, and would have been grossly insulted by such a description. Again, to take an opposite, perhaps obvious example, 'fool' was often used, as it is today, in a literal or pejorative sense of someone who was not very bright in the head or behaved foolishly; the professional fool, whether of the natural or artificial kind, is clearly of a special stamp. The expression 'amateur minstrel' is thus a contradiction in terms and wholly anachronistic.

This brings us to the second of our distinguishing marks: the matter of social status.

It is not just that the status of the minstrel was low; for very many of his contemporaries, he was altogether beyond the pale of social acceptance.

4

In this respect, he was worse off than a serf; if the serf occupied the lowest place in the medieval hierarchy, the minstrel had no place at all. Not only was he excluded – or more correctly, perhaps, had excluded himself – from the normal web of ties and responsibilities that constituted medieval society, but even his membership of the universal church, the fellowship of baptised Christians, was at one time in serious dispute.

A minstrel could rise. One way – open only to those who served the king or one of his greater magnates – was by a grant of land or property, normally on retirement, in which event he (and more especially his descendants) were enabled to join the ranks of 'serjeants' and of the minor landed gentry. Another way, if he was willing to reform and was literate – and among the minstrel-*trouvères* and harpers were many with command of not just one, but several written languages – he might become a clerk, even a priest. As Miss Waddell pointed out, 'It was a clerk's business to sing' and that he was already trained to do. (Unfortunately, the reverse might also happen and clerks sink to the level of a *jongleur*, an occupation 'disgusting even in a layman'.) [3]

The twelfth-century scholar, John of Salisbury – contemporary and friend of the martyr, Thomas Becket – puts the matter most harshly.

> Concerning actors and mimes, buffoons and harlots, panders and other like human monsters, which the prince ought rather to exterminate entirely than to foster, there needed no mention to be made in the law; which indeed not only excludes such abominations from the court of the prince, but banishes them from among the people of God. [4]

And if this should be thought to apply only to the mimetic functions of the minstrel and not to his music, here is what the same writer says about that. The sole purpose of music, he maintains, is to serve God. However, anyone who

> expresses passion or vanity, who prostitutes the voice to his own desires, who makes music the medium of pandering, is indeed ignorant of the song of the Lord and is revelling with Babylonian strains in a foreign land.

In former days – the time of Plautus, Menander and 'our favourite Terence' – it may have been different.

> But our own age, descending to romances and similar folly, prostitutes not only the ear and heart to vanity but also delights its idleness with the pleasures of eye and ear. It inflames its own wantonness, seeking everywhere incentives to vice. Does not the shiftless man divert his idleness and court slumber with the sweet tones

of instruments and vocal melody, with gaiety inspired by musicians and with the pleasure he finds in the narrator of tales...?[5]

John of Salisbury was a scholar of classical, continental outlook, trained in the Roman curia. To that extent, his uncompromising views are not to be taken as representative of clerical opinion in England. They derive from his identification of contemporary performers with their pagan precursors, whom a whole series of ecumenical councils had condemned and excluded from the Sacraments for the obscene and blasphemous nature of their performances.

There is more here than a correspondence of names, of official terminology. An element of obscenity – occasionally, even blasphemy – was often present in medieval popular entertainment. John of Salisbury and those who thought like him were not prudes, indulging in moral rhetoric. When they complain of obscenity, they mean obscenity. One admired, eleventh-century *ludus histrionum* (play performed by actors) is reported to have featured a tame bear, an actor's naked *membra* and honey![6] John's extraordinary procession of contemporary performers – 'mimics, jumping or leaping priests, buffoons, Aemilian and other gladiators, wrestlers, sorcerers, jugglers, magicians, *tota joculatorum scena*' – is so much in vogue, he complains, that 'even those whose exposures are so indecent that they make a cynic blush are not barred from distinguished houses'.

He spells it out for us, 'they are not even turned out when with more hellish tumult they defile the air and more shamelessly disclose that which in shame they had concealed'.[7] (By 'Aemilian and other gladiators' does he mean boxers, pro fighters of various kinds? The jumping and leaping priests may be an early reference to thirteenth-century ring dances or *caroles*, the so-called 'Devil's mill', which newly-elected Masters of the University of Paris are alleged, in 1230, to have led through the streets in unseemly revelry.)[8]

Such fears are understandable in the context of a European civilization still emerging from barbarian anarchy veined with the old Roman decadence; but could easily lead to the sort of obsessive mania displayed by the English monastic reformer, Gilbert of Sempringham, cited by John of Salisbury with evident approval: 'We do not permit our nuns to sing. We absolutely forbid it, preferring with the Blessed Virgin to hymn indirectly in a spirit of humility rather than with Herod's notorious daughter to pervert the minds of the weak with lascivious strains'.[9] Salome is often portrayed by medieval artists as a minstrel doing handstands or sword-juggling. (See the twelfth-century example below.)

Salome as acrobatic dancer with two swords.
Cambridge, Pembroke College MS 120, f.5v.

Fortunately, in England at least – where another, very different tradition of minstelsy was also at work – wiser and more discriminating counsels prevailed. [10]

The third and final distinctive feature that *mimi* and minstrels held in common was their versatility as performers, which (as I have said) invariably encompassed at least one instrumental skill, more usually several. What is now the exception – admired or otherwise – was then the rule.

We shall encounter very many examples of this in the pages that follow: Taillefer juggling with his sword as he chants verses from the Song of Roland at Hastings, fools who pipe and play the tabor, a taborer fooling to entertain the royal children or blowing a trumpet in battle, a King of Heralds famed as a fiddler. Such flexibility of function will even be found to extend to activities with little or no apparent connection with entertainment at all: minstrels delivering diplomatic messages or going on business trips on behalf of their patrons; waferers who combined the baking of biscuits with after-dinner minstrelsy; the huntsmen-fools, the watchmen and waits. Here, the nature of the relationship between minstrel and lord will be seen as the determining factor. Such versatility is confirmed and supported by contemporary evidence from France, Italy and elsewhere. A poem by the thirteenth-century Provençal troubadour, Giraud de Calanson, defines a true *jongleur* as one who is able to 'speak and rhyme well, be witty, know the story of Troy, balance apples on the points of knives, juggle, jump through hoops, play the citole, mandora, harp, fiddle, psaltery...' [11] He is further advised (for good measure) to learn the arts of imitating birds, putting performing asses and dogs through their paces and of operating marionettes. [12] The Princes of Achaia in their castle at Pinerlo, near Turin, 'employed two *goliardis* in 1295, a *menestrerio* with a performing monkey in 1379, and in 1395, in Milan, saw minstrels dancing, leaping and playing with swords, performing with a dog, and also heard funny stories and two women *menestrerie* singing'. [13]

The nature of the English evidence is such that inevitably we shall be drawn (especially in the early centuries) to that select group already mentioned, those attached to kings and other great people as their personal retainers. So far as contemporary chroniclers and later political historians are concerned, we must face the fact that the mass of minstrels are mentioned (if at all) merely to give colour to a narrative or throw a gleam of light on the foibles of the rich and powerful. They exist – sometimes quite literally – in the margins of history, and creep into its pages on the coattails of those who employed them. It will be important to see them as they really were – even at the cost of some cherished legends.

I make no apology for attempting to place the minstrels we shall meet in an historical context or spending some words on their patrons; for (like Lear's fool) the servant can only properly be seen and understood in relation to his master, and both in the concrete circumstances of their particular world.

But before we can start on this journey of discovery, I must first describe the background to it: *tota joculatorum scena*, that bustling panorama of medieval entertainment at the popular level of street and fair which comprises the deepest and most ancient stratum of minstrel activity.

2

Tota Joculatorum Scena

Fourteenth-century minstrels from *Roman de
Fauvel*. Bibliothèque Nationale fr.146, f.34r.

When we widen our view to encompass the broad sweep of the medieval
'entertainment scene', we find that, for all the variety of names used, few
distinctions are made by the chroniclers between the different types of
entertainer. The consequent, terminological confusion undoubtedly re-
flects a large degree of versatility and flexibility of role on the part of the
performers, but is also an indication of the low esteem in which they were

Contortionist on bar. Oxford, Bodleian Library MS 264, f.108v.

generally held – especially by clerics. One gets an impression from many of the records that as all such people are considered equally unworthy of attention, it would simply be a waste of time to bother with exact descriptions.

One thing that the medieval names do tell us, however, is that the traditions of popular entertainment to which they point are ancient in origin, probably classical. Medieval churchmen took this for granted, and it is the main reason for their censorious attitude.

Histrio and *scenicus* derive from the Roman theatre, where they were applied more particularly to actors; *mimi* were originally performers of the improvised 'mime' plays that succeeded the literary drama of Plautus and Terence in the later centuries of the Empire; they were not, however, silent, as the word now implies. Indeed, we can trace these same traditions further back still to classical Greece. Zenophon, for example, tells of a performance in a private house attended by Socrates, in which a girl, having impressed the company by her skill in the sword-dance, was joined by a male partner for a representation in words and gesture of the love of Dionysus and Ariadne[1] – a pattern of play, dance and physical dexterity which was to be repeated by small groups of *mimi* and minstrels down the ages.

In the course of an entertainment given by the Roman emperor, Carinus, in the third century AD, rope-dancers 'seemed to hang in the air; an animal–trainer performed with a bear, and other bears "acted a mime" (*ursos mimum agentes*); a hundred trumpeters sounded their instruments at one time; there were hundreds of flute-players and thousands of

Balancing on two swords. British Library, MS Royal 10 E iv, f.58.

pantomimes and acrobats; while a firework "machine" succeeded in destroying the scenic buildings of the theatre'.[2]

There can be little doubt that many of the English minstrels we are to meet in the following chapters – fools, acrobats and mimes as well as musicians – are in a direct line of descent from these Greek and Roman performers.

The traditional motley of the medieval fool (more French than English in use) makes its first appearance in the patch-work jacket (*centunculus*) worn by the mimes, and in the eared hoods of the *derisores* and *scurrae* of imperial Rome.

The cone-shaped hat of the Roman *stupidas* will be remembered by older readers as a dunce's cap, and is still worn by white-faced clowns in circuses.

The Romans too had specialised terms for trapeze artistes (*petauristae*), jugglers with balls (*pilarii*), jugglers with swords or daggers (*ventilatores*), stilt-walkers (*grallatores*) and rope-walkers (*funambuli* or *neurobatae* according to the thickness of the rope); fire-spitters and sword-swallowers are also mentioned.[3] All had their medieval and later successors.

In the thirteenth century, a rope-walker made an aerial descent from the cathedral at Basle. *Tumbleres* 'twisted themselves into incredible attitudes, leapt through hoops, turned somersaults, walked on their hands, balanced themselves in perilous positions'.[4] If the evidence of an early fourteenth-century manuscript is to be believed, *tornatrices* or female tumblers balanced dangerously on the points of swords. Musical accompaniment is provided by tabor and pipe, played simultaneously, and double recorder. (See illustration on page 12.)

Animal acts have already featured in the Roman spectacle sponsored by Carinus; Juvenal has a reference to a street entertainment in which monkeys ride on the backs of goats (*Satires*, V, 55). Such acts were equally common and equally popular in the middle ages, as the manuscript drawings amply demonstrate. Horses dance, box and beat drums.

Tutored horses. Oxford, Bodleian Library MS 264, ff.73r, 96v.

Some minstrels specialised in the imitation of animal and bird sounds. Dogs, bears and horses had featured largely, not only in the Roman circus, but also in the performances of *mimi* of imperial times. In the middle ages, animals continued to appear in plays (*ludi*) of the same, improvised kind. (Some, as we saw in the first chapter, were, like those of their pagan antecedents, grossly indecent.) The practice of including them was continued by Shakespeare, as in *The Two Gentlemen of Verona* (III.ii.) where Launce's dog, Crab, refuses to weep – a reference to the weeping dogs of medieval tradition [5] – and as in the famous exit of Autolycus in *The Winter's Tale*, 'pursued by a bear'.

Most of these medieval 'acts and specialities' – whether of the animal or human variety – are shown in the manuscript drawings as having a musical accompaniment. In one tenth-century performance, a bear ' plays dead' while the bearward's assistant dances over and around it to the music of double recorder. In a fourteenth-century manuscript, a dancing dog and stilt-walking cock appear to respond to the sounds of tabor and pipe. Sometimes, the human performers are seen to provide their own instrumental accompaniment; acrobats stand on each other's shoulders or balance on stilts while playing the bagpipes!

These street musicans are not to be thought of as a separate species from the minstrels already mentioned. Though each performer would have had his or her special skills, the instrumentalists among them would as readily have lent a hand or leg with an acrobatic turn, or filled a part in a sketch, as acrobats and actors doubled in wind or brass. In other words, they remained pre-eminently *minstrels*. The musician or instrumentalist 'pure and simple' belongs to a rather distant future. A twelfth-century drawing depicting 'Profane Music' (reproduced by Galpin, Pl.43) sums it up in graphic form; accompanied by bugle and rebec (an early type of fiddle), a large bear at the centre beats a drum with one paw while the other paw indicates a pair of tumblers.

Public statues were erected in ancient Greece by city communes to honour favourite conjurors, depicted with a traditional pebble in their hands; a reference to what is now known as the 'cups and balls' trick, in which small balls or pebbles placed under inverted cups or dishes are made to disappear or travel from one container to another. This most basic of conjuring tricks reappears c. 1470 in a painting by Hieronymus Bosch, and is explained in Reginald Scot's *Discoverie of Witchcraft* of 1584.

The Roman term for conjurors was *acetabularii* from *acetabulum*, the Latin word for a small cup to contain vinegar. In the middle ages, practitioners of sleight of hand – when not lumped together, as they often were, with other entertainers as *mimi* or minstrels – were known as *prestigiatores* or *tregetours*, and attributed their special powers to *nigremance* or sorcery – a dangerous claim in the prevailing climate of belief. A girl who tore a handkerchief apart and then restored it in front of a large crowd in Cologne in the fifteenth century was taken at her word and put on trial for witchcraft!

Chaucer's *tregetour* in his *House of Fame*, Colle (possibly a real person), practises an illusion whereby a windmill appears to shrink to the size of a

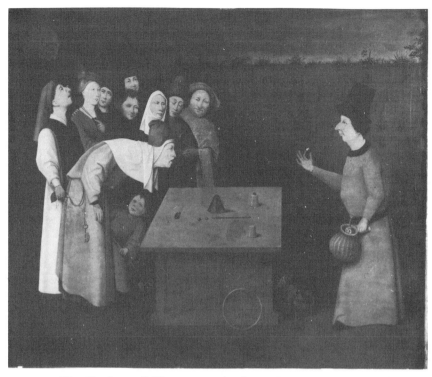

The Conjuror (L'Escamoteur). Saint Germain-en-Laye,
Musée Municipal.

hazel-nut. The fifteenth-century poet, Lydgate, has an intriguing reference
to Henry V's *tregetour* in his *Daunce de Macabre*:

> Maister John Rykell, sometyme tregitoure Of noble Henry kynge of
> Englonde And of Fraunce the myghty conqueroure, For all the
> sleightes and turnyngs of thyne honde, Thou must come nere this
> daunce to understonde. [6]

Puppets and marionettes have an equally ancient lineage going back to
the fifth century BC, when Xenophon mentions a mimic actor supporting
himself by the manipulation of 'little cord-controlled figures'. [7] In the
middle ages, the puppeteers are known as *bastaxi* or *jouers des basteax*, and
their performances and booths (as illustrated in the Jehans de Grise mini-
atures of the Bodleian *Romans d'Alexandre*) bear a striking resemblance to
our present-day Punch and Judy shows. In traditional puppet-theatre
terminology, the stage set depicted in the lower part of the drawing
shown below is known as a 'castello'.

Puppet shows.   Oxford, Bodleian Library MS 264, ff.54v and 76r.

Histrionic ability is but one more of a bundle of skills that minstrels might possess in varying combination. (Indeed, the gradual emergence of specialised actors in the Tudor period will be seen to correspond exactly with the decline of the minstrels. Take away any one of the minstrel's skills and you diminish that which makes him uniquely a minstrel.) But this is not to say that – as with their other skills – a popular tradition of professional playing may not have survived from late classical times through the 'dark ages' to Anglo-Saxon England and beyond.

I am speaking here of an oral tradition of improvised acting which, by definition, is not recorded in the form of a written text. In contrast to the liturgical drama with its basis in 'anamnesis' – a recovery of the mythic past through carefully constructed patterns of symbolic action, words and music intended for ritual repetition, which thus require to be recorded in the greatest possible detail in the service books – the art of the professional mime is spontaneous. As such, his performances are rarely , if ever, repeated in the same form, and never recorded. [8] The analogy with music is close. Not a note of the music we see being played in the manuscript drawings I have reproduced has been recorded in its original form, but we can hardly doubt that it existed.

Visits of *mimi* and *histriones* to monastic houses had been a subject of episcopal censure from the eighth century onwards and, in 789, one of Charlemagnes's laws decreed that 'If any player (*scenicus*) shall be dressed

16

in a priestly or monastic robe, or that of a nun or any other clerical garb, let him undergo corporal punishment and be condemned to exile';[9] an echo, perhaps, of those sacrilegious parodies that had landed the Greek and Roman *mimi* in such trouble with the early Christians.

In about 960, King Edgar was complaining that 'now a house of clerks is considered a meeting place for *histriones (conciliabulum histrionum)'*, and that while the military men shout and the common people whisper the monks' shortcomings, 'the *mimi* sing and dance them in the market-places (*mimi cantant et saltant in triviis)'.*[10] The implications of this are clear enough. The *mimi* were taking advantage of the monks' hospitality to gather fresh material for the satiric shows which they later performed for the salacious enjoyment of the laity.

Within fifteen years (between 965–75), the English bishops were to meet at Winchester to draw up their great programme of monastic reform, *Regularis Concordia*, with its earliest account of a liturgical 'play': the Easter trope of *Quem Quaeritis* (The Three Marys).[11] So our evidence for a popular tradition of professional playing pre-dates the liturgical drama – the renaissance of dramatic form in the West – and may even have stimulated its development.

In the history of early theatre, singing and dancing are everywhere found to accompany impersonation. The three go together. Athenian drama of the fifth century BC had developed from a 'still flourishing art of choral song', and remained within a unifying framework of choral odes which were sung and danced; the spoken dialogues of the Roman playwrights, Plautus and Terence, were pitched to a musical accompaniment; *saltator* (literally dancer or acrobat) is often used by Roman writers to denote a mime actor. The liturgical drama itself was sung and accompanied by an elaborate ritual of symbolic movement. Neither in classical nor medieval Latin is there any exact term to distinguish 'straight acting' as we know it today. And as for the performers' customary venue, several medieval glosses equate *theatrum* with the market place.[12]

One rare, thirteenth-century attempt to classify the different types of medieval performer – albeit from an ethical point of view – describes the lowest and most reprehensible kind as 'those who transform and transfigure their bodies with indecent dance and gesture, now indecently unclothing themselves, now putting on horrible masks'.[13]

The *histrio*'s use of such masks in the impersonation of dogs, birds, asses and monkeys is recorded by the Bishop of Salisbury, c. 1300, and illustrated in the fourteenth-century manuscript, the *Romans d'Alexandre*.[14] (See below.) Here again, the performers are joining hands in a dance, accompanied by a gittern, an early form of guitar.

If the singing and dancing *histriones* of the market place, with their burlesques of clerical misbehaviour, represent the old 'mimic' tradition of Roman popular theatre (associated with the cities), these animal impersonators may possibly derive from the Atellani, small bands of profes-

Dancing minstrels wearing masks. Oxford, Bodleian Library MS 264, f.21v.

sional players who toured the countryside, and whose improvised performances are known to have been based on farcical situations of an earthy kind which often featured animals. Unlike the *mimi*, they invariably wore masks. Juvenal describes them as cheerfully staging on public holidays 'the same old shows as last year...

> In the grassgrown theatre, when peasant children, sitting
> On their mothers' laps, shrink back in terror at the sight
> Of those gaping, whitened masks...' [15]

Dr. Axton's re-examination of evidence for the celebrated Play of the Resurrection at Beverley c. 1220, has revealed that the play in question is unlikely to have been liturgical at all as it was performed out of its due season (Easter) on the north, unhallowed side of the church by 'masked performers, *as usual (larvatorum, ut assolet)*'. [16] (The masks would probably have included devil-masks.) This sounds more like professional *mimi* muscling in on the popularity of the religious drama than like a religious play in process of becoming secular. While the liturgical drama continued to be enacted in churches in its traditional form and due season until the Reformation, the drama of the streets is now seen to owe its significant impetus to the institution of the feast of *Corpus Christi* in 1311 [17] – where minstrels will also have a part to play. The secular drama does not have to be explained as a by-product of religious drama because it already existed in embryonic form in the reprobate hands of the *mimi* and their successors, the minstrels. (We shall find further evidence of it later on when we come to look at the activities of the court minstrels.)

One stock character whose origins are obscure but without which no medieval fair or street festival would have been complete is the *woodwose* or wild man – still to be seen in the roofs and misericords of medieval churches. Probably adopted – along with his cousin, Green Man or Jack in

18

the Green – from folk legend, he was to be taken up by the Court as a fashionable disguise at tournaments and masques; but his natural habitat is that of the village fair and street procession where he rushes about amongst the crowd, scaring the children.

We may seem to have spread ourselves very far in this chapter in attempting to delineate the features of that *tota joculatorum scena* of which John of Salisbury wrote with such contempt. But very many of the varied skills and specialities I have sketched might well have been contained within a single group of itinerant minstrels. In a remarkable set of drawings from the fourteenth-century *Roman de Fauvel* – one of which is reproduced at the head of the chapter – we see exactly such a minstrel troupe entering a village.

The minstrels step out gaily to the beating of drums and the clanging of a bell, wearing the most colourful and striking costumes from their wardrobe.

Some are dressed as monks and nuns; there is a wild man and a devil. The animal masks complained of by the Bishop of Salisbury are well in evidence. Two or three of the performers are naked, and some are showing a bare behind.

Such drawings present a vivid pictorial image of one aspect of medieval minstrelsy in all its diversity and rough, popular appeal; it will remain in the background of all that follows. But there was another, very different kind of minstrelsy in England, virtually concurrent in time and perhaps more truly indigenous. It is to this that we must now turn our attention.

3

The Anglo-Saxon Tradition: Widsith and the Early Harpers

While one aspect of the minstrel tradition in England can be seen as deriving from the Roman circus or the masked mimi of the Atellane farces, the other will be found to have had its beginnings in Anglo-Saxon England in the harsh world of the Celtic bard and the Germanic scôp. It is with the harpers who celebrated the heroic exploits of their lords and their warrior bands that this chapter is particularly concerned.

The bard was a valued member of Anglo-Saxon society for his skill in perpetuating the fame of the heroes, past and present, whose courage and prowess in battle established an ideal for future generations. It seems, however, that among all classes of society above the lowest slaves, proficiency in harping and singing was taken for granted. In *Beowulf* the king himself performs on the harp, but at the other end of the social scale, Bede's *Ecclesiastical History* (Book IV, 24) tells of how the humble Northumbrian layman, Caedmon, miraculously acquired the art of song. Caedmon had all his life felt himself incompetent as a singer, so that when at feasts the harp was passed around the table for each guest to take his turn in entertaining the others, he would always find some excuse for withdrawing before the harp reached him. One night, when to avoid humiliation in the hall, he had gone to the stable to look after the animals, he fell asleep and dreamed that he was ordered to sing a song to celebrate the beginnings of creation. In his dream, he had sung the song which, remembered on waking, has ever since been associated with him. From then on, he was always able to take his due turn with harp and song. The illustration below is from an eleventh-century manuscript of verses attributed to Caedmon.

In the Anglo-Saxon period, the harp seems to have been the dominant musical instrument for the accompaniment of singing. In 764, Cuthbert, abbot of Jarrow, wrote to his friend Lull, archbishop of Mainz, asking for a *cytharista* (harper) to be sent to him, as he has an instrument (*rotta*) but no one to play it.[1] *Rotta* here could mean either a harp or a form of lyre.[2] Performers on both instruments are referred to in the Latin as *cytharistae*.

From this time, lyres appear as frequently as harps in Anglo-Saxon manuscript illuminations. The English and Welsh harps were generally small and portable with rarely more than twenty strings, and often only

Eleventh-century harper. Oxford,
Bodleian Library MS Junius ii, f.54r.

twelve, which were tuned by means of a key. They continued in this form
for many centuries.

In a pre-literate age, poetry and music are almost invariably associated;
poet and composer are often the same person, and he may well be his
own performer. The harper-poet of the oral tradition was also a story-teller and historian; the stories and songs that he sang were the people's
remembrance of their past. As Tacitus wrote of the Franks, 'their ancient
songs are their only history' (*Germanica*, 2). This was the characteristic
mark of the northern tradition of minstrelsy, separating it absolutely from
the Roman, Mediterranean kind, which was concerned only with entertainment and the giving of pleasure. The Germanic scôp, like the Celtic
bard and the Anglo-Saxon gleoman, was the guardian of those links with
the past which were essential to the identity and coherence of the *cym*
(kin).

The significance of the bard's role in Anglo-Saxon society is very much
apparent in *Beowulf*, but although Hrothgar has an official bard (who of
course accompanies himself on the harp) and, in addition, minstrels who
sing 'clear-voiced in Heorot', the warriors who surround him are also able
to recount the tales which celebrate the achievements of the past. One of
the king's thanes is a warrior who has the gift of poetic eloquence and
remembers many lays, but who is also able to compose a new story. The
poem emphasises the importance of the 'store of words' on which the
singer can draw in order to praise his lord. When in *Beowulf* the lord's
harper rises in his accustomed place –

21

> a fellow of the king's
> whose head was a storehouse of the storied verse,
> whose tongue gave gold to the language
> of the treasured repertory...

a respectful silence fills the hall and a different quality of attention is his to command.

> The man struck up,
> found the phrase, framed rightly
> the deed of Beowulf, drove the tale,
> rang word-changes. [3]

He is his lord's memory, the keeper of his genealogy and of the valiant deeds of his ancestors, of which his guests are to be suitably informed or reminded. Through him the tradition is 'made new, the common fund of experience... brought to bear on the present. Knowing the past, he (can) interpret life as it come(s), making it a part of the tale of the tribe'. [4]

In the ancient Welsh code of laws, the *penkerd* or 'chief of song' has his land free and sits next to the *edling* (king's heir) in the hall. The *bard teulu*, 'bard of the royal entourage', also has his land free and his horse from the king, as well as his harp and a gold ring from the queen, but he sings only after the *penkerd* and his seat in the hall is lower. [5] In the courts of the Anglo-Saxon kings, such men were probably of the noble rank of thane. [6]

They were the precursors of the 'king's harpers' whom we are to encounter in the courts of the Plantagenets. They had their equivalents at each descending rung of the social hierarchy, down to the 'ale minstrels' who mingled with and became indistinguishable from the *mimi* of the market place. Their prototype is Widsith, the wandering minstrel-*scôp* of the Myrgings.

> This is the testimony of Widsith,
>   traveller through
> kindreds and countries;
>   in courts he stood often,
> knelt for the lovely stone,
>   no living man more often.
> Unlocks his word-hoard. [7]

His 'word-hoard' – the earliest recorded song in Anglo-Saxon English – survives in a single, scorched manuscript of the eleventh century, given by Leofric, first bishop of Exeter, to his cathedral library. We do not know who put it in writing, but its original composer was clearly a minstrel of the old, oral tradition. Was he speaking in his own name or through an assumed identity? Again, we do not know. But along with genealogies and legendary histories – some sixty-nine heroes and seventy tribes are catalogued as he journeys across Europe – the poet is surely giving us a glimpse into his own thought and experience, rare fragments of minstrel autobiography.

Widsith, 'the wide-traveller', has been commissioned to accompany Ealhhild, daughter of Edwin, king of the Lombards, to her bridegroom-to-be, the formidable Eormanric, tyrant of the Ostrogoths. Fortunately, on arrival, he says,

> the Goth King was kind towards me:
> lord over cities and they who lived in them.
> Six hundred shillings' worth of sheer gold
> were wound into the ring he reached to my hand.
> (I owed it to Eadgils, overlord of the Myrgings,
> my king and keeper, and at my coming home
> I gave it him against a grant of land
> formerly bestowed on me, the estate of my father.)

Ealhhild is also kind with the gift of another ring, and will receive in return due honour and renown. For afterwards,

> when the name was asked of the noblest girl,
> gold-hung queen, gift-dealer,
> beneath the sky's shifting – the most shining lady –
> I sang Ealhhild; in every land
> I spoke her name, spread her fame.
> When we struck up the lay before our lord in war,
> Shilling and I, with sheer-rising voices,
> the song swelling to the sweet-touched harp,
> many men there of unmelting hearts,
> who well knew, worded their thought,
> said this was the best song sung in their hearing. [8]

Here is an important point. The rewards that Widsith receives from his patrons are not given only, even primarily, out of aesthetic appreciation of his performance, or as a recompense for services rendered, but also in expectation of a future benefit to themselves: praise, the widest possible dissemination of the givers' royal virtue of magnanimity. And the greater the gift, the more is expected in the way of praise.

The relationship here of minstrel to patron is not therefore – as John of Salisbury saw it – one of pandering to an ignoble desire for diversion or sensual pleasure; but of mutual interest, involving (on the part of the minstrel) a future obligation close to that of feudal enfeoffment. (In relation to his own lord, Eadgils, Widsith's position would indeed seem to have been just that; Eormanric's gift is passed to Eadgils as a 'fine' by which he is granted 'seisin' of his father's estate.)

That is why in William of Malmesbury's story of the visit of the Danish king Anlaf to the English camp of Athelstan in the disguise of a harper, Anlaf surreptitiously buries the coin that Athelstan gives him, as reward for his performance, in the earth at his feet. To have left Athelstan's tent with the money in his pouch would have implied an obligation of future service which – as in truth a spy and Athelstan's sworn enemy – he cannot accept without dishonour. (Alfred is earlier reported to have visited a Danish camp in the same disguise, and for the same purpose – to reconnoitre the strength and dispositions of an opposing army.)[9]

There is a debt to be re-paid – however passing the relationship. Though he is unlikely to see his 'noblest girl' ever again, Widsith 'spoke her name, spread her fame' – striking up with his companion or accompanist Shilling even before the battle-host of his 'lord in war', Eadgils. He fulfils his part of the bargain. To do otherwise would be dishonourable and risk professional disgrace.

But if, on his part, Widsith depends utterly on the largesse of Eormanric and Ealhhild as recompense for his long and arduous mission – as well as on the continuing favour of Eadgils – all three of them may also be said to depend on him for the fame on which their own position rests. And in a pre-literate age, they have no other more effective means of achieving it.

All this may help to explain the disparity of rewards given to later minstrels. It is not wholly explicable in terms of what is likely to have been a wide difference between them in quality of performance; their varying abilities to extol their patrons' generosity in the places where such publicity mattered is also a factor. Values change. To the mind of the middle ages, fame was something glorious: a due flowering of noble and generous acts. Great people, whether kings or bishops – and we should remember that bishops, however pious, were temporal magnates as well as spiritual pastors – were expected both to be magnanimous in their rewards and to seek to trumpet the fact.

In the final, moving verses of his song, Widsith speaks for all his fellow minstrel-scôps and gleomen; perhaps, unknowingly too, for many of their later successors.

> The maker's wierd is to be a wanderer:
> the poets of mankind go through the many countries,
> speak their needs, say their thanks.
> Always they meet with someone, in the south lands or the north,
> who understands their art, an open-handed man
> who would not have his fame fail among the guard
> nor rest from an earl's deeds before the end cuts off
> light and life together.

> Lasting honour shall be his,
> a name that shall never die beneath the heavens. [10]

The old tradition of oral minstrelsy survived the coming of Christianity. The new language of record was predominantly Latin, and Latin was the exclusive preserve of the Church, of clerks, but it was in English that the mass of the people continued to communicate; and it was to the harpers that they naturally turned to express their deepest feelings about the changing world in which they found themselves, and to keep alive – for a time at least – the old stories.

Beowulf of course belongs to this age of transition; as does the Sutton Hoo ship burial with its strange cargo of Christian and pagan artefacts. It should no longer surprise us to find among them the remains of a broken lyre. [11] William of Malmesbury tells an anecdote of the seventh-century abbot of his own monastery of Malmesbury, St Aldhelm, which he claimed to have found in the *Handboc* of King Alfred – a personal anthology of favourite psalms and quotations for which there is supporting contemporary evidence, though the book itself has been lost.

Arriving at a church to give a sermon, the old man found no one at all had turned up to hear him. Nothing daunted, he took up a harp and went to the town bridge where – assuming the role of a gleoman – he played and sang some of the old, English songs. Having collected a sizeable crowd, he laid the harp aside and delivered his sermon. [12]

Alfred himself was a key figure in the process whereby the gleomen came to terms with Christianity and found a new role. We know on the authority of his contemporary biographer, Bishop Asser, that the king had learnt 'by heart' some English songs before he could either read or write, and that later he was to insist on his children learning them too. [13]

Faced by the imminent collapse of Latin culture in his kingdom of Wessex under the recurring tide of Danish incursions, and by the illiteracy of his earls and leading men, he imported scholars from the continent and, with their assistance, set to work to translate the Psalms of David and other classic Latin texts into English. (Among these was *The Consolation of Philosophy* by the Roman Christian author Boethius, with its eloquent verses on Orpheus' subjection of the powers of Hades by his 'sweet song' and 'loud harp's delightful string', which Alfred glosses to nearly twice their original length. [14])

He is frequently pictured in tenth and eleventh-century manuscripts in the likeness of David. In this one – which comes from a copy of his English version of the Psalter – he appears as a divinely-inspired harper accompanied by three musicians and a juggler.

Royal Psalmist.   British Library,
MS Cotton Tiberius C vi, f.30.

At the foot of an earlier painting of the mid-eighth century, in which the royal psalmist is playing a lyre, we find two gleomen dancing and clapping their hands to an accompaniment of horns.

Gleemen dancing.   British Library, MS Cotton Vespasian
A i, f.30b.

The influence of this Anglo-Saxon, Celtic tradition of minstrelsy, especially harping with its Biblical echoes and links with an heroic past, was not, of course, confined to Britain. Through the missionary journeys of early Irish and English monks – men such as Columbanus, Boniface and Alcuin – the whole of western Europe, the cradle of medieval Christianity, was affected by it. Only the shadowy navigator, Brendan, is said to have listened to 'no harping', but that was because the Archangel Gabriel had once sat on his altar and sung to him in the likeness of a white bird, 'leaving him deaf to all earthlier music'. [15]

It would seem that because these men and their spiritual descendants had never experienced Roman culture in its final, decadent phase – as had Augustine and, to a lesser extent, Gregory – they were the better able to reach back through their knowledge of surviving Greek and Latin texts to a truer and finer seam of classical culture and learning in its golden age; an inheritance which the middle ages never ceased to reverence. [16] And for the Greeks, music was the supreme expression of the harmony of the universe; its practice – as a 'muse-descended' art – forbidden to slaves.

Dunstan, chief architect of those tenth-century monastic reforms codified in *Regularis Concordia* with its 'Play of the Three Marys', is said to have constructed an Aeolian harp solely from his reading of ancient Greek authors. It stood in a niche of his cell and – when presumably the wind was in the right direction – made its own mysterious music. Not surprisingly, it brought down on his head accusations of witchcraft.

One of the last of the Saxon kings, Edmund Ironside, gave the hills of Chartham and Walworth to his *joculator*, Hitardus – probably a harper. Hitardus, wishing to visit Rome, donated this considerable property to Christ Church, Canterbury – Canterbury Cathedral. [17] Nearly three hundred years later (1296–7), Edward I was to reward no less than fourteen harpers for 'making their minstrelsy before the statue of the Blessed Virgin' in the crypt of the same cathedral. [18] One is reminded of the legend of *Le Jongleur de Notre Dame*, a former minstrel become a monk who, in the secrecy of night, is discovered by his disapproving superiors in church, performing his old tumbling act before a statue of the Virgin – as the best gift that he has to offer her.

4

Norman Jongleurs and Buffoons: Taillefer and Rahere

There are very few occasions – perhaps half-a-dozen at most – when individual minstrels may be said to have affected the course of history in the larger sense. As it happens, two of them come to light in the dawn of the Norman period of English history.The first concerns a fool.[1]

William the Bastard, duke of Normandy – the future Conqueror – was no more than eighteen or nineteen in 1046 when his authority in Normandy was threatened by a revolt of *vicomtes*, of which the prime mover was Guy of Burgundy, who sought to make himself duke in William's place. According to later tradition, the revolt began with an attempt on William's life while he was at Valognes, in the far west of the duchy – the heart of his enemies' territory. Let Sir John Hayward, a contemporary of Shakespeare, take up the story.

> A certaine foole (nothing regarded for his want of wit), observing their preparations, secretly got away and in the dead of night came to Valogne, where the Duke then lay; no lesse slenderly guarded with men than the place it selfe was sleight for defence. Here he continued rapping at the gate and crying out untill it was opened, and hee brought to the presence of the Duke. To whom he declared the conspiracie, with circumstances of such moment, that the Duke foorthwith tooke his horse and posted alone towards Falais, an especial place for strength of defence.[2]

From there, William appealed to his overlord, Henry I of France, with whose assistance the revolt was crushed and his ducal authority restored. The episode derives from Wace, who tells us that the fool's name was Goles.[3]

Wace's narrative, the *Roman de Rou* (written between 1160 and 1174), has not a good reputation among historians, which may explain Goles' absence from the indices of recent biographies of the Conqueror. And yet we must allow the story a certain feasibility. Unlike some of Wace's more fanciful passages, it fits the historical facts so far as these are known, and casts a true light on the extreme vulnerability of the young duke at what was certainly a turning point in his early career. Moreover, Goles being, as

Sir John has it, 'nothing regarded for his want of wit', was just the sort of person whose absence – having got wind of a conspiracy and set out on his hazardous journey to warn the Duke – might not have been noticed.

If for no other reason, the enormous consequences which would have ensued for the history of England if the assassination attempt had succeeded surely entitles Goles – about whom nothing else is known – to a place in the footnotes of history; the first in a long series of royal fools, of whom we shall have more to say in subsequent chapters.

The next occasion when a minstrel takes centre-stage in big events is much more fully reported by the chroniclers; though here too modern historians have been sceptical, if not totally dismissive – I think unfairly. This is the famous charge of the minstrel Taillefer at the Battle of Hastings.

In so far as all the medieval kings, from William onwards, were required as a first priority to have at least some competence in the arts of war, and their households were thus (among other things) standing headquarter staffs for military operations, actual or potential, the minstrels who formed an integral part of the household establishment were able to turn their individual skills to warlike purposes as naturally and easily as everyone else – especially if they were Normans.

Surprisingly enough, even juggling could take on a flavour of combat. In the story of Havelok as told by Gaimar, its Danish hero is described as a *jongleur* because of his skill in overturning and throwing opponents in wrestling matches, staged for the amusement of the court.[4] (John of Salisbury, it will be remembered, includes wrestlers in his list of *joculatores*.) Though formal marching has a much more recent origin, the drum-major of today who casts his ceremonial mace in the air and catches it again in front of a marching band is doing something that a medieval spectator would instantly identify as 'juggling'.

On the occasion of Taillefer's exploit, the two armies at Hastings were drawn up in their opposing formations: the English behind their shield-wall in tight order along a ridge of the Sussex Downs, later to be marked by the building of Battle Abbey; the Normans in a more extended line of three divisions, over half a mile in width, facing them across the valley from the forward slope of Telham Hill. The English, on foot, were armed with spears and axes. The Normans fielded a mixed force of cavalry and foot in three lines: infantry with short bows in front, heavy infantry behind; cavalry with lances and swords in the rear. Between six and seven thousand men on either side confronted each other at 9 o'clock in the early morning sunshine of October 14, 1066.

Geoffrey Gaimar, writing about 1140 in Norman French, has the fullest account of what seems to have happened next.

One of the French then hasted,
Before the others he rode.
Taillefer was he named.
He was a minstrel (*ioglere*), and bold enough.
Arms he had and a good horse.
He was a bold and noble warrior.
Before the others he set himself.
Before the English he did wonders.
He took his lance by the butt
As if it had been a truncheon.
Up high he threw it,
And by the head he caught it.

Three times he threw his lance in the air; then, advancing towards the English, hurled it among them, wounding an English soldier.

Then he drew his sword, retreated,
Threw the sword which he held
On high, then caught it.
One said to the other, who saw this,
That this was enchantment
Which he did before the folk.[5]

Three times he threw the sword, then charged into the English line and was engulfed. All this is expressed, of course, in the language of poetry – specifically that of the *chansons de geste*, the jongleur's *métier*. But Gaimar's is not our only account.

Henry of Huntingdon in his Latin *History of the English* (c.1150) gives a briefer and more prosaic version of what is basically the same story;[6] but the *Carmen (Song) of the Battle of Hastings* – formerly attributed to Guy, bishop of Amiens, before 1068, but now given a later, possibly twelfth-century, date by some historians – adds significantly to Gaimar's account by putting it into context.

According to the *Carmen* (a more respectable source than Gaimar, irrespective of date), Taillefer's action was preceded by a period of uncertainty on the part of the Normans, which gave their opponents a welcome opportunity to re-group. Faced by the formidable sight of the English on their commanding ridge, which the attackers would be obliged to charge uphill, the Normans experienced an understandable loss of confidence. (I quote from a prose translation of the Latin verse of the original.)

Meantime, while the battle hung in ominous suspense... a player (*histrio*), whom his most valiant soul greatly ennobled, rode out before the countless army of the duke. He heartened the men of

France and terrified the English, and, tossing his sword high, he sported with it.

An English soldier came out to challenge Taillefer, now described as *mimus*. Taillefer defeated him and cut off his head, which he displayed to his comrades to show that the beginning of the battle favoured them. 'All rejoiced and at the same time called upon the Lord.' (The Norman battle-cry was *Dex aie.*) 'They exulted that the first blow was theirs... and at once the men hastened to close shields'.[7] As the *Carmen's* editor comments, the Taillefer of this account is a 'man with a job, not a figure of high romance. His ride is necessary because of the events which have preceded it. He heartens his own side and confounds the enemy whom he insults by juggling with his sword – an invitation to the insulted to break ranks and chastise such impudence'.[8] (Neither Henry of Huntingdon nor the *Carmen* mention Taillefer's juggling with a lance.)

Gaimar and the *Carmen* elaborate the story in different ways, but the core of each of their narratives is the same – Taillefer's defiant juggling before the English host; the point that Henry of Huntingdon fastens on also. But there is a fourth account, and this one introduces quite a new element into the story. I return to Wace and his *Roman de Rou* (again, using a prose translation).

> Then Taillefer who sang right well, rode mounted on a swift horse before the duke, singing of Karlemaine, and of Rollant, of Oliver and the vassals who died in Renchevals.

He asked permission to strike the first blow in the battle, which the Duke gave.

> Then Taillefer put his horse to a gallop, charging before all the rest, and struck an Englishman dead, driving his lance below the breast into his body, and stretching him upon the ground.

After more blows, the English pushed forward and surrounded him. 'Forthwith arose the noise and cry of war, and on either side the people put themselves in motion'.[9]

Wace's reference to Taillefer singing of Roland and Oliver, of Charlemagne and the heroes of Roncesvals, might be disregarded as a typical flight of fancy – along with the unlikely interview with the Duke – were it not supported by William of Malmesbury who, as a youth, would have been able to talk to survivors of the battle; he wrote about 1125. William does not mention Taillefer by name, but says that a song of Roland (*cantilena Rollandi*) was sung as an inspiration to the Norman soldiers as the battle began.[10] Both accounts imply that inspiration was needed; neither has anything to say of Taillefer's juggling.

So altogether we have five separate testimonies to a jongleur's decisive intervention in the Battle – all written within a hundred years of the event – of which four refer to him by name. The differences between them at least indicate that they are drawing on more than one primary source. But are they contradictory? If historians continue to be sceptical, it is partly because of the difficulty of combining the accounts of Taillefer's juggling with those of his singing (and the apparent oddity of his doing both), and partly because neither of the two main, contemporary sources for our knowledge of what happened at Hastings – the treatise of William of Poitiers and the pictorial record of the Bayeux Tapestry – refer to him at all. I shall come back to the second objection in a moment. Drawing on the extant text of *The Song of Roland* – of late eleventh or early twelfth-century date, but thought to derive from an earlier, lost original – let me first attempt a reconciliation of the varied accounts, which may help to rescue Taillefer from the realm of myth and romance to which he is often consigned, and put the whole episode on a more credible basis of solid, flesh-and-blood reality.

Accepting the *Carmen*'s report of an uneasy pause after the two armies had taken up their positions and before the battle began, during which there was uncertainty and some loss of nerve among the Normans, a jongleur called Taillefer rode out from his place at the rear of the Norman line, where he was stationed with other members of the ducal household, into the deserted no man's land of the valley floor. He would have been armed with the normal lance and sword of the cavalry. (In battle, there is no reason to suppose that a minstrel would wear anything different to other mounted men, i.e. hauberk and pointed helmet.)

He begins a high, unaccompanied chanting of *The Song of Roland* at the passage where the dying and defeated Roland is addressing his sword, which is named Durendal.

> Oh Durendal, how dazzling bright you are –
> you blaze with light and shimmer in the sun!

He has drawn his own sword, and now throws it in the air where it catches the October sun before returning to his hand. (Juggling with swords and knives is a recognised skill among both Saxon and Norman minstrels.)

> King Charles was in the Vales of Moriane
> when God in heaven had His angel tell him
> that he should give you to a captain-count:
> the great and noble king then girded me.

Again, the sword goes twisting and turning up into the air.

> With this I won Anjou and Brittany,
> and then I won him both Poitou and Maine,
> with this I won him Normandy the Proud –

His voice carries up the hill to the forward ranks of the waiting English but, as he sings in French, the words are not understood. The Normans immediately behind him catch enough of them to recognise their source and murmur appreciatively at the reference to 'Normandy the Proud'; it is his *singing* that these will remember and report, rather than his 'juggling', which is the normal acting-out of his text expected of a jongleur or *mimus*. But those on the far wings of the Norman line – up to a quarter of a mile away – hear little or nothing. To them and to the bemused English, Taillefer's actions – divorced from their poetic context – cast an incomprehensible spell of their own: an 'enchantment before the folk'; it is the *juggling* that they will remember and speak about afterwards. Taillefer's performance continues and now approaches its climax.

> With this I won him Scotland, Ireland too,
> and England, which he held as his demesne.
> With this I've won him so many lands and countries
> which now are held by Charles, whose beard is white.
> I'm full of pain and sorrow for this sword;
> I'd rather die than leave it to the pagans.

The sword is sheathed as he brings up his lance to the throwing position. And with a final –

> Oh God, my Father, don't let France be shamed! [11]

he spurs his horse up the hill towards the English.

Seeing a solitary, seemingly mad Norman approaching them, an English soldier – Henry of Huntingdon refers to him as a standard-bearer – emerges from the shield-wall to confront him. Taillefer hurls his lance which pierces the soldier's shield and, as the jongleur draws his sword, the English line surges forward to engulf him.

Apart from the scuffle of bodies where Taillefer has now vanished from view and the English line is re-forming behind him, several moments of horrified silence pass in which both armies appear transfixed by what has just happened. Then an angry shout of *Dex aie* goes up as the Norman cavalry charge forward between the intervening lines of infantry in a first, determined assault. Battle is joined. [12]

As to William of Poitiers' failure even to mention Taillefer's exploit and his apparent absence from the Bayeux Tapestry, the unavoidable implication that it needed a *jongleur*, a *mimus* of all people, to spur the Norman knights into effective action may be enough in itself to explain why these semi-official Norman records look the other way; especially as those responsible for them – Bishop Odo of Bayeux, who is thought to have commissioned the Tapestry, and William of Poitiers, a former knight who became the Conqueror's chaplain – were clerics. However courageous, Taillefer's solitary charge was also a clear infraction of the strict chivalric code which forbade men of inferior rank (let alone minstrels) to advance against the enemy ahead of their betters; such behaviour was viewed as a snatching of honour from those who were properly entitled to it – in this case, the nobles appointed by the Duke to lead his divisions, Odo among them. (The author of the *Carmen* makes the point that through the bravery of his actions – his 'valiant soul' – Taillefer is enabled to transcend his lowly status to achieve a kind of *de facto* nobility.)

Taillefer is one of only a handful of names mentioned by the chroniclers in all their varied reports of the Battle; to most of these he was simply a hero. That the differing accounts contain elements of myth is undoubted; but can we really dismiss him from the historical record for no other reason than that? Is there any report of the Battle of Hastings from either side that does *not* contain 'elements of myth'?

The existence of a third minstrel associated with William I is attested by the Domesday Book. He was Berdic, described in the Latin text as *joculator Regis*: the king's jongleur or minstrel.

Berdic is recorded as being in possession of land in Wales. He has '3 villages; 5 ploughs there. He pays nothing'.[13] Whether this modest property was enjoyed as a form of 'serjeanty' (in return for Berdic's continuing service and that of his heirs), or as an outright gift, the Domesday record provides hard evidence that, right from the start of the Norman domination of England, minstrels had a recognised standing at court, and that one of them was honoured by an official title known to the Domesday surveyors, *joculator Regis*, 'royal minstrel'.[14]

Berdic is not the only minstrel to appear in the *Domesday Book*. Within twenty years of Hastings, William's Norman magnates are seen to be following his example in their patronage of minstrels – even to the granting of land. In 1086, Adelinda, a *joculatrix* or female minstrel – probably a dancer – possesses a virgate (a villein holding of, typically, about thirty acres) in Hampshire, given to her by Earl Roger, William's cousin who had commanded the French right at Hastings.[15]

If, as seems likely, Taillefer and Berdic were, like Widsith, singers of *gestes*, what instrument would they normally have used to accompany themselves? Harps and lyres were not, of course, confined to Britain; they are found from an early date across the whole of continental Europe. But what the harp had been for the English gleomen and Welsh bards, the *vielle* or viol was soon to become for the French jongleur. Though we should not forget that the Normans had Viking blood in their veins and may have inherited older traditions from the Scandinavian *scôp*, it would seem, in fact, to have been the viol – ancestor of our present violin – that they brought with them across the Channel; it makes its first appearance in an English manuscript illumination early in the twelfth century (Galpin, p.64).

From the point of view of a performer of *gestes*, the viol had certain advantages over its rival, the harp, in that it was more easily capable of producing a sustained drone to underlie and give a continuous tone or colour to recited or chanted verse. It could not, of course, in those circumstances, be played as it is today, tucked under the chin, as this would have interfered too much with the performer's 'singing' or chanted recitation of his *geste*, but was rested on a knee and played something like a modern cello.

The extent to which the harp persisted in England after the Conquest as the normal instrument used to accompany the singing of *gestes* is a measure of the degree to which the Anglo-Saxon tradition in minstrelsy survived, and was adopted by the Norman invaders. But it was now joined by the *vielle*, and the players of this new instrument – whether *gestours* or not – soon became a regular feature of English minstrelsy, especially at court and in the households of the French-speaking nobility.

Life in the bachelor household of William Rufus – the Conqueror's second surviving son who succeeded him in 1087 – was wild and rough, if enjoyable for those who had a taste for it.

William of Malmesbury paints a vivid portrait. Rufus was 'thick-set and muscular with a protruding belly; a dandy dressed in the height of fashion... in his red, choleric face were lively eyes of changeable colour, speckled with flecks of light'. [16] Though small in stature and every inch a soldier, he could, when crossed, be 'dangerous like an animal. Archbishop Anselm once likened him to a wild bull'. [17]

The outrageous fashions affected by the king and his companions – long hair swept back from the forehead, luxurious clothes revealing the thighs, shoes with pointed and curled toes – were a constant provocation to the clergy of his time, and prompted unfavourable comparisons with the clean-cut heroes of Hastings. They bring us another reference to a court fool, described here as a *nebulo*, literally a 'nobody'.

It seems that a particular fashion for shoes with long points like scorpions' tails was attributed to an old enemy of Rufus, Fulk of Anjou, who – according to malicious gossip – wore them to disguise the unshapely appearance of his feet, deformed by bunions. The *nebulo*, called Robert, had stuffed the points of his own shoes with tow and curled them back like a ram's horn, and in consequence was given the nickname, Horny (*cornadus*) [18] – an indication of the tone of Rufus' court in its lighter moments.

Another, 'below stairs' member of the same dissolute band was Rahere who, in a later, reformed phase of his life, was to achieve more lasting fame as the founder of St Bartholomew's Hospital and Fair. His first biographer – an Austin Canon of Bartholomew's – describes him at this time as having –

> hawntid the kyngis palice and amonge the noysefull prese (press) of that tumultuouse courte, inforsid hymself with iolite (jollity) and carnale suavyte by the whiche he myght drawe to hym the hertys of many oone ther, yn spectaclis, yn metys (banquets), yn playes and othir courtly mokkys (nonsense) and trifyllys.. [19]

On this evidence, Rahere would seem to have belonged to that category of entertainers later defined by Thomas de Chabham as *scurrae*: buffoons or hangers-on 'who frequent the courts of the great and talk scandal', who are 'good for nothing except gluttony and scandal-mongering'. [20] The destructive progresses of Rufus and his entourage through the English countryside are described by Eadmus, biographer of Anselm.

The chroniclers, of course, are invariably clerics, and their occasional references to fools and *mimi* – associated, as they nearly always are, with wastrels and whores – reflect an inevitable distaste. Orderic Vitalis, an English monk who had joined the Norman monastery of St Evroul as a boy and remained there for the rest of his life, describes Hugh of Avranches, earl of Chester, as 'lavish to the point of prodigality, a lover of games and luxuries, actors, horses and dogs'. (The Latin has an even more contemptuous ring to it: *ludis et luxibus, mimis, equis et canibus.*) [21]

But like his contemporary, William of Malmesbury, Orderic is too professional a writer to allow his outraged feelings to get in the way of a good story. In the course of a legendary acount of the early history of his own abbey of Evroul, he tells how the abbey had been attacked and despoiled of its relics by an invading force from France, led by the Duke of Orleans. The relics – including the precious remains of its founder, Evroul, and his saintly companions – were then transported back to Orleans by the retreating raiders as loot, while the dispossessed monks followed disconsolately behind at a safe distance.

> On the first night after leaving Normandy the army encamped in a place called Champs, and after supper an altercation and harsh words arose among some of the hangers-on (*parasitis*). So one of the *mimi* said jokingly to the duke, 'My lord duke, do you know what Herluin the chancellor and Ralph the chamberlain have done? They have dug up the bodies of some peasants in Normandy and, deceived into thinking that they are holy relics, have placed them in your chapel and are reverently carrying them with them into Gaul.' When the duke enquired their names, the *joculator* said, 'Evroul, Evremond, and Ansbert.' Then the Franks, because the names were unfamiliar to them and they little knew how great was the glory of

these men in the sight of God in heaven, burst out laughing and made coarse jokes.

Given the context of Orderic's story, the sequel, with its stern warning of the consequences of such behaviour, is only to be expected. In the first vigil of the night, when everyone had settled down to sleep, a thunderball of fire descended on the *joculator* and on the idle wretches (*sociis nebulonibus*) who had shared in his mockery, and annihilated them. From then on, of course, the relics were treated with greater respect, and the homeless monks brought in from the cold and damp of the forest. [22]

Though it is probable that French-speaking jongleurs of the more dignified kind were already employed in the English halls of the newly-established Norman barons, and that minstrel-*scôps* of the Widsith tradition were still operating in the diminishing enclaves where Saxon influence held its ground, the sound of the harp is silent in the chronicles. Other than in churches and abbeys, the only music to be heard is the blaring of trumpets, ordered by Rufus to mock the rebels of 1088, as they emerged defeated from Rochester Castle. [23]

The arrow that prematurely ended Rufus' life in the New Forest in 1100, with the implications placed upon it of divine retribution for his cavalier treatment of the Church and dissolute private life – as well as for the sins of his father in the creation of the New Forest – has ensured for him a bad press from subsequent historians; but near-contemporaries held a more balanced view. As a soldier, John of Salisbury (not a man to be easily impressed) rated him above his father; William of Malmesbury praised him for his magnanimity and for a certain greatness of soul; while Geoffrey of Monmouth is even said to have drawn on Rufus in his portrayal of the pseudo-historical Arthur. [24]

His most recent biographer describes him as 'a buffoon with a purpose, a jester who accepted his father's mantle but spread it in extravagant caprice'. [25] With such a person centre-stage, it is not surprising that the professional entertainers of his time (Rahere among them) remain in the background; shadowy figures by a soldiers' camp-fire, a butt for disorderly pranks in the candle-lit royal hall.

Rufus' younger brother Henry, who was present at his death (and has been suspected of conspiracy in a murder plot), lost no time in securing the throne for himself – circumventing any such move on the part of the elder brother Robert.

Henry's early marriage to Eadgyth – through her saintly mother, Margaret, a descendant of Alfred and Edmund Ironside – helped to foster a sense of national unity. Unexpectedly, it was through Eadgyth – renamed Matilda on her marriage but more usually known as 'Good Queen Maud' – that French poetry and music continued to make their way across the Channel. Maud was a woman of extraordinary piety, who walked barefoot through the streets in Lent to attend Mass and washed the leprous sores of beggars in the privacy of her own chamber. According to William of Malmesbury – who has otherwise nothing but good to say of her – her one weakness lay in the extravagance of her rewards to musicians and poets, recklessly providing –

> for sweet-singing clerks, speaking well of them all, making
> generous gifts, providing more. Thence, as news of her
> liberality spread world-wide, clerks famed in song and
> poetry flocked thither; he who charmed the queen's ears
> with the novelty of song considered himself lucky.

But, more to the point, she contributed payment not only to these clerks but to 'all kinds of men, especially foreigners: so that, having accepted the rewards, they might sing her praises in all lands' – a striking echo of Ealhhild's gifts to Widsith and the attitudes that lay behind them for, as William goes on to say, 'the desire for glory is so innate in the minds of men that scarcely anyone eager for the precious fruits of a good conscience, if he has done any good, does not find it sweet to be extolled to the crowds'. But while the 'foreigners' (i.e. Frenchmen) were rewarded to a man, the 'others' – presumably native harpers of her own race and tongue – were 'kept in suspense, sometimes with effectual, but oftener with empty promises'. [26]

One of those rewarded – probably at Matilda's prompting – was William Le Harpur, who received four and a half bovates of land (perhaps ninety acres) at Wiston for a rent of 16d. a year, though it was worth 10s. (The property descended to his heirs and is recorded with details of the original grant in a Book of Fees of the reign of John. [27])

We are given no clues as to the nature of the foreigners' material; but it may be relevant to note in passing that the oldest surviving version of *The Song of Roland* (the Oxford Manuscript) was made in England at about this time – the turn of the twelfth century – and scholars agree that it was composed for oral performance by a single poet of genius, whose name may have been Turoldus. [28] The *Song's* four thousand lines are divided into *laisses*, verse paragraphs of variable length, among which are dispersed – especially, it would seem, at moments of heightened tension – the mysterious letters AOI, for which no wholly satisfactory explanation has yet been given. If, as I believe, the *Song* – or this version of it – was originally recited to the accompaniment of a viol or harp, they may well have had a musical significance – cues for a change of key or note or for a short passage of improvisation; a musical punctuation of the narrative.

The circulation at this period of *The Song of Roland*, of Arthurian stories and early versions of the Tristan legend, reminds us that we are entering the age of chivalry, with important consequences for the minstrels which we shall be examining in the following chapter. But the twelfth century in western Europe also saw a renaissance of classical learning and literature (St Bernard, William of Malmesbury, John of Salisbury), and a sweeping movement of spiritual renewal and monastic reform. It is in this latter context, surprisingly enough, that I must now take up and complete the story of Rahere, whom we briefly encountered as a *scurra* or buffoon at the dissolute court of Rufus.

It is not known exactly when or in what circumstances Rahere became a priest. Legend has it that he was 'King Henry's jester', and that his conversion was influenced by Good Queen Maud or, alternatively, by the catastrophic sinking of the White Ship in 1120, when Henry's heir, William, and his companions were drowned. But this is far too late as, shortly after 1115, his name is already recorded as a prebendary Canon of St. Paul's. (I have found no evidence linking Rahere with Henry in his first profession as *scurra*.)

Like most of Rufus' original following, he was French, probably from La Perche in the south-east corner of Normandy, where his feudal lord would have been a certain Richard de Belmeis. (Rahere's name appears as a witness to several charters of that region.) In 1108, Belmeis was appointed by Henry Bishop of London, where he was to found a grammar school attached to his cathedral, the statutes of which provided for a *magister scholae cantus* (Master of the Song School). [29] It was probably then through Belmeis' influence that the former royal buffoon arrived at St. Paul's, where his minstrel skills as musician and singer would have stood him in good stead.

But it was on a pilgrimage to Rome, shortly after 1120, that Rahere was to receive a second and even more decisive calling. Visiting the holy places, he contracted malarial fever; near to death and feeling the sins and vacuity of his former life lying heavily upon him, he made a vow that, if his health was restored, he would return to England and build a hospital 'yn recreacion of poure men'. In a subsequent vision, the apostle Bartholomew is said to have appeared to him in person and instructed him that the site of the new foundation was to be Smithfield in London, and that he was also to build a Priory there. He was not to worry about money; that would be provided.

It must have been while still in Rome that Rahere joined the Austin Canons (Canons Regular of St Augustine), the earliest of the new, reforming orders of priests and monks to have reached England. (The Austin Canons were priests, not monks, living together in small communities, engaging in parish or charitable works.)

Rahere returned from Rome a new man, and lost no time in explaining his mission to the citizens of London; they promised support but pointed out that Smithfield lay within the king's 'farm', over which they had no rights or control. Again through Belmeis' influence, Rahere obtained an audience with Henry; he came away with the promise of a royal charter

Rahere's tomb in St Bartholomew the Great (National Monuments Record). The effigy and elaborate canopy date only from 1405.

and the title deeds of an extensive site; his powers of persuasion were clearly phenomenal. In 1123, he began building the hospital, and shortly afterwards, the Priory. Both were completed by 1127, and his first patient was a man called Aldwynne from Dunwich in Suffolk. In 1133, Rahere got from the king an additional 'charter of privileges', confirming the previous grant and giving 'protection' (immunity from arrest for previous misdemeanors and crimes) to all comers to the Fair, which was already being held about the Priory on the feast of St Bartholomew, August 24. In the tolls and rents it produced, the fair was to be an important source of income for the upkeep of the hospital; but it is not impossible that Rahere saw it also as contributing to that larger aim of his: 'yn recreacion of poure men'. If so, he was merely anticipating Franciscan teaching on the nature of recreation – 'the rest, the mirth, the ese and the welfare that god hath ordeyned in the halidayes' – as a figure or token of that 'endlesse reste, joye and myrthe and welfare in hevenes blisse that we hope to have withouten ende'.[30]

Rahere's three-fold legacy of Hospital, Priory and Fair was to prove remarkably resilient to the winds of change. Bart's Hospital continues his work of healing on the same site to the present day. The Priory – at least, the heart of it, the chancel – somehow survived the Dissolution of the monasteries, the Great Fire and two world wars to become the only surviving medieval parish church in the City of London: St Bartholomew the Great. Most remarkably of all, perhaps, there Rahere's body still lies in the usual founder's position to the north of the Sanctuary.

As to the Fair – Bartle-my Fair, as it was known to Londoners – it was to provide an annual, safe haven for minstrels, puppeteers and players for centuries to come, and survive long enough to be celebrated by Ben Jonson.

> Hey, now the Fair's a-filling!
> O, for a tune to startle
> The Birds o' the booths here billing
> Yearly with old Saint Bartle!

5

Minstrels in the Age of Chivalry: Stephen to John

There can have been little space for minstrelsy in the anarchic reign of Stephen. The apocalyptic horror of the conflict between Stephen and Matilda is well conveyed in the chronicles.

In the first year of the new reign (1136), Gerald of Wales tells how Richard FitzGilbert set out from Clare in Suffolk with a large force of men-at-arms to quell a rising on his Welsh estate of Cardiganshire. Travelling through Wales, he was obliged to traverse a dense forest. Warned by his guide of the danger of ambush, he decided to go on alone, preceded only by a singer to announce his coming, and a fiddler 'who replied to the notes of the song in an *alternatim* fashion' – an established minstrel technique. Perhaps there was an element of insurance in the plan; in the case of trouble ahead, the stopping of the music might give time to escape. But, if so, the Welsh were too canny for him; they let the minstrels through unharmed, still playing and singing, and picked off their lord as he followed behind.[1]

An episode recounted by Jean, a French-speaking minstrel-poet, redounds to Stephen's credit . A little boy, left with the king as a hostage by his father, and abandoned to his fate when the man defaulted on his promises, wandered unknowingly into the royal tent. Here he was later discovered unharmed, playing conkers with the king. He was to grow up to become William Marshal, the 'Flower of Chivalry' and, some sixty years later, the guardian and protector of the young Henry III. The minstrel was commissioned to put the memories of Marshal's family and former squire into verse.[2]

The story helps to mark the transition between the old *chanson de geste*, which dealt exclusively with stern matters of war and the heroes of battle, and the softer genre of romance, as represented by the Tristan poems of Thomas of Britain and Beroul, and Arthurian romances of Chrétien de Troyes. Chrétien looks down with a degree of contempt (real or assumed as a literary pose) on those who 'earn a living by telling stories' which 'they mutilate and spoil in the presence of kings and counts' – in other words, the minstrels.[3]

We are reminded here of the European dimensions of English, aristocratic culture at this period. Its kings and leading magnates were, of course, wholly French and French-speaking. Stephen had been count of Blois; Henry FitzEmpress duke of Normandy, as well as count of Anjou,

Maine and Touraine. With Henry's marriage to Eleanor of Aquitaine and subsequent accession to the English throne as Henry II, the 'Angevin Empire' extended from the Cheviots to the Pyrenees.

Eleanor was a key figure in the dissemination of the new chivalric ideas, music and poetry.[4] She was a granddaughter of William, ninth duke of Aquitaine (1071–1127), the first known troubadour – a notorious womaniser who kept a harem of Saracen girls for his personal use, and was more than once excommunicated by the Pope. (His compositions ring true to character: highly-wrought, literary conceits in which women are idealised as the remote objects of courtly love, along with coarse ballads.[5]) On the death of her father (the tenth duke) in 1137, the fifteen-year-old Eleanor – now duchess of Aquitaine in her own right – had been married to Louis VII of France. The high-spirited, good-looking girl from the south and the pious, increasingly ascetic king made an ill-matched pair; but more importantly, after ten years of marriage, Eleanor had borne two daughters but failed to provide the male heir that Louis desperately needed to perpetuate his line. In 1152, with the connivance of the French clergy, the marriage was dissolved on the specious grounds of consanguinity. Barely eight weeks later – to the shock and alarm of the French – she married her equally close relation, Henry of Anjou, then nineteen years old and ten years her junior. Within three years, Stephen was dead, and Henry and Eleanor were crowned together as King and Queen of England at Westminster on 19 December, 1154.

The chronicles speak of the great joy of the occasion and the many bishops who were present; but to gain a more detailed picture of the ceremony and the celebrations that followed it – to discover what part, if any, the minstrels had to play in them and in the subsequent life of the court – we need to look further afield. Robert Wace, in a passage of his *Roman de Brut* published the following year and dedicated to Eleanor, describes the coronation of the legendary Arthur in terms that may well reflect a personal knowledge of the contemporary event.[6]

In the Coronation Mass, which was of exceptional splendour, the sound of the organ was heard –

> And clerics chanted in polyphony,
> With voices subsiding and lifting,
> Song falling and rising.[7]

The kind of music that John of Salisbury describes in his *Policraticus* of 1159 as having such a disturbing effect: 'Before the face of the Lord, in the very recesses of the sanctuary, showing off in a riot of wanton sound... caressing melodies, starting, chiming in, resounding, falling away, intertwining and twittering ... the high or even the highest notes are so tempered by the lower and the lowest that the ear loses its power to distinguish, and the mind, soothed by such sweetness, is unable to judge of that which it has heard'.[8]

Afterwards, the court was invaded by

> jugleürs,
> Singers and instrumentalists;
> ......
> Vielle-players, noted lais,   *(lais de notes)*
> Lais for vielle, lais for *rotes*,
> Lais for harp, lais for pipes,
> Lyres, cymbals and shawms,
> *Symphonies*, psalteries,   (hurdy-gurdies)
> Monochords, timbrels, bagpipes.
> There were also magicians,   *(tresgeteürs)*
> Performers and jugglers;   *(Joeresses et jugleürs)*
> Some tell tales and fables,
> Others ask for dice and *tables*.[9]   (backgammon)

(The shawm was a wind instrument of the oboe type with double reed; the psaltery a zither-like instrument, plucked on one side. The monochord had a single string of changeable note, also plucked; timbrels are tambourines.)

If this is not merely romantic fancy on the part of Wace, Henry and Eleanor's Coronation party was a good deal livelier than many that were follow, when the dead hand of an over-elaborate ritual had descended on every move and gesture.

But who were these minstrels, and where might they have come from? Many of Henry's magnates and greater vassals – summoned to the ceremony as a matter of duty – had minstrels in their households who normally accompanied them on such occasions. Of the lords, few were more powerful or wealthy than Roger de Mowbray, earl of Warwick. In the period 1147–57, there is charter evidence that Roger employed a *gigator* called Bartholomew – the gigue was a small fiddle, often used to accompany dancing – a singer, Luke, and a man called Warin who is variously described in the Latin as *vielator* (vielle-player) and *joculator*.[10] There is no reason to suppose then that Wace's minstrels were brought in from the street; many, if not all, would already have been present at Westminster in the retinues of their respective lords.

Writing somewhat later (about 1170), Chrétien de Troyes – who also had links with the English court – describes a similar scene of celebration following a wedding. After a blessing by the Archbishop of Canterbury –

> There was not a minstrel in all the land
> Who could offer any entertainment
> Who did not flock to the court.

Great was the joy in the hall:
Each performed his service:
One leaps, one tumbles, one conjures,
One tells tales, the other sings,
One whistles, the other plays tunes,
This one plays the harp, this the rote,
This the gigue, this the fiddle,
This the flute and this the shawm.
Maidens carol and dance.
All strive to make joy. [11]

In chivalric language, *joie* is usually associated by the poets with music and with the conferring of honour. As Laurence Wright explains, 'joy is always made *for* someone, to give them honour... And the more jugglers, instruments etc., the more joy and hence the more honour'. The equation of joy and music is taken so literally by some poets that they can speak of *seeing* joy and *hearing* joy; the carols and dances of the courtiers are joy in motion. [12] The minstrels 'strive to make joy' and, in so doing, honour the givers of the feast; in our case, the newly-crowned King and Queen. Each performs his or her service; a service that is handsomely rewarded by gifts of money, clothes, even horses, each 'according to his skill'. [13] And not only on special occasions such as this; but in a more regular and substantial way implying – despite the disapproval of churchmen – recognition of the minstrels' permanent and valued place in a feudal, chivalric society. Warin, Mowbray's viol-playing jongleur, received a life interest from his lord in a small estate for an annual rent of a pound of pepper; Bartholomew, the gigue-player, was given the village of Little Wildon, but was later persuaded to relinquish it in favour of a newly-established priory of Austin Canons in return for some sixty acres of land (a carucate) at Thirsk, which he was to hold in perpetuity; it was to pass to his heirs. [14]

That *histriones* and other minstrels had a permanent presence at Henry II's court – and further, that they were on terms of some intimacy with the king (or were thought to be) – is attested by a letter of the former royal secretary, Peter de Blois, writing to court chaplains of what they might expect to suffer in Henry's service.

If the king has announced that he will go early next morning to a certain place, the decision is sure to be changed: and so you know he will sleep till midday. You will see pack-animals waiting under their loads, teams of horses standing in silence, heralds sleeping, court traders fretting, and everyone in turn grumbling. One runs to whores and pavilioners of the court to ask them where the king is going. For this breed of courtier often knows the palace secrets. For the king's court has an assiduous following of entertainers (*histriones*), female singers, dice-players, flatterers, taverners (*caupones*), waferers (*nebulatores*), actors (*mimi*), barbers – gluttons the whole lot of them! [15]

(Nearly all these people – even the waferers and barbers – are listed as *minstrelli* in later, wardrobe accounts. The mention of heralds is particularly interesting at so early a date.)

As a cleric writing to clerics, Peter de Blois' tone is sour, but we should not allow the prejudice of a disgruntled civil servant to obscure the fact that many of those he disparages as camp-followers and gluttons – a frequent complaint – had a useful and recognised place in the royal household. In the *Dialogus de Scaccario,* an authoritative account of the workings of the Exchequer dating from the 1170s, pipers (*tibicines* – a term which embraces a wide variety of wind instruments) are instanced along with keepers of the royal palaces and wolf-takers as receiving 'liveries', i.e. regular daily payments for food and clothing in lieu of wages. [16] The waferers (mentioned above) were officials of the bakery responsible for the making of a special kind of thin biscuit eaten with sweet wine after dinner, often to the accompaniment of their own minstrelsy. Henry's personal waferer, whose name was Godfrey, was rewarded for his services by a gift of the manor of Liston Overhall in Essex, which was to remain in the same family for many centuries. [17]

If Peter de Blois was disgruntled when he wrote his now famous letter, he had reason to be. Henry II was a man of restless energy whose unpredictability was notorious; Gerald of Wales (a member of his household for many years) tells us that he rarely sat down 'either before or after supper. And... would wear out the whole court by remaining on his feet'. [18] As Peter de Blois goes on to suggest, there was an element of mischievous humour in the King's changes of plan: 'I hardly dare say it, but I believe that in truth he took a delight in seeing what a fix he put us in'. [19]

The same glint of devilish humour appears in Henry's gift of another serjeanty – a convenient way of rewarding the humbler sort of royal servants when the king had more land than ready cash at his disposal – to a *joculator* named Roland le Pettour. His estate consisted of thirty acres at Hemingstone, near Ipswich in Suffolk; but, instead of the usual pound of pepper or pair of spurs, the service enjoined was to make a leap, a whistle and a fart (*saltum, siffletum et pettum* or *bumbulum*), presumably a special trick of Roland's that had taken the king' fancy, to be performed annually in his presence on Christmas day. [20] When we first hear of it, in 1185, Roland's son Herbert was in possession of the property, and the grant with its extraordinary service was solemnly repeated for his descendants down the years. [21] When Chétien de Troyes writes of the individual services performed by minstrels, 'one leaps, one tumbles', he is not indulging in poetic exaggeration but telling the exact truth.

Another aspect of minstrelsy, typical of the whole Plantagenet period, is the minstrelsy of the chase. In a schedule of royal household servants and their entitlement to wages drawn up c.1136 for the benefit of Stephen, four hornblowers are listed among the hunting staff as receiving three-pence a day. [22] 'In the forests', says Richard FitzNigel in his *Dialogus* 'are the secret places of kings and their great delight'. This was never more true than of Henry II. Large areas of the country, including most of Essex, were designated as King's forest and subjected to an arbitrary and repressive law. The protected beasts were red, fallow and roe deer, and wild boar.

The king and his companions hunted on horseback to hounds of various kinds in both scenting and coursing, using bows to bring down the game. The job of the hornblowers – then as now – was one of communication between horsemen and dog-handlers in forest country where they might easily lose sight of one another and, when the prey was sighted, to rally the hunt for the chase and the kill. There are elaborate descriptions of the hunt and its music – the 'halowing on highe' and 'blawyng of prys in mony breme horne' – in the fourteenth-century *Sir Gawain and the Green Knight*.

It is in connection with the hunt that the only mention of a court fool from this reign occurs. In 1178–9, the master of Henry's otter-hounds was a man called Roger Follus, and he too is awarded a serjeanty; a house and outbuildings with not less than fifty acres of land (a messuage and three virgates) in Aylesbury,

> by the service of finding straw (*literiam*) for the king's bed, and straw (*stramen*) or grass for decking his chamber (*hospicium*) thrice a year, straw if he should come (to Aylesbury) in winter and grass if in summer, and of rendering two geese (*gantas*) in the latter case, and three eels in the former, that is to say, six geese or nine eels a year, if he came thrice a year, by which service the said Roger and his heirs are to hold the land and the office of otter-hunter (*lutracionem*). [23]

In the following year, he receives money to join his royal master with horses and dogs. [24] There were originally eight hounds in the pack, and – apart from the occasional sport they provided – their chief task was that of protecting the royal fishstews on which the household depended for supplies of freshwater fish in Lent; these, of course, were especially inviting to otters, the 'vermin of the water'. [25]

It is possible that 'Follus' here is simply an early example of an occupational surname that has been handed down from an antecedent in the royal service; but, if so, it is not used of any of Roger's known successors in the serjeanty or office of otter-hunter, [26] and there is really no good reason to doubt that the two occupations of fool and master of otter-hounds were successfully combined in the same person – given, of course, that Roger was a fool of the 'artificial' kind.

There are hints indeed of a more general association of hunting and fooling, the origins of which are now lost to us.[27] In the reigns of John and Henry III, we shall shortly encounter a royal huntsman variously named as John le Follus, John Stultus and John Fatuus, who also has charge of a pack of hounds. The two professions (of huntsman and fool) are linked, not only by the patronage and favours heaped upon both by a succession of kings from Henry II to Edward II, but, throughout the same period, by an equally marked antipathy on the part of churchmen. In the course of one, typical diatribe against huntsmen and foresters, Walter Map lets fall the enigmatic remark, 'They get no nearer to mirth than murder'.[28]

It is time to return to Eleanor. Though it would seem she was able to give a certain amount of encouragement and patronage to French-speaking poets like Geoffrey Gaimar and the Jerseyman Wace, and is confidently stated to have brought over from France *trouvères* (poets or composers of songs, presumably of the minstrel kind), it may be doubted whether the conditions of her early married life with Henry – giving birth to five children in a matter of seven years and, when not occupied in childbirth, riding behind him on a mule as he made his relentless progresses through the often wild terrain of his vast domains – would have afforded her much leisure or opportunity for cultural pursuits. As relations with her husband deteriorated under these and other strains, it was in Poitiers that Eleanor came to settle and to spend most of her time, ruling over her duchy of Aquitaine with her favourite son Richard at her side. It was in Poitiers that she became the presiding genius over that 'society of troubadours and knights who lived for chivalry and war',[29] and established her famous 'courts of love'.

The word *trouvère* – so far as I have been able to determine – is absent from the English records; its nearest equivalent is probably *citharista*, harper. But only one harper comes to light in the whole of Henry's reign of over thirty years. This is a man called Henry, who – we learn again from a later book of fees – had been given an heiress, Emma, in marriage, along with her inheritance from her father (William de Grandune), and the manor of Chaugrave in Wallingford.[30] As it would be highly unusual for a native minstrel – even a royal harper – to be given a bride of Norman blood, the man is more likely to have been a French immigrant of the *trouvère* type.

However, the life-span of such immigrants was naturally short and, if they married like Henry the harper, their descendants would soon have been naturalised; while retaining the name 'Le Harpour', many are seen to have passed out of the minstrel profession altogether, joining the swelling ranks of minor landed gentry – a process which the more divided nature of English society can only have encouraged. It may be significant that when, in the following reign, Richard's chancellor and regent, William Longchamp, felt the need of *trouvères* to boost his flagging reputation in England, it was again to France that he had to send for them.

Eleanor's influence on English minstrelsy appears to have been small. But there is one distinction that cannot be denied her: that of bearing and raising the only known English troubadour, Richard Coeur de Lion. (It may, however, be questioned whether 'troubadour' here means anything more than that he composed occasional songs in the language and style of Aquitaine and Provence.)

Richard's reputation as crusader and king is encrusted with legend. Though English by birth he was in every other respect – upbringing, culture, language and tastes – the most foreign of kings. There can be little doubt of where his heart really lay; – in the land where he had spent his formative years under the tutelage of his mother – Aquitaine.

The story of Blondel – the faithful minstrel who went in search of his master when Richard was captured by the German Emperor on his return from the East – is part and parcel of the Lionheart legend and, as such, invites a large degree of scepticism. It is hardly necessary to repeat the details of the story which first appears in the work of a fourteenth-century French minstrel known as the Ménestrel de Reims.[31] Briefly, a minstrel called Blondel, whom the king had known intimately since childhood, resolved to learn the whereabouts of the imprisoned monarch and went in search of him. Hearing of a certain German castle where a mysterious prisoner was kept in secret, he made his way there, ingratiated himself with its lord by means of his minstrel skills, and was invited to stay for the winter. One day, at Easter, he happened to be in a garden at the base of the tower in which Richard was imprisoned; the king saw him from a window of his cell and, to attract the minstrel's attention, sang the opening of a song which the two of them had formerly composed together. Blondel, recognising his master, responded by completing the song. Blondel then returned quickly to England and informed Richard's friends of his whereabouts. By their means, the necessary ransom was raised and he was released.

Clearly, much of this is pure invention. Historically, the king was never really lost; the difficulty of effecting his release lay not in any doubt as to his whereabouts but simply in the magnitude of the ransom demanded – which invalidates the story of Blondel's search and discovery. Whatever the name of Richard's loyal minstrel, it is unlikely to have been Blondel, which is that of a well-authenticated French troubadour poet of the time, Blondel de Neele, whose works have been published but of whom much scholarly research has failed to provide any hint of a role in Richard's rescue. It has been suggested that the whole episode was invented by the Minstrel of Rheims to 'glorify a fellow poet and a famous patron of troubadours, Richard I'.[32]

But, like most of the other legends that have gathered about the person of Richard and which now tend only to obscure him from view, there may be a grain or two of truth in this one. Richard *did* write and compose songs; the suggestion in the story that the one used as a recognition signal between the king and Blondel had been composed by the two of them in collaboration has an authentic ring. And Richard *had* left behind him in England a favoured singer for whom he provided a London home during his absence:-

RICHARD by the grace of God King of England, Duke of Normandy (and) Aquitaine, Count of Anjou, to his Archbishops, Bishops, Barons, Justices, Sheriffs and all his officers and faithful (subjects) of his whole land, salvation. Know ye that we have given granted and confirmed to Vassall our singer (*Vassallo cantori nostro*) and his heirs the land of Erberie which was wont to render five shillings a year, with a house in Oldestret which belongs to the same land, for a half pound of cummin to be rendered yearly. Wherefore we will and firmly ordain (etc. etc.). Witnesses: Hugh, bishop of Durham, William Marshal and sixteen other names. Given at Dover the sixth day of December by the hand of William (bishop of) Ely elect, our Chancellor, and in the first year of our reign. [33]

The fact that this was done at Dover in the last, hectic days before Richard set sail for Normandy and the East, suggests a last-minute decision. Perhaps Vassall had intended to go with him but was found to be too ill or too old.

If it is fitting that the only extant royal charter granting land to a minstrel from the reign of Richard should be in favour of a singer, it is perhaps equally appropriate that its equivalent in the reign of his younger brother John, who succeeded him, should benefit a fool. It dates from the first year of his reign – before his Coronation – as we can tell from the omission from the preamble of the phrase, 'King of England'.

JOHN, by the grace of God. Know ye that we have given, and by this present charter have confirmed to William Picol, our fool, *Fons Ossanne* with all the appurtenances to have and to hold to him and his heirs by doing therefor to us yearly the service of a fool as long as he shall live, and after his decease his heirs shall hold the same by rendering unto us yearly the service of one pair of gilt spurs etc. etc. [34]

This sounds like a retirement grant. As his 'serjeanty service', William is to continue to perform as a fool but now on only one occasion yearly, probably at Christmas; after his death, his heirs are considerably allowed to present instead a pair of spurs. The man plagued all his life to this point by lack of an adequate inheritance – John 'Lackland' as his father jokingly called him – thus takes the first available opportunity to reward his even more landless and looked-down-upon fool.

That John was no saint is immediately obvious. That he could be cruel and avaricious with a child-like greed for gold, jewels and the good things of life generally, is beyond dispute. And nowhere is this unscrupulous side of his character more apparent than in his treatment of the Jews. In 1198–9, the year of John's accession, we learn from a later Book of Fees that 'the land of Moses, the Jew, was confiscated by the lord King; and Vitalis the Vielle-player has it, on the authority of the lord King John; its value is half a mark'. [35]

There appears, however, to have been another and better side to John: a vitality, a refreshing lack of humbug and hypocrisy in his view of himself and others, an accessibility and – where gold was not involved – an apparently genuine concern for justice which did not exclude the interests of the common people.

In spite of the paucity of records, there can be little doubt of his liking for minstrels and minstrelsy – in line with his hedonistic philosophy of life. Though there are occasional references to harpers, it is not always clear whether they were his own or survivors from a previous reign. Thus, in 1203, Alexander the harper receives a 'prebend which Passemer had' and, in about 1211, another harper called Roger is given five shillings for 'carrying the mantle while the King is in Cornwall' – a serjeanty service of the less arduous kind; in spite of which, it is interesting to see that Roger is paid for its performance. [36] But John's personal tastes would seem to have lain more in the direction of fiddlers and fools. Vitalis having retired and been settled on the former property of the unfortunate Moses, he is replaced as the king's violist by a man called Vyelet, who is recorded as receiving wages of a whole mark (13s. 4d.) on four occasions in 1210–1, while the king was on a series of progresses taking in Bridge-north in Somerset and Ipswich in Suffolk. [37]

John shared to the full his father's enthusiasm for the hunt; it is in this reign that we first have notice of that other huntsman-fool already referred to, John le Fol (Stultus etc.). The first mention of him is in 1210 when, in partnership with an Irishman called Brian, he is in charge of forty-four dogs. In the following year, a total of a hundred dogs are accounted for, of which John has personal charge of twenty-nine; a little later, the number is down to fourteen. [38] This is not demotion. The huntsmen and their packs move about the country freely, from forest to forest, in varying combinations of men and dogs, in response to the particular requirements of the job in hand. The venison and other meat which their labours provide is especially on demand at the three principal crown-wearings of the year – Easter, Whitsun and Christmas – when the king's magnates gather in force (wherever he has appointed) to pay him homage and enjoy his hospitality, consuming vast quantities of food. In 1232 (in the following reign), John and his current partner, Philip de Candever, are authorised to take forty beasts – 'as many does as deer' – from the forest of Whitlewod; and, in 1240, sixty swine and sows from St Briavels, and 'to cause it to be well salted, kept, and carried to Winchester against Christmas'.[39] This produce of the forests is thus of considerable economic importance to the crown – quite apart from the occasional sport it provides.

In May 1242, John le Fol was receiving 21d. daily from Henry III for himself, his horses and dogs. Two years later, he was rewarded with about twenty acres of land (a virgate) in Sutton for his maintenance till 'he should otherwise be provided for', and was ordered to hand over his hounds to the Bishop of Carlisle. It seems that he failed to do so – or the order was rescinded. At any rate, he remained active as a huntsman, in partnership with another long-serving colleague, Walter Luvel, till 1247, when – after thirty-seven years service – he was finally awarded a pension of 7½d. per day – the wages of a royal squire or master minstrel.[40]

Another fool in the service of King John, Ralph Stultus, is recorded in 1210 as being jointly responsible for twelve greyhounds;[41] but I have found no other reference to him.

The extent to which these huntsmen were also active as fools, as their names indicate, remains an open question. Clearly, John and his predecessor, Roger the otter-hunter, were men of ability and intelligence, living rough, peripatetic lives, but capable of receiving and carrying out written instructions. If fools they were, they were fools of a very different kind from the spoilt playthings of later Renaissance courts. They must have been more like present-day travelling circus people – useful with their hands, good with animals, putting on their finery only at the day's end; versatile as performers, skilled in the playing of musical instruments, specialising in broad comedy of the slapstick kind. (The linking of fools and minstrels generally with *feasts* is notable throughout the whole of the middle ages. The waferers come to mind: providing wafers for the *issue de table* – the final stage of feasts – doubling as after-dinner entertainers. Did the fools come in with the meat?)

We can supplement our knowledge of how minstrels were regarded at this time by looking at some surviving sculptural representations.They are rarely complimentary. A rather dignified figure of a man playing a viol held between his knees in Oakham Castle is partnered by a rote-player in the form of an ass.[42] In the crypt of Canterbury Cathedral, a series of grotesque reliefs includes among its subjects goats playing the shawm, cornett and gigue.

Goat playing gigue. Crypt of Canterbury Cathedral.

We are reminded of John of Salisbury's strange procession of *joculatores* and his attitude to them, which belong precisely to this period. Most eloquent of all, perhaps, are the figures of a dancer, a fiddler, and two men fighting monsters – again belonging to Canterbury Cathedral – which recent restoration reveals as having been deliberately carved with one ear missing; a sign of their degraded status as petty criminals.[43] (Mutilation by severance of an ear was a common medieval punishment for trespass and other misdemeanours.)

One-eared gigator. Photo: *The Independent*.

Such figures as these are a stark reminder that the lot of the majority of minstrels in the twelfth century was as harsh and brutal as it could be, and that – in the eyes of most educated people, Norman or English – minstrels remained beyond the pale – if not actually diabolical!

These impressions are confirmed by an extraordinary episode from John's reign which, though lacking support from contemporary sources, appears from its historical consequences to have a reasonably factual basis. A fair had been founded by Ranulph, first earl of Chester, in honour of the city's patron, St Werburgh, which – like Bartholomew's – offered to all comers protection from arrest for previously-committed crimes – an obvious magnet to rogues and minstrels of the less reputable kind. In about the year 1212 or a little later, Ranulph's descendant, the last earl whose name was also Ranulph, found himself besieged by the Welsh and in dire straits in his castle of Rhuddlan in North Wales, and sent to his Constable back in Chester, Roger de Lacy, for reinforcements. Having no other men at his disposal, de Lacy (nicknamed 'Hell' because of his fiery temperament), remembering that St Werburgh's Fair was then in progress, recruited an army of minstrels and other 'loose people' he found at the Fair and – by allurement of the minstrels' music – led then to the relief of the besieged earl. The Welsh – who, it should be said, had the contemporary reputation of being brave and ferocious fighters – were so alarmed by the appearance of Lacy's motley rabble as they approached that they immediately raised the siege and took to the hills. [44]

6

The King's Minstrels: Henry III to Edward II

The character of Henry III, as portrayed in some older biographies and political histories of the thirteenth century, is of an obstinate but fundamentally weak man, ruled by superstition, who is invariably on the wrong side in the constitutional conflicts of his time; a man whose reign is only saved from ultimate shipwreck by the intervention of his 'strong' son, Edward of Monmouth. But Henry's long reign – especially from 1227 when he took power into his own hands after a ten-year minority – has been justly described as the spring-time of the new Gothic style in English art and architecture, a style instinct with life, energy and nervous tension. [1] Divorced from their political context, such developments can easily be made to appear as almost inevitable, as somehow bound to happen in response to mysterious, evolutionary forces implicit in their own aesthetic forms. By examining the State records – especially the more detailed and intimate entries of the Wardrobe and Liberate rolls which now, for the first time, become available – we see, on the contrary, the outline of a very human process whereby one man, with almost obsessive determination and singlemindedness, wrests into his own hands the initiative of patronage that had so far lain with the Church, and uses it to bring those very developments into being on English soil; a man who was so enamoured of Sainte Chapelle in Paris that it was said of him that he would like to have taken it off in a cart if he could. [2]

Henry's personal involvement in the great building works of his reign, especially at Westminster, is well-documented; much less so is his encouragement of literature, music and minstrelsy. From the beginning, he surrounded himself with artists of every description – poets, painters, musicians and harpers – irrespective of their origin or nationality; and though individuals came and went, he continued to do so – in spite of the unpopularity that they often brought him. His son Edward I, who (unlike so many royal heirs) never ceased to love and respect his father, inherited this cultural legacy and brought it to splendid fruition. From the mass of detailed information about Edward's patronage of minstrels – which the researches of Dr Bullock-Davies have done so much to uncover and elucidate – I shall take a cross-section at a wedding-feast in 1297. The effects of this continuous royal patronage through the century, in terms of a steady rise in both the social status of minstrels in general, and the significance of their contribution as performers and creative artists to the cultural life of the nation, will, I hope, become gradually apparent; effects which not even the amiable but politically-disastrous eccentricities of Henry's grandson, Edward II, could wholly dispel.

Beginning with Henry himself, it is not so much the fact of his patronage of minstrels that is unusual but the importance that he gives to it, and the intimate nature of the relationships that he is seen to have with these men, extending also to their families. There is nothing out of the way, for example, about the pension he grants to a fiddler called John de Metz in 1238; the amount (2½d. per day) is not even especially generous; what is unusual is to find him, a couple of years later, ordering a fine new outfit for John's wife: tunic, supertunic and cloak, with lining and trimmings of rabbit-fur.[3]

In 1243, new robes for Christmas are provided for the singer Lorea and his wife; and when, in the following year, Lorea dies, an embroidered pall is ordered from Mabel of Saint Edmund, at a cost of ten pounds, to cover his coffin. A payment on the same occasion of five shillings to Edward, son of Odo (Edward of Westminster, 'keeper of the king's works'), suggests that Lorea was one of very few performers – and certainly the first – to have been given the honour of a funeral and internment in Westminster Abbey, which the king was then engaged in re-building.[4] There are robes too for a German minstrel (*istrio*) called Aleman, who is first mentioned (in 1247) as attached to one of Henry's half-brothers, Geoffrey de Lusignan, and then, in the following year, as *istrio regis*, 'entertainer to the king'.[5] Two other *istriones* of Geoffrey's rewarded by the king have the unusual names of Clarin and Lancelot.[6] Payment of 16s. in 1237 for 'clasps, hasps and nails of silver for the King's great book of Romances' reminds us of Henry's interest in literature, and that he was probably the only medieval king to have employed a full-time poet (*versificator*) as one of his household staff. This was Master Henry of Avranches. He may well have been a contributor to the king's book, but the first mention of him is in 1244, when he is asked to compose a Latin verse for a ring to be offered in honour of St Thomas of Westminster. While in the king's service, he receives 20s. a month; and, in 1251, a peremptory writ goes out to the effect that he is to have 100s. of his arrears of wages 'without delay or objection – *even if the exchequer is closed*'. In the same year, he is rewarded with two jars of the best wine – the first of many – and five years later is granted 6d. daily 'for life'. Sad to say, with the single exception of the little verse he wrote for the ring, nothing of his literary labours over nearly twenty years has survived – or has been identified . All we know is that he was a clerk, and that he gave offence in one of his writings to a Cornish poet named Michael Blaunpayne, who reciprocated with some Latin verses of his own; these have survived, but are so scurrilous and, at the same time, so completely uninformative that I shall not do Master Henry the injustice of quoting them here. He is last mentioned – as receiving a new robe – in 1262.[7]

The pervasive influence at court of Henry's adored queen, Eleanor of Provence whom he married in 1236, cannot be overlooked; not only was she the daughter of a famous troubadour poet, Berenger, count of Provence, but her mother is reputed to have exchanged verses with Richard Coeur de Lion, and Eleanor first brought herself to the attention of the English royal house by sending a poem of her own composition in Occitan to Henry's brother, Richard of Cornwall.[8]

The musical establishment of the king's chapel – where he attended Mass several times each day – was modest, consisting of three singing clerks whose names were Walter de Lanches, Peter of Beddington and Robert of Canterbury; but Henry takes the same personal interest in their welfare as in that of his minstrels. Robert was a married clerk; his wife Isabel receives a robe of green cloth priced at 2s. a yard, with the usual trimmings, and Robert is given 40s. to buy a robe for his daughter.[9] (It should be added that the king was equally generous – even prodigal – to the poor; his gifts were not limited to a small clique of royal favourites. The great hall of Westminster was regularly filled at his order with poor folk to be fed and provided with shoes and clothes.)[10]

It is to this reign that the earliest notated secular song – *Sumer is icumen in, Lhude sing cuccu!* – has been dated, and the way in which the simple charm of its lyric is set to music of elaborate sophistication makes it an appropriate *leitmotiv* for the age. Summer was indeed coming in – not least, for the minstrels; not only does the phrase *istrio regis* first appear in these years – implying an officially-recognised status at court for the king's musicians and entertainers – but the Latin *ministrallus* also now occurs for the first time, as applied to a Frenchman called Eustace de Reyns (Rennes?) for whom a robe is ordered in 1266.[11]

There was, of course, a lighter, not to say frivolous, side to the life of Henry's court. In 1254, John de Blavia, *istrio regis*, is given a good robe to replace one that the king had 'torn up'; and three years later, Fortunatus de Luca is similarly rehabilitated after Henry had 'pushed him into the water (*projecit in aquam*)'. What is highly unusual about Fortunatus is that he is described in the Close Roll as *miles istrio noster*, 'our minstrel knight'; and the many robes that he receives during his ten years of service (from 1247) are specified *sicut uni de militibus regis*, 'just as for one of the king's knights', with the appropriate trimmings of squirrel-fur and other accessories. I suggest he was a court buffoon (*scurra*) of the type defined by Thomas de Chabham in the early years of the century, who 'frequent the courts of the great and say shameful things concerning those who are not present so as to delight the rest'; a precursor of the court buffoons of Renaissance Italy.[12] Fortunatus' successor, Jacominus, is described, not as 'miles', but as *stultus et istrione regis*, 'the king's fool and minstrel' – a person, doubtless, who the king could push in the water whenever he felt like it without too much consequent fuss![13]

But the longest-serving and most generously-rewarded of all Henry's minstrels was Richard the Harper.

Richard is first heard of in 1230, when he receives 'protection' to accompany the young king – now three years his own master – overseas.[14] Then, after a silence of twelve years – during which he probably alternated service at court with the harpers' more usual touring – Richard is retained to entertain the king's children at Windsor, their permanent nursery.[15] As Prince Edward (the future Edward I) was only three at this time and his sister Margaret little more than a year, the choice of a harper as children's entertainer may appear a trifle odd; I take it as a demonstration of Henry's good sense, and faith in the educative powers of music and poetry. From the fact that Edward grew up to have a marked partiality for the harp, and is invariably found to have had at least one harper closely at hand throughout the whole of his life, we may safely assume that Richard's appointment was a success. In the same year (perhaps as a reward), the harper – now named as Master Richard – is exempted from 'suits of counties and hundreds and from being put on assizes, juries and recognitions'; a rare privilege and, at the same time, an indication of his growing prosperity, as only men of property would qualify for such duties in the first place. The title *Magister* was given as a matter of right to clerks and graduates (usually the same thing); but this is the first instance I have come across of its being awarded to a minstrel, and it has clearly been earned. It carries with it a social rank equivalent to that of a squire (the first degree of knighthood) and, of course, a correspondingly higher rate of pay.[16]

In 1246, for the celebration of his wife Beatrice's 'purification' (after childbirth), he receives from the king a tun of good wine;[17] a quantity which would have amounted to about 250 gallons! By 1250, Richard is involved in a legal dispute over tenements in Devon and, two years later, a further tun of wine is ordered to be carried to his house in Bury St Edmunds; for some reason this failed to arrive, and a sharp reminder is sent to the Sheriff of Suffolk to deliver it without delay.[18] In 1260, there is a mandate to provide Master Richard, described as one of the king' serjeants, along with Master Thomas, king's surgeon – 'who have served the King long and have not yet had whereof to sustain themselves in his service' – with 'lands of wards or escheats' worth £7 10s. a year.[19] In the same year, he turns up in a list of distinguished names – actually between the Archbishop of York and the Abbess of Lacock – as exempted from jury service in Gloucestershire, indicating that he had acquired property there too.[20]

If Richard was looking forward now to a peaceful retirement in Suffolk after thirty years' service, it was probably denied him. 1260 saw the beginnings of the Barons' Revolt; and a scrap of paper attached to the Close

Roll for that year suggests that along with two fiddlers – Gylet of Ipswich and a man called Raulinus, who was a retainer of John Walerand – and other of the king's oldest friends and servants, he was actively involved in defence of the royal interest. [21] There were to be times in the next few years when Henry was to find himself with little other support than that of his immediate family and the loyal servants of his household.

At Christmas 1296, Edward I, known as 'Longshanks' – he was tall and imposing in stature – visited Ipswich in Suffolk for the marriage of his youngest daughter, Elizabeth, to the Count of Holland; it was the occasion of a remarkable display of professional entertainment, of which the details are preserved in an official record of the fees that were paid. [22] The bride Elizabeth, born at Rhuddlan Castle in Wales, was fourteen at the time. Her bridegroom – John I, count of Holland and Zeeland – was but two years older, and had succeeded to his title only in June when his predecessor had been assassinated. Why was the small but flourishing east-coast port of Ipswich chosen for such an important royal event? Perhaps because it was a diplomatically convenient middle-ground between the capital London and the Low Countries, for which the newly-weds were afterwards due to depart.

Militarily, it was a moment of triumph for the king; only a few weeks earlier he had returned from a short and brutal campaign in Scotland, during which opposition to his claim to over-lordship had been crushed and a projected alliance between the Scots and his old enemy, Philip IV of France, nipped in the bud. It was thus as the effective ruler of a newly-united England, Scotland and Wales – with the Stone of Destiny in his baggage train – that Edward entered Ipswich. Now he could turn his mind again to the implementation of his grand strategy for allying the princes of the Low Countries against the French king, a plan which the marriage of Elizabeth and John of Holland was intended to further. (His third daughter, Margaret, had married the Duke of Brabant in 1290.)

Shortage of cash in the exchequer rarely inhibited Edward from whatever he regarded as politically necessary expenditure. While the Dutch prince and his party waited with as much patience as they could muster in nearby Colchester, the king entered the town liberties on December 23, 1296, and began a leisurely and wholesale distribution of alms. [23] In the Christmas week following his arrival, four thousand poor people were fed at a cost of more than fifty pounds, a very large amount in medieval terms when the wages of a labourer were twopence a day. There was frantic activity behind the scenes; much coming and going of horses and carts to Colchester, while Elizabeth's robemaker Henry, with thirty-five locally-recruited assistants, laboured to complete the bridal trousseau, which traditionally included hangings for the marriage bed.

Meanwhile, entertainers and minstrels of every kind had been gathering in their hundreds. (At Margaret's wedding in 1290, Walter de

Stertone, the king's harper, had distributed £100 among 426 minstrels. [24])
Of the Ipswich minstrels, the names, specialities and fees of about thirty
are recorded; I shall say what I know about each.

The formal entertainment began in earnest on the evening of St John's
day (December 27) with a solo performance for the young Prince Edward
– the future Edward II, now thirteen years-old – by a *saltatrix* or female
acrobat with the charming and appropriate name of Matilda Makejoy:
'making her vaults in the presence of the Lord Edward, the King's son, in
the King's Hall, at Ipswich, *ijs.*' [25]

Matilda was not one of the king's regular minstrels, but was a representative of that mass of popular entertainers of the streets and fairs we
have already glimpsed at work in chapter two – where one of her sisters
was seen balancing on swords. All the same, she seems to have become
something of a favourite with the royal children. Her three recorded court
appearances – of which this was the first – cover fourteen years, so she
was probably now in her early teens. (She was also at the great Pentecost
feast of 1306 at Westminster, where Prince Edward was knighted; and, in
1311, at Framlingham Castle, again in Suffolk, to give a special performance for Edward I's children by his second wife, Margaret of France, the
ten and eleven-year-old princes Edmund and Thomas. Edward's first
wife, the beloved Eleanor of Castile, had died in 1290.)

In what did Matilda's act consist, and what did she wear for it?
Graphic evidence of the manuscript drawings suggests two broad
categories of *saltatrix*. [26] Performers of the first type wear long, ample
skirts – as shown on page 12 – which would clearly make running or
vaulting movements impossible; their long hair is braided in elaborate
coiffures and they specialise in strange poses and balancing acts. Matilda
then – especially at this early stage of her career – would seem to have
belonged to a second category, more precisely defined as *tornatrices*, female tumblers, who wore little more than a 'kirtle' or brief tunic.

By the thirteenth century, the art of the acrobatic dancer was already at
an advanced stage of technique, and employed an internationally-recog-
nised terminology. Of vaults, there were *le tor francois, le tor Champenois, le
tor d'Espaigne, les tors c'on fait en Bretaigne, le tor Loheraine* and *le tor
romain.* [27] To have enjoyed the royal patronage over so many years, we can
be sure that Matilda was exceptionally gifted, probably the outstanding
exponent of her art within the span of her active career. [28]

We can only guess at the reason why her performance before the boy
prince took place in advance of the wedding banquet. Perhaps it was
considered inappropriate for a formal feast – or maybe Matilda simply
needed more space than would then be available. She is the only female
performer mentioned in the record; but the fact that her fee was only two
shillings – the wages of a labourer for twelve days, but meagre indeed
compared to the amounts that follow – had more to do with her being also

the only unattached minstrel to appear there. Such fees, as we have already seen, have more to do with status than performance.

William Bruges, Garter King.   British Library MS Stowe 594, f.5b.

Matilda Makejoy's energetic display was but a prelude to the mixed bill of
entertainment to follow on January 7, the day of the wedding. In contrast

to Matilda, the performers were either members of the king's regular company of minstrels or had travelled to Ipswich in the retinues of visiting nobles and bishops.

The king's minstrels received a daily rate of pay for the times they were in attendance at court. They belonged to a class of servants who, in John Pecham's phrase, *vont et vient*.[29] As a group, they had a permanent presence; as individuals, it was expected and allowed that they should absent themselves at irregular intervals and for irregular periods to look to their personal affairs. For the minstrels, this meant touring – either on their own behalf, as 'the King's Harper' or 'the King's Piper', or as a group, 'the King's Minstrels' etc. As the court itself was constantly on the move at this period, accompanying the king on his endless progresses – dispensing justice, receiving petitions or pursuing his wars – to re-establish contact cannot always have been easy. It will be remembered, however, that at this particular point in time, the household had only recently come to rest after its return from the Scottish campaign of the autumn; we catch it at what must have been near its full, war-time strength. (Even in peace, the household constituted a standing HQ staff for potential military operations, and the minstrels were an integral part of that establishment.)

The senior men among them – those like Richard the Harper in the previous reign who were styled *Magister* or *Monsire* - get 7½d. per day, the others 4½d. The substantial rewards that came their way on occasions such as this were therefore bonuses, *largesse*. While on duty, they also benefitted from free board and lodging, stabling for their horses and twice-yearly issues of clothing – but they had to be there on the appointed day to collect it. The 'masters' in particular were men of some standing at court; they had a servant to attend them, and usually had families and permanent establishments of their own in the city; they were the trusted servants and companions of the king; their function as entertainers was secondary to that or rather, was an aspect of it – and may sometimes have been combined with other services as watchmen, messengers or waferers. Their 'minstrelsy' was not defined by their musical or other skills, but by the nature of their relationship with the king.

A few among them were further honoured by the title 'Le Roy' (King) – a style which now only survives among officers of the College of Heralds such as 'Garter King of Arms'. The heralds and minstrels were so closely associated at this period that it is difficult to be sure of their precise relationship one to the other, or where, indeed, the distinction between them lay. (In the Ipswich manuscript, their names are thoroughly mixed under the general heading of 'Minstrels'.) Le Roy Robert (Robert Parvus) – absent from Ipswich, probably on garrison duty in Scotland, and undoubtedly the senior King Herald – is also described in contemporary records as 'King's Trumpeter', 'King Robert the Taborer' and 'Robert, King of Minstrels': a man of many talents in the true minstrel tradition. Of the five 'Kings' present at Ipswich, Le Roy Druet was mainly known as a fiddler and Le Roy Capenny as a harper. In the Celtic tradition, the *Arwyddfardd* (heralds) had formed a regular division of Welsh minstrelsy.[30] As propagandist of his lord's ancestry and exploits, the harper-minstrel required the genealogical and military knowledge of the herald; as *alter ego* of the monarch in his function as royal ambassador on the field of battle, the herald was distinguished by the surrogate title of 'King'. (It is interesting that when, in Shakespeare's play, Henry V wishes to disguise his identity in the English camp at Agincourt, he should give his name as 'Harry le roi' (IV.i. 49–50). 'Le Roy?', returns Pistol, 'a Cornish name: art thou of Cornish crew?') The honour is thought to have been conferred by a ceremony in which the monarch rested his crown for a moment on the head of the recipient, thus imparting something of his own unique charisma and authority. Its sacramental nature is brought out by the fact that a cup of wine was then passed from sovereign to servant, and shared between them. (In 1472, the creation of a 'Richmond King of Arms' involved a 'baptism'.[31]) The illustration given above of a later 'Garter King' (William Bruges) shows him actually wearing a crown as the symbol of his office, kneeling before the patron of his order, St George. The herald/minstrel thus became bound to the king in a very personal way, and the records show that – even in the time of the unpredictable Edward II – it was a bond that was rarely betrayed on either side.

If the entertainment of January 7 was in the nature of a command performance, the form that it took was that of a cabaret at a great state banquet – the royal wedding feast. We have to picture the king and the newly-wedded couple seated at the top table of a crowded hall, with a space kept clear in front of them for the performers; other tables were fitted along the sides and at the back of the hall, where the Ipswich Bailiffs and senior Portmen were probably allotted places. In the manuscript – as we might expect in what is, after all, a financial statement – the minstrels are listed according to the size of their fees, in roughly descending order of magnitude; not, as here, by speciality.

I take the heralds first. I have found no contemporary pictures of heralds, but the self-portrait given below of Gelre, a later king of Arms to the Count of Holland (from 1390), may stand as representative of the best of the type: thrusting forwards with characteristic energy, his tabard flying in the wind, poet and heraldic artist *par excellence* – and every inch a soldier!

Of the five heralds present – all *Reges Haraldorum* (King heralds) – we know the minstrel skills of only two, Capenny and Druet. Le Roy Page, who heads the original list receiving fifty shillings, is *de Hollandia*. The heralds are also known to have had an entrepreneurial function at court as arrangers of state entertainment, as of pageantry and tournaments.

Self-portrait of the herald Gelre.
Bibliothèque Royale Albert 1er, Brussels.

(The latter were, in fact, banned throughout most of Edward's reign; he had too many real wars to fight.) The precedence given to Page may be no more than courtesy to a distinguished visiting herald; the hard work of organisation and 'stage management' is likely to have fallen to Le Roy Robert's acknowledged deputy as senior King herald, Nicholas Morel. Morel was a Norfolk man, a former tenant there of Sir Robert Clifford, later Marshal of England, and it is probably through Sir Robert's influence that he had come into the king's service. [32] At the end of the month, he was to be sent off with a letter of recommendation to the Prior of Merton for a period of recuperation. (The letter has a sting in its tail; if he behaves other than 'courteously and honestly', the king is to be fully informed!) [33]

John de Monhaut, minstrel and King herald, is linked with Druet and Capenny as receiving forty shillings, but we are not told what instrument he played. [34]

Of the thirty, named 'Ipswich minstrels', no less than ten are harpers. Le Roy Capenny (James de Cowpen) is a fascinating figure. He is first heard of in 1290 at the wedding feast of Princess Joan and Gilbert of Clare at Westminster, where he appears in the record along with 'King' Grey of England – a *Rex haraldorum* who has since disappeared from the scene – as 'King Caupenny de Scotia'. [35]

Since then, disaster had overtaken the Scots' throne. Alexander III – who is most likely to have given Capenny his original commision as King herald – had died in 1284 without a male heir. All hopes had thus come to rest on the Maid of Norway, Alexander's young grandaughter, who was affianced to Prince Edward. Then, in October 1290, had come the terrible news of her death in Orkney. In thirteenth-century political ethics, a kingdom which found itself in the unfortunate condition of having no acknowledged ruler or heir to the throne was in grave danger. After a period of uncertainty, in which Edward interposed himself as referee between a number of claimants of whom John Balliol and Robert Bruce were the only serious contenders, Balliol had been enthroned with Edward's support in return for his acceptance of the English king's claim to over-lordship; it proved too high a price to pay, and Edward made his client's position in Scotland impossible by pushing his demands to the utmost. Predictably perhaps, Balliol was rejected by most of his own magnates, who turned for assistance to Philip IV of France. War with England had thus become inevitable. In a determined drive north, Edward had taken Berwick-on-Tweed, the Scots' feudal host had been decisively defeated, and Balliol was forced to abdicate and was humiliated – the royal arms literally stripped from his coat. [36] Thereafter, the Scots' King herald was without a patron or employer.

Capenny's birthplace, Cowpen, was not in Scotland at all as we know it now, but in Northumberland, close to Morphen, then part of the 'disputed lands'. As it happens, we know that Edward had been in that area as recently as the end of September; he had set out from Morphen on his journey south on October 1. [37] Perhaps Capenny had come to him there, or Edward – remembering his performance at Joan's wedding feast six years earlier – sought him out. In the circumstances, the unattached minstrel would have needed little persuasion to accompany the king to Ipswich. That is speculation; all we know for sure is that Capenny's next appearance in the records is at the Ipswich wedding, and that he was taken on to Edward's regular payroll shortly afterwards.

There can be little doubt of his usefulness to the king, both as herald for the military intelligence he possessed – his knowledge of the Scots nobility and their relative strengths and weaknesses – and, as former harper to the kings of Scotland whose throne Edward had now abrogated, for his propaganda value. In 1305, the king was to give him a gold clasp worth £4 10s. He is then named as 'King Copyn, herald', which illustrates both the happy inconsistency of the wardrobe clerks in matters of spelling – other variants are Caupenny, Capyn, Capigny, Capainy and Copiny – and that he was still regarded and employed to some extent as herald as well as minstrel. At the Pentecost feast of 1306, he received £4 15s. (in today's money, something over £2,000) as his own reward, and was further entrusted with the payment of the king's largesse to several distinguished foreign visitors, including Philip de Cambrai and Le Roy de Champagne. Two years later, when Edward lay dying at Lanercost, exhausted by his efforts to launch yet another campaign against the Scots, he was prominent in 'helping to organise stage plays (*miracula*) to amuse the queen, now taking his turn with the other minstrels in easing the king's long hours of pain'. [38]

Of two other harpers who may also have been attached to the king, there is less to be said; these are Henry le Harpur and Laurence le Harpour, who receive ten shillings each, along with the harpers of the Earl of Oxford and Lord Thomas de Multon. Laurence re-appears at the Pentecost feast of 1306, and that is all we know about him. [39] Henry may be the 'Henricus de Blida' who also appears in 1306 but, three years earlier, is reported as entertaining the Prince at Newcastle, where he is described (in one of the prince's wardrobe books) as 'the old king's minstrel', and receives 6s. 8d. to buy himself a tunic. [40]

Robert de Vere, fifth earl of Oxford, had died on August 25 while the king was besieging Berwick-on-Tweed. His body was interred in the family church at Earls Coln in Essex, and his heart separately – as was sometimes then the custom – at Ipswich Greyfriars. The earl's eldest son and heir, also called Robert, was serving the king in Gascony at the time of his father's death. When the news reached him, he returned to England and did homage to Edward at Nayland on December 5. This is how he came to be invited with his mother to the wedding, bringing his harper with him. [41] The man's name was Nicholas. There are 'letters of protection' for him when he accompanied his lord to Scotland in 1298. When, in the following year, de Vere was sent overseas again (perhaps back to Gascony), Nicholas remained behind and was appointed de Vere's 'general attorney' to represent him in a legal case which the Abbot of St Alban's was bringing against him and several others for trespass; a strong indication of the harper's literacy. [42]

Thomas Multon, a minor in the wardship of the king, had been married a few days earlier (January 3) to Elizabeth's maid-in-waiting, Eleanor, the eldest daughter of Richard de Burgh, earl of Ulster. Like the Princess and her groom, it would seem that they were little more than children. [43] But Thomas was not too young to have a personal harper, who took his turn with the others.

Capenny was not the only minstrel from north of the Tyne to have performed at the feast; we have also the *citharista* of Lord John Comyn. This was John Comyn of Badenoch the elder; called 'the Black' to distinguish him from his son of the same name, 'the Red', who was to be brutally murdered by Robert Bruce in 1306. Himself a former claimant to the Scots' throne, though never a very credible one – his title derived remotely from the fugitive Donalbane familiar to us from Shakespeare's *Macbeth* – Comyn senior was a supporter of the unfortunate Balliol who was his brother-in-law, and had opposed Edward's invasion of Scotland. Having submitted to the king at Montrose in July, he had now been exiled with other Scots' magnates to live in the south of England, where Edward could keep a watchful eye on him. The Scots' nobility, like the English, were part-Norman in blood and spoke French; the harper – though probably a native Celt – would, like the other harpers at the feast, have had command of French and would probably have performed in it. In a multilingual age, linguistic versatility was a basic requirement for the successful minstrel. (Edward is reported to have spoken English on only two occasions; once in an irreverent pun on the name of the Earl Marshal, Bigod; the other when attacked in his tent by an emissary of the Old Man of the Mountains, while crusading in 1271. It was on this latter occasion that his harper, hearing the scuffle, rushed in and proceeded to attack the assailant with a stool, although by this time the man was already dead, having been despatched by the king. [44]) The old Scots' lord and his minstrel must have attracted curious attention in Ipswich. And the minstrel may have been in some difficulty when called upon to take a turn with his instrument. In his lord's present circumstances, he had not much to sing about! Doubtless he swallowed his pride – as his master had been obliged to do – and tuned his harp to the prevailing, celebratory key; apparently with some success, for the king rewarded him with a mark.

That the Bishop of Durham should bring two harpers to Ipswich may at first surprise us. In the early years of the thirteenth century, Thomas de Chabham, sub-dean of Salisbury, wrote a penitentiary in which the minstrels of his time were categorised and graded from an ethical point of view for the guidance of confessors. His lowest category – those who expose themselves in indecent dances wearing horrible masks – were utterly condemned, as has already been mentioned. The next group – not quite so bad but still beyond the pale of what is morally acceptable – included the *scurrae* (buffoons, hangers-on) and 'those who sing stanzas to move men to lasciviousness' – perhaps referring to the singers of troubadour songs. The final group and the only one to be approved (though with a significant condition) was that of the *joculatores* who 'sing of the *gestes* of princes and the lives of the saints' – the harpers' usual matter. [45] In view of what has already been said about the attitude of the Church to minstrels generally, it is useful to be reminded that in English practice at least exceptions were made; that even the severest critic could view the harpers with a degree of tolerance, even favour.

According to the Gilbertine Canon, Robert Mannying of Brunne (no friend to the general run of minstrels), the saintly scholar and bishop Robert Grosseteste (c.1168–1253) enjoyed the services of a personal harper.

> Next hys chaumbre, besyde hys stody,
> Hys harpers chaumbre was fast therby.
> Many tymes, be nyghtys and dayys,
> He had solace of notes and layys. [46]

And Grosseteste has been described as 'in many ways the noblest Englishman of his age', scourge of the folk *ludi* and plays called *miracula* within his diocese of Lincoln. [47]

Mannying's lines were written about 1303, some fifty years after the good bishop's death, but there is contemporary evidence of such patronage by eminent and pious churchmen down the years; it is not a simple matter of clerical backsliding.

During the course of 1289 and 1290 (from which years detailed accounts of his household expenses survive), Richard de Swinfield of Hereford – a scholar, renowned in his time as an especially conscientious bishop – is entertained by a succession of harpers as he goes about his diocese. Master Henry, harper to Sir Edmund Mortimer at Wigmore, is rewarded with a shilling, and the harpers of Sir Ralph Pippard and Sir John Tregoz (a neighbour of the Bishop's at Sugwas) with two shillings each. On a rare visit to the court of Edward I at Westminster, he stops for two nights at Reading Abbey where Hugh, the Abbot's harper (*cithariste domini Abbatis Rading*), receives a relatively modest shilling. [48]

Antony Bek of Durham was a bishop of a very different type from Grosseteste and Swinfield. Though pious and obsessively chaste – he is said never to have looked a woman in the face – his appointment was none-the-less political; more a reward for devoted service as a former fellow-crusader of the young Edward, and as a royal official, than for any spiritual qualities he may have possessed. As Bishop-Palatine of Durham, he had considerable secular power at his disposal, and was expected to use it in support of the king. For the recent campaign in Scotland, he had provided a force of a thousand foot and five hundred horse and led them in person behind the sacred banner of St Cuthbert. His peacetime retinue numbered no less than a hundred and forty knights – more than that of the king. It was his pride that was to be his undoing, and the presence of this very following of knights that was to set in motion a train of events that, in 1300, led to his fall from favour. In 1296, he was on the crest of a wave. Leaving his regiment behind him in Durham, he had accompanied the king south – first to Bury for the Parliament of Clergy – and now to Ipswich. We do not know how many of his precious retinue Edward allowed him to bring, but they included his two harpers.

In 1306 (for the Pentecost feast) they are named as Guilleme le Harpour and John de Grendon. Like Edward himself, Bek was an enthusiastic falconer; he is said to have played with a falcon on his wrist during his interviews in Rome with Pope Boniface VIII. We know that a William ('Gillot the harper') was with him in 1304 because in that year he was sent with the gift of a goshawk to the king, who rewarded the minstrel with five shillings for looking after the bird and bringing it safely to him. [49] This is typical of the confidential missions with which minstrels were often entrusted by their lords. In Ipswich, the Bishop's harpers received twenty shillings each as their reward. Another minstrel on the list, named simply as 'Dureme', was probably also in the Bishop's retinue.

Fiddler playing at a feast.
British Library, MS Royal 2 B vii, ff.185v–187.

One function of the five fiddlers who were present at the feast will be apparent from the illustration above (taken from an early fourteenth-century manuscript in the British Library); they 'play in' the various courses of the meal. With the other instrumentalists, they would then have provided a musical accompaniment for the serious eating that followed, and for the non-musical acts that were interspersed between the courses as 'interludes'. If dancing were to follow the feast, they provided the music

Two minstrels playing the citole and fiddle.
British Library, MS Royal 2 B vii, f.174.

for that too – as we see them doing in the near-contemporary manuscript reproduced above. (The use of citole and fiddle together shows that instruments of different kinds are already being played in combination.)

However, though I have brought them together on the page for the sake of convenience, our five fiddlers do not make an ensemble – any more than they, with the other musicians, make an orchestra. We have to remember too that none of the music played at the feast had been scored for particular instruments; the players were expected to improvise within the range and tonal qualities of each instrument to their own or 'standard' tunes and melodies, transposing, or finding chordal harmonies in tune with other instruments or with a singer, on the pattern of the more highly developed religious music of the time, requiring skill and creative musicianship of a high order.

Master Richard Rounlo was the king's principal violist and a man of property in London; he was to remain in the royal service for a total of thirty-five years. Later in this year (1297), he was on hand to help entertain the famous composer Adenet le Roy, minstrel to the Count of Flanders, when he visited England to perform for the king; and doubtless took the opportunity of enriching his repertoire.[50] It was in ways such as this that the latest developments in music were transmitted from country to country; contacts between England and Flanders were especially close at this time. (Adenet was to be followed in 1306 by the composer and playwright, Adam de la Hale, from the French Court of Naples, who appears under his popular name of Adam le Bossu in a list of entertainers at the Pentecost feast at Westminster in that year.[51])

Since 1293, William of Roos had been semi-retired and in receipt of an annual pension from the king of five pounds; he was also exempted from jury service and from payment of certain taxes on land that he owned. If his hometown was Roos in Yorkshire, he might have travelled south with the king to contribute to the wedding festivities.[52] The third string-player is impossible to identify with certainty because he is named simply as 'John Vidulator', John the viol-player; this may have been John of Brabant who was later to find service with the Despensers. [53] Along with Richard and William, he received the top fee of fifty shillings. Le Roy Druet comes next in order of largesse; in spite of his kingly rank, he receives the lesser but still considerable fee of forty shillings. [54] (In the Ipswich manuscript, he is grouped with two other 'kings' – John de Monhaut and the harper, Capenny – and all three receive the same amount of forty shillings.) The last of the fiddlers is Thomas of Tunly (a village near Stroud in Gloucestershire) who gets a more modest twenty shillings. Thomas is another visitor, and may have come to Ipswich in the retinue of Humphrey de Bohun, earl of Hereford and Constable of England. [55]

Master John the Lutenist (Janin Le Lutour') is the only player of a plucked-string instrument (other than the harp) to be specified, and was one of the king's most favoured minstrels. He was a citizen of London and, in 1299, wealthy enough to be a founder of the Guildhall Chapel, where Mass was to be said daily for, among others, 'John Luter and Isabel his wife'. He had some special relationship with the king's brother, Edmund, and it was partly at Edmund's prompting that, in 1295, he had been exempted from all taxes and civic duties whatsoever. (When, nine years later, through a clerical error, payment of a special tax voted by Parliament was demanded of him, he complained both personally at the Guildhall and by letter to the king, then on campaign in Scotland. A royal missive was immediately despatched to the assessors in which they were duly reprimanded and instructed to remove John's name from the roll.) There would have been an appreciative silence for his Ipswich performance, not only on account of the softness of his instrument and the quality of his playing, but because of the lute's rarity in England at this time. John, in fact, is the first and only player of the lute recorded in the wardrobe books from his own earliest appearance in 1285 to as late as 1327. Almost certainly, he would have come originally from Spain and may well have owed his early advancement to Edward's first queen, Eleanor of Castile, which would help to explain the great regard which the king continued to have for him. [56]

The Anglo-Norman forms in which the names of the minstrels are given in the manuscript tend always to conceal their countries of origin; but there can be no mistaking the English ring of Hammond in the French 'Hamon Lestiuour': Hammond the estive-player.

The estive is now believed by experts to have been a form of bagpipe; perhaps a smaller, courtlier version of the cornemeuse which was played out of doors – as shown below in an illustration from the fourteenth-century Luttrell Psalter. Hammond was chiefly employed as a groom of the Wardrobe, acting as valet to one of the king's officials, delivering letters. [57] He seems to have made himself generally useful and, for his playing at the feast, received twenty shillings.

Bagpiper. British Library, MS Add
42130, f.176 (detail).

The two 'Trumpeters of the King' are unnamed at Ipswich but were almost certainly Edward's personal trumpeters, John Depe and his son, John of London. They too receive twenty shillings each. Their regular duty was to precede the king on all his formal appearances – in the thick of battle as well as at court – announcing his presence with their fanfares; they may also have heralded the entrance into the hall of the various courses. Their instruments were four feet long and more, and for ceremonial use, of silver. In 1302–3, John Depe was paid £5 'to buy his gear for the Scottish war'. [58]

For woodwind at the feast, we must turn to the king's four *vigiles* or watchmen.

Medieval nights were filled with the music of pipes, flutes and other wind and string instruments. It was provided by those minstrels whose special duty it was to watch over the king and his subjects during the hours of darkness, later to be known as 'waits'.

They were required to blow or pipe the hour four times during the long winter nights, and three times in summer. As well as guarding against thieves and other malefactors, they had to keep a careful look-out for fire – an ever-present threat to life and property in an age of timber-framed buildings and the naked lights of candle and torch. Their music – as well as telling the hours – would have been reassuring to all who heard it; and it may also have served to keep the watchers themselves awake and alert. They played a variety of instruments.

In the *Roman de la Rose*, the watchman, Male Bouche, takes pipes, horns and trumpets with him to the battlements to sound the hours, and Cornish bagpipes and flutes to amuse himself.[59] But the waits most usual instrument, and the one with which they are generally associated (it became known as a 'wayt'), was the double-reeded shawm, the somewhat harsh, oboe-like sound of which was well suited to penetrate the night and the ears of all but the soundest sleepers.

Silence at night could carry a sinister message. When, in the romance of *Richard Coeur de Lion*, Richard's fleet approaches in the night under the walls of Joppa, which is besieged on the land side by a Saracen army, the unaccustomed silence leads the relievers to fear the worst.

> They looked up to the castel,
> They heard no pipe, ne flagel,   (flageolet, flute)
> They drew em nigh to land,
> If they mighten understand,
> And they could ne nought espie,
> Ne by no voice of minstralcie,
> That quick man in the castle were.

They hold back in uncertainty until the dawn, when happily

> A wait there came, in a kernel,   (battlement)
> And piped a nott in a flagel.[60]

Like their successors the town waits, the royal watchmen were often called upon to play at feasts, in addition to their other duties. The names of the four men rewarded at Ipswich are not given, but may well have included Geoffrey and Alexander de Windsor – two of the king's regular watchmen at this time who were based in Windsor Castle. The 'Prince's watchman', who is also listed as appearing at Ipswich, was another Windsor man, Richard. In 1306, when fire broke out in the Castle while the Prince and his entourage were in residence, Richard was to save them from being burned in their beds by raising the alarm, helping to extinguish the flames and evacuate the building. His minstrel skills were such that, a month later, he was to be especially summoned to Byfleet in Surrey 'to make his minstrelsy in the presence of the lord prince and his nobles'.[61] Combining, as they did, the functions of firemen, security patrol and minstrels, they must have earned every penny of their largesse of ten shillings each, which was over and above a daily wage of 4½d.

If the Ipswich burgesses were inclined to nod off as course followed course of the protracted feast, they would have been pleasantly awakened by the beat of the tabor, or the antics of Tom the fool.

The tabor was a two-skin drum, most usually played in combination with a three-holed or tabor-pipe. (See figure L of the drawing on page 12.)

Though there are illustrations of tabor and pipe being played separately on occasion, the peculiar skill of the taborer lay in his performance of the two instruments simultaneously. As an English monk was to put it in 1360, 'the Tympanum maketh the better melody yf there is a pype therewyth'.[62] Their main use was as a kind of one-man band for the accompaniment of dancing, the tabor providing the beat and the pipe a jigging tune; but, as we have seen in the example just cited (page 12), they were also used to accompany acrobatic and other turns; here the player might use his hands or fingers, or utilise the pipe itself to produce short exciting rolls and other rhythmic effects. Though both instruments were of remote origin, their use together by a single performer had been introduced from the continent only during the course of the thirteenth century – probably by visiting court minstrels. Tabor and pipe brought a characteristic note of gaiety to the late medieval scene – to courts and castles, and thence, by a process of assimilation, to town fairs and village greens. (They survive in the folk-dancing world as a 'whistle and dub'.) Canon Galpin cites an account of a famous performer of the countryside, Old Hall of Herefordshire, who "born soon after Henry VIII came to the throne, was still at his play in 1609 though nearly ninety-seven years of age, 'giving the men light hearts by thy pipe and the women light heels by thy tabor. O wonderful piper! O admirable tabor man" '.[63]

Taborers will even be found on the battlefield – like the French 'taberette' (as he was then called) who deserted his own side to serve the 'Kingmaker' Warwick in 1463; a 'manly man' who

> stode a-pon an hylle with hys tabyr and hys pype, taberyng and pyping as merely (merrily) as any man myght, stondyng by hym selfe, tylle my lorde (Warwick) come unto hym he wold not lesse hys grownd; and there he be-come my lordys man.[64]

Our three 'Ipswich' taborers – Baudet, Lambyn Clay and Martinet – have a good deal in common with each other; they all make their earliest recorded appearances at the wedding feast, while Baudet and Clay are seen thereafter to move freely between the King's and Prince's households, and go on to serve Edward II for many more years to come.

'Baudet' may derive from an old French word, *baud* or *baldé*, meaning 'boldness', 'sprightliness'. His Christian name is unknown, but there is a contemporary reference to a Roger Baudet who held land in Suffolk by serjeanty of 'paying the ancient fee of 100 arrows to the King'; in spite of his French-sounding name, our Ipswich Baudet may well have been a Suffolker. In 1306, he is dignified with the title of 'Master', and is entrusted with the payment of largesse to a group of visiting minstrels. When on campaign with Edward II in 1312, he is called 'Baudet the trumpeter'[65] – a further reminder of the minstrels' versatility. Lambyn (Lambert) Clay was almost certainly English. He was a citizen of London and, in 1299, contributed to a loan of a thousand pounds, which the aldermen and other citizens were called upon to raise among themselves to tide the king over one of his recurrent financial crises. Lambyn was a favourite performer of the Prince's, and when in 1305, he fell ill and was unable to travel with the court into Hampshire – thus losing his attendance fee of 7½d. per day – the Prince came to his aid with a gift of five shillings. By the following year, he would seem to have been transferred permanently to the Prince's household, and he and Richard the violist received 6s. 8d. for the hire of two hackneys to take them in the Prince's entourage from London to Dover. After the old king's death, Lambyn was again troubled by illness and received a further dole from Edward II for 'having to stay behind'. What happened to him then is unclear. A minstrel called Cley (and Clays) le Taborer was still receiving the king's livery in the early years of Edward III, 1328 and 1330. If this was the same person, he would then have been in royal service for thirty-three years.[66] (At Crécy in 1345, Edward's taborer is a man called Lambkin or Lambert de Stokerode.)

Both Baudet and Clay received twenty shillings at Ipswich; the third man, Martinet, got only ten shillings, and may then have been an apprentice. In 1301–2, Martinet was transferred to the household of the two young princes Thomas and Edmund, the children of Edward I's second marriage, in their permanent nursery at Windsor. (Matilda Makejoy, it will be remembered, was to be sent to entertain them at Framlingham a few years later. We begin to form a clearer picture of the intimate nature of this privileged milieu, in which the royal minstrels move easily from household to household and are sometimes passed on from parents to children like the Edwardian nanny.)

Dr Bullock-Davies gives a charming account of the scenes at Windsor, where the two boys (now four and three years old) were shortly to be joined by the king's baby granddaughter, Margaret, the child of Elizabeth, countess of Hereford.

At first, when they were very tiny, they played with his drum – and broke it. 'To Martinet, the minstrel, making his minstrelsy in the presence of Thomas and Edmund, the two sons of the King; and for repairing his tabor, broken by them, 2s.' And after baby Margaret arrived, '. . . for repairing his tabor, broken by them, 7s.' It needs no effort of the imagination to visualise the scene and hear the row... A year later, in 1305–6, they were old enough to have their own drums and burst them to their hearts' content: 'To Martinet the Taborer, for repairing the little drums of the King's sons; and for money paid by him for parchment for covering the same drums, 11d.' The change to toy drums was of great benefit to the household economy, if nothing else. [67]

The children's excited laughter rings down the years. It is interesting that both Baudet and Lambyn Clay were associated throughout their careers with Prince Edward, and that, in later years when he had succeeded to the throne as Edward II, he was to remain so loyal to them, and they to him. Had they known the same kind of relationship with him as a child as Richard the Harper has been seen to have enjoyed with his father, and Martinet with his young step-brothers? In view of the unnatural circumstances in which royal children were raised at that time, a special bond of affection and loyalty between the monarch and his former childhood companions is easily comprehensible.

Tom the fool (Thom le Fol, as he appears in the manuscript) was definitely a Suffolk man; he came from the village of Stratford St Andrew, which is about eighteen miles from Ipswich, and had been in royal service since, at latest, 1287–8, when he was with the king in Gascony. [68] In 1292, he is recorded as having been in debt to a certain Roger Mygnot. This, and the fact that no 'keeper' is ever mentioned, suggests that he was a fool of the competent or artificial kind. In 1294, he received 'protection', going with the king on campaign in Wales, and, in the following year, was granted respite from payment of tax of a 'tenth'; on this last occasion, he is described in the Roll as 'king's yeoman'. [69] In November 1296 (only two months before the Ipswich feast), he is reported as leading a 'courser and two greyhounds' (hunting dogs) from the King, who was then in Bury, to the Prince. [70] At Ipswich, he received, not alms, but the top fee of fifty shillings.

There are no contemporary illustrations of English court fools, so we have little idea of what Tom wore for his Ipswich appearance. (The drawings from the *Romans d'Alexandre* usually reproduced, showing lines of linked figures wearing a sort of knickerbockers and caped hoods with pointed 'ears' ending in bells, are Flemish in origin and show, not professional fools at all, but members of the *Sociétés Joyeuses*. These 'fool societies' flourished in many continental towns from an early date, comprising men and women of the bourgeoisie who dressed up in a uniform costume – imitated in part from classical models but deriving also from the ecclesiastical Feast of Fools – to take part *en famille* in festival processions and plays. [71] Though important for their influence on later secular drama in France, they had no English counterparts so far as is known, and no connection at all with men like Tom, who belong to a quite different tradition, going back, as we have seen, to the huntsmen-fools of Henry II and King John. As Chambers pointed out many years ago, it is doubtful, in fact, if the French *habit de fou* – with its eared hood and bells, so familiar in later medieval art as a type or symbol of Folly – ever crossed the Channel;[72] certainly, it cannot have done so at this early period. Even much later Tudor and Elizabethan fools such as Tarleton and Kempe appear in their portraits either in country gear or the court dress of their period.)

The most likely supposition we can make as to Tom's outfit in 1297 is that he aped the latest fashions of his time, and preened himself in whatever rich hand-me-downs he had acquired as gifts; not from the king himself who, like Henry II, was noted for the plainness of his clothes, but from the wealthy magnates who attended him – as so many of his famous successors were to do. It is one of the reproaches that Langland brings against minstrels in general in his *Piers Plowman*: they dress above their station.

As for the content of Tom's act, we have virtually nothing to go on. Retrospective evidence of later folk survivals can be notoriously misleading; but as Tom is of Suffolk, I refer the reader (for what it is worth) to the rather remarkable, nineteenth-century account of a Horkey celebration given in the Raynbirds' *Suffolk Agriculture* (1849, pp.306–7), which combines parody of hunting rituals, 'hallooing largess' – the Anglo-Norman word is still in use – and a farcical tooth-pulling sketch featuring a transvestite 'female' patient and a Doctor. As George Ewart Evans has shown, the life of rural Suffolk was to change very little from medieval times to as late as the First World War.

After this, Tom disappears from the scene – or at least from the records. (It is just possible that he is to be identified with the 'Thom fatuus' known to have been resident at Durham Abbey between 1330 and 1356, when he died and was buried at the Prior's expense.[73] One other distinction I can claim for him: he is the first 'Tom-fool' to appear in the historical record.)

A further group of minstrels whose speciality remains unknown, and some others who are known only by the names of the lords they accompanied to Ipswich, may now be mentioned.

Of the former, the most notable is John de Cressin or Cressy who received twenty shillings, and was one of those who, in 1307, when the king lay dying at Lanercost, helped to put on plays to amuse the young queen Margaret.[74]

Of those whose names have not been recorded, the most highly paid were the two 'Earl Fitz Simon minstrels' who receive fifty shillings between them, and are mentioned third in the manuscript after Le Roy Page and John Vidulator. They were clearly of some importance, but I have been unable to identify a Fitz Simon among Edward's earls; perhaps, like the first two, they were visitors from overseas. Finally, we have two minstrels 'of the Earl Marshal'. This was that Roger Bigod who had provoked the king's only English pun, and who lived nearby at Nayland.

The remaining two groups of minstrels at Ipswich are both associated with the final stages of the feast.

The royal waferers – whom we first encountered in the person of Godfrey in the reign of Henry II – combined the production of wafers with after-dinner minstrelsy. The wafers were made in a special wafer-iron from a stiff dough of flour, sugar and sometimes, eggs, served with a sweet, spiced wine called Hippocras at the close of a meal. (The hosts used at Mass – then, as now – were a variety of wafer made from especially pure ingredients.) The office was represented in the households of most of the great men of this and later times down to the sixteenth century, though by the reign of Edward IV it had begun to decline in importance.[75]

Master John Drake had been appointed in 1290 and was to serve Edward for seventeen years, and his son, Edward II, for a further six. Prince Edward's waferer at this time was a man called Reginald. Their inclusion in the Ipswich record, where they are named as receiving twenty and ten shillings respectively, is itself an indication that their duties were not confined to the making and serving of the wafers (for which they received regular wages of 7½d. and 4½d. per day); but the connection with minstrelsy in the sense of entertainment is made more specific in the case of their successor, a certain Richard Pilke. In 1311, he and his wife Elena were sent to the royal nursery, then at Framlingham – along with Matilda Makejoy – perhaps as part of the young princes' education in courtly etiquette. The record of their payment reads: 'To Pilke, King's Waferer, and Elena his wife, minstrels, serving their wafers at the tables of the two young princes, Thomas and Edmund, and making their minstrelsy in the presence of the said two princes...20s.[76] Ten waferer-minstrels are included in a list of touring entertainers who appear before the Chamberlains of York in 1447.[77]

It is doubtful whether waferers specialised in any particular form of minstrelsy. (Wodderspoon, in his own account of the Ipswich manuscript, translated *waffrarius* as 'conjuror', but this was based on a mistaken etymology. But the notion remains attractive, as conjuring and sleight-of-hand are traditionally associated with the final stage of a meal: the 'nuts and crackers'.)

How the art of making wafers came to be linked with minstrelsy in the first place remains unclear – perhaps it lay simply in the fact that both services were performed by the same kind of people, i.e. minstrels in the sense of 'little servants of the king' – but that there was such a link is supported by an otherwise obscure passage in *Piers Plowman* of c. 1380. As Piers goes on his way, he meets a man (Haukyn) who looks like a minstrel. When asked to state his calling, he replies,

I am a minstrel, and my name is *Activa Vita*;
I abhor an idle man, for Active Life is my name.
If you want to know, I'm a waferer, and work for many lords;
But they furnish me with few robes or furred gowns.
Could I lie to make people laugh, I should latch on
To mantles and money among the lords' minstrels;
But I play neither tabor nor trumpet, and cannot tell romances,
Or harp or fiddle or fart in tune at feasts,
Or tell jokes, or juggle, or pipe a jig,
Nor tumble, neither, nor dance, nor sing to the gittern.
So I get no good gifts from those great lords. [78]

(The reference above to farting 'in tune at feasts' will remind us of Henry II's Roland le Pettour, later named as 'le Fartere'. The actuality of this extraordinary talent among the Greek and Roman *mimi* of his own day is attested by no less an authority than St Augustine. [79] No wonder John of Salisbury complained of such people 'defiling the air'!)

Chaucer in *The Pardoner's Tale* puts 'waferers' in the company of 'Syngeres with harpes, and bandes', as those who kindle and blow the fire of lechery (C.479–81). Though waferers in the service of great lords certainly counted as 'minstrels' in the general sense of 'little servants' and dressed as such, not all waferers so employed had the additional skills as entertainers – which, it would seem from Langland, might be of various kinds – to attract 'good gifts', and had to be content with more modest rewards. The disparity rankles.

The wedding feast has now been in progress for many hours. All but three of the minstrels have taken their turn in the cleared space before the top table. It is time for the bride and her attendant ladies to withdraw.

Enter the three mimes. All we really know about them are their names, which are those of the characters they play, but these are suggestive: Griscote, Visage and Magote. Griscote (Greyside), greybeard, the traditional cuckold figure of marital farce; Visage (Face), the girl, beautiful but perhaps, like Jonson's Face in *The Alchemist*, double-faced and double-dealing; Magote (Ape), the girl's young lover in a grotesque, animal disguise? Something surely along these lines. The use of masks – as described in chapter two – is strongly indicated. As the names are unrecorded elsewhere, the actors were probably three of the king's regular minstrels appearing here anonymously; two who are known to have been involved in plays elsewhere are Le Roy Capenny and John de Cressin. They receive a total largesse of sixty shillings.

As for the probable content and style of the piece that was performed, we are fortunate to have a rare, surviving fragment of text which is contemporary in date: *Interludium de Clerico et Puella*, 'Interlude of the Student and the Girl'. This also has three characters; a student in minor orders, a young girl and a bawd, Mother Eloise. When the student approaches the bawd to enlist her services in arranging an assignation with the girl, with whom he has fallen violently in love at first sight, Mother Eloise protests her rheumatism and religious devotion in a way that suggests Shakespeare may well have been drawing on a comedic type already familiar to the 'groundlings' when he came to create the Nurse in *Romeo and Juliet*.

> Eh, son? What do you say? Bless us!
> Lift up your hand and bless yourself,
> For it is both sin and shame
> That you should have lain this blame on me;
> For I am an old crone and a cripple.
> I lead my life under the wrath of God.
> With my distaff I earn my food;
> I can do nothing over and above reciting
> Both my *Pater Noster* and my *Credo*...[80]

And so on. Here again are the traditional targets of the professional *mimi* as defined in chapter two: sexual misbehaviour and religious hypocrisy. The Ipswich interlude may well have been of a similar farcical and broadly indecent kind.

(While the mimes were bringing the Ipswich feast to a doubtless uproarious end, behind the scenes, another real-life drama was developing: a kind of anti-comedy, though deadly serious in its personal and political consequences. It would seem that either Elizabeth found her young husband repellent, or that the prospect of shortly leaving her family and homeland for a foreign country with a man she had only just met, was too much for her to bear. In either case, she played the only card left to her in the situation in which she found herself, and refused consummation of the marriage. A furious confrontation between father and fourteen year-old daughter ensued, in the course of which Edward snatched a golden coronet from her head – it had been his wedding gift to her – and threw it in the fire. But Elizabeth stood her ground, and the king – who, in spite of his sudden rages, had a real affection for his children – was obliged to make the best of a bad job and defer matters; the disconsolate Count departed for Holland brideless, and two carriages with Elizabeth's tailor, Henry, and the marriage bed were to be seen trundling their way sadly over the Cattawade bridge to London. In the event, Edward himself accompanied Elizabeth to Holland in 1298; but, within another year, she was back in England again, a childless widow, her husband having meanwhile died of dysentery. In 1302, she was to marry Humphrey de Bohun, earl of Hereford – perhaps her original choice. He had been present at Ipswich with his father. It was their baby, Margaret, who joined the young princes in their play with Martinet at Windsor. Even medieval princesses – if they were determined enough – sometimes triumphed over circumstances!)

Edward of Caernarvon, who succeeded his father as Edward II in 1307, is inevitably measured against Edward I, and, as he lacked nearly all of his father's exceptional qualities – his energy, drive, political skills and ambition – is found badly wanting. But Edward Longshanks left his son a Treasury virtually bankrupt, the 'problem' of Scotland unsolved, a war-weary population, and a set of powerful magnates restless of the constraints they had had to suffer so long, and determined to assert themselves. As Dr Denholm-Young neatly sums it up, 'Edward II sat down to the game of kingship with a remarkably poor hand, and he played it very badly'. [81]

It is interesting, however, to see that many of the criticisms of the young king that soon began to flow from his contemporaries bear a more than passing resemblance to those that still hang about his grandfather: the 'foreign favourites', whose company he prefers to that of his English peers who are his natural and properly-constituted companions and advisers, his extravagance, and the fact that he surrounds himself with 'buffoons, singers, actors'. [82] It is ironic to find that interests which today are accepted as perfectly normal – indeed, as evidence of a healthy, heterosexual outlook on life, with due regard for cultural values and a certain liking for the 'stage' – were then regarded as eccentric to the point of mental and moral degeneracy. In January 1316, a chronicler sneers over the fact that the king had taken a wintry holiday in the fens 'that he might refresh his soul with the solace of many waters'. He had had a narrow escape from drowning while 'rowing about on various lakes' before 'he set off with all speed, he and his silly company of swimmers, for the parliament which he had ridiculously caused to be summoned to Lincoln'. [83] He is never happier than when 'messing about in boats' – which becomes the subject of a popular, satirical ditty – and when, in 1312, news reached him of the brutal murder of his friend Gaveston, he seeks to console himself in digging a ditch around his favourite estate.

In view of all the evidence we have now seen of his father's extravagant partiality in that direction, which had raised not a breath of criticism, the accusations against Edward of an inordinate fondness for minstrelsy and play-acting appear unjustified. The real reproach is that – unlike his father – he failed to subordinate these interests to the main job of a medieval king, which was to keep his magnates in check by one means or another in asserting the national interest, and that he allowed them instead to gain ascendancy over him, with the terrible results for the country and for himself which are familiar to everyone.

At the very beginning of this study, I suggested that the minstrels could only properly be understood in relation to their patrons, and especially the king, the fount of all such patronage in the middle ages. The king and his household (of which the minstrels are an integral part) can be seen to stand or fall together, and the weakness of a king soon redounds upon his following. Moves to remove from Edward's court the 'unnecessary members of his household' are reported from 1315,[84] and the York Ordinance of 1318 strikes at the very roots of minstrelsy in attacking the 'undifferentiated household establishment... in which every royal officer was jack of all trades'.[85] The minstrels, it appears, were not the *only* people at court to combine a variety of functions; but in so far as they are viewed, along with artists in general, by succeeding generations of bureaucrats and administrative reformers down to the present as, almost by definition, 'unnecessary', and often 'unworthy' into the bargain, it is clear that they will always be prime targets of such 'reform'. There is now (in 1318) to be an exact job description for each of the household's members. Thus, 'There shalbe ij trompeters & two other minstrels, & sometime more and sometime lesse, who shal play before the kinge when it shal please him'.[86] That 'sometime more, sometime lesse' is still vague enough – though it could hardly have been much less – but the pressure is on, and will be renewed repeatedly through this and succeeding reigns.

In 1316, Stow reports an incident which must have had considerable impact on the king and his friends. A female minstrel – or rather, 'a woman adorned like a minstrel then used' – was sent into the great hall of Westminster at Pentecost, when the king was sitting at table with his peers. Having circled the other tables, 'showing pastime', she rode up to the king's table, 'laid before him a letter, and forthwith turning her horse, saluted every one, and departed'. The letter contained a riddling remonstrance to the king, the gist of which was that he was heaping undue favours on foreigners to the neglect of his faithful subjects. When the doorkeepers were admonished for letting her in, they replied 'that it was never the custom of the king's palace to deny admission to Minstrels, especially on such high solemnities and feast days'.[87] What better way to strike at the king than through the very people – a *female* minstrel into the bargain – with whom he was criticised for spending his time.

The extent to which these and similar moves were successful in actually reducing the number of the king's minstrels and other members of his household, and in thus restricting his patronage, can only be determined by more detailed research into the unpublished wardrobe accounts, and doubtless will be found to fluctuate with the rise and fall of the king's political fortunes. That Edward continued to enjoy the company of his minstrels, and to treat them with generosity, has already been shown in his loyalty to the taborers Baudet and Clay, and other of his father's former retainers; it will be confirmed by the following anecdotes, gathered from both before and after his accession.

There is first a record of the young Prince of Wales on a Christmas holiday in Hampshire in 1302–3, sending for 'three clerks of the town of Windsor' to perform interludes on the vigil of Epiphany, requiring purchases from a London merchant of gilded skins and a quantity of *wire*. [88] (Probably for an Epiphany play featuring the Three Magi, in which the wire would be needed to operate a moving star – as happened every year in parish churches throughout the land.)

There is also an account of a visit along with his father to Roxburgh in Scotland in 1303 when a fool called Robert Buffard is compensated with four shillings 'for the trick the Prince played him in the water that day' [89] – *projecit in aquam*? This, be it noted, was Scotland in February. (Buffard may have been the former fool of Queen Eleanor, also called Robert. He was 'retired' to the Yorkshire abbey of Meaux before the old king's death in 1307.) [90]

Preparations for another Scottish campaign were then in progress and, among other purchases of armour and field equipment, four 'pennoncells' (banners) of gold painted with the prince's arms were provided for his two trumpeters, John Garsie and John of Cateloyne, to attach to their instruments. On the same occasion, John the Nakerer received three shillings for skin to cover and repair his drums. [91]

This is our first mention of nakers, which consisted of a pair of small kettle-drums that could be attached by a strap around the waist, and were of Arabian or Saracenic origin. The earliest notice of John – or of his instrument in England – is in 1302 when the Prince bought a sorrel hack for him to ride. Of the trumpeters, John Garsie was a Londoner and John of Cateloyne (Catalonia) a Spaniard. These three Johns are often mentioned together in the Prince's company. Though John Garsie died in 1307, leaving a little boy of eight (also called John) who was then entrusted to a London skinner, the other two appear to have remained at Edwards's side through most of his reign as king. John the Nakerer eventually retired in 1323, and was found a home in the abbey of Burton-on-Trent. [92] (See below for a contemporary drawing of nakers in use.)

It is at this period that another instrument makes its appearance: the Welsh *crwth* or croude – a type of bowed or plucked lyre, usually with three strings, sometimes double-coursed, which was still in use among some country people and gypsies in the early years of the present century. The Prince had heard that the abbey of Shrewsbury had a good crouder in residence and, in 1305, wrote a letter of introduction for Richard the Rhymer to take with him, addressed to the Abbot, asking permission for Richard to stay there until he had learned how to play it. In 1306-7, Richard returned, and there were visits from two other crouders to play for the prince, one at Windsor and the other – a minstrel of his sister's, Elizabeth, now countess of Hereford – at Wetheral. [93] (Richard the Rhymer may perhaps have been an author of some of the rhymed romances of the period. It is interesting that he is here seeking an additional, instrumental skill. He had formerly been one of the prince's five boy choristers, all of whom grew up to be king's minstrels.) [94]

From the time of Edward's accession, there are a number of references

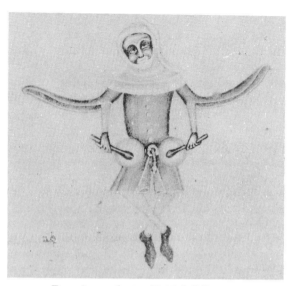

Dancing nakerer. British Library,
MS Add 42130, f.176.

to payments to minstrels, though many more must lie hidden in unpublished records.

In 1311, John the Nakerer was entrusted with payment of a reward to Janin le Tregettur (John the Conjuror) for making his minstrelsy for the king in a private room of Swineshead Priory.[95]

In 1312, on a visit to France, Edward was entertained by 'Bernard le Fol and fifty-four of his companions coming naked (*nudis*) before the King, with dancing (*tripudio*) at Pontoise'.[96] In the same year, at Canterbury, John de Colon, a Lombard minstrel, makes his minstrelsy before the king *with snakes (cum serpentibus)*.[97]

In the course of 1316-7, he rewarded William de Horsham and three companions for their singing with a gift of twenty-five yards of striped cloth, costing twenty shillings, to make garments for themselves; the Boy-Bishop of St Mary's church, Nottingham, was rewarded for coming into his presence on the feast of the Holy Innocents (December 28); Robert Daverouns, violist of the Prince of Tarentum, was given the princely sum of £5 at Newburgh; and, in the year following, Edward was visited at Baldock by Dulcia Witherstaf, 'mother of Robert, the King's fool' – presumably Robert Buffard's successor.[98]

Finally, there is a nicely human glimpse of this sad, often lonely man convulsed with mirth ('beyond all measure') at the suprising antics of his court painter, Jack of St Albans, dancing on a table top. In gratitude, Edward presses upon him '50 shillings in aid of Jack himself, his wife, and his children'.[99]

7

Sir Orfeo: Later Harpers and the English Romances

Harper in hall. British Library, MS Royal 2 B vii, f.71v.

With the Norman Conquest, the native tradition of oral English verse, along with the livelihood of its professional guardians, was almost extinguished. That a few recorded examples of the early poems such as *Widsith* and *Beowulf* survived at all is a fortunate chance; yet the tradition was somehow kept alive during two centuries of French domination, to emerge Phoenix-like with undiminished vitality in the thirteenth century, in the form of some hundred and twenty surviving poems, once known as Minstrel Lays, but more prosaically referred to now as the Middle English Metrical Romances. These became the stock-in-trade of the English harpers, whose long history I began to trace in chapter three and will continue here.

The harpers were still involved in warfare: of the ten appearing at Ipswich, most had probably been engaged in Edward's punitive raid into Scotland of a few months earlier. We cannot exclude the possibility that, like Taillefer, they may even have taken part in the fighting. But their main task on campaign was to take note of those individual acts of prowess that were afterwards recorded in the form of *sirventois* or 'duty' songs to be recited after the battle, and then, in a more polished state, on occasions such as the Ipswich feast.

One such poem that has survived is the *Song of Carlaverock*, which tells the story of the siege of a not very important Scottish castle by Edward I and his knights in 1300. This poem, written in Old French, has been described as 'perhaps the last attempt by anyone in England to be a herald as well as a minstrel'.[1] It has something in common with *Widsith* in its comprehensive listing of over a hundred knights, for each of whom a quick portrait is given along with a description of his heraldic blazon. The poet manages to pack a surprising amount of vivid observation into his 120 stanzas of variable length:

> Adam de la Forde mines at the wall
> As well as he can,
> For as thick as rain rains
> These stones fly in and out,
> By which was much crushed the gold
> Of three lioncels crowned,
> Which he bore rampant in clear blue.[2]

At the battle of Falkirk in 1298, all the great lords who were present were accompanied by harpers: John le Harpur with Norfolk, Nicholas le Harpour with Oxford (the same Nicholas who had accompanied his young lord to the Ipswich wedding), John le Harpur with William de Cantelupe, John le Harper with Lancaster, and Richard le Harpour with Walter de Beauchamp, Steward of the Royal Household; only Percy has a 'King' in his retinue.[3]

While publicly the harper was required to celebrate his lord's military prowess, privately he had to fulfill a very different function, that of soothing and healing the troubled mind and soul, and it is here that his instrumental skills would have come to the fore. Robert Mannying in *Handlyng Synne*, where he speaks of Bishop Grosseteste and his harper-companion, has the bishop explain:

The virtu of the harpe thurgh skylle and ryght	
Wyl destroye the fendes myght,	*fiend's*
And to the croys by gode skylle	*Cross*
Ys the harpe lykened weyle...	
Tharfor, gode men, ye shall lere	*learn*
Whan ye any gleman here	*hear*
To wurchep God at youre powere,	
As Dauyd seyth yn the sautere...[4]	*David, psalter*

These words echo both the Psalter, traditionally attributed to David which Mannying goes on to quote, and, more especially, the *Book of Kings*. For when Saul is troubled by an 'evil mood' that gives him no rest, his servants offer to find 'some skilful player on the harp' to relieve him, and return with David. 'And whenever Saul was taken with this evil mood of his, David would fetch his harp and play; whereupon Saul was comforted and felt easier, till at last the evil mood left him'.[5]

In David – harper-poet and warrior – the medieval harper could have had no more powerful or appropriate patron. But more than that; by providing this form of musical therapy for the men and women who employed him, as David had done for Saul, we see how once again the harper was able to escape that narrow definition of the minstrels' function which critics like John of Salisbury might otherwise have used against him. Thus, in 1253, Richard the Harper is sent by his master, Henry III, to console his son Edmund when he lay sick, and is instructed to stay with the boy until he recovers.[6] And later, when Henry's eldest son, Edward, has succeeded him as king, Melior, harper of Lord John Mautravers at Plympton in Devon, is rewarded with twenty shillings for 'making his minstrelsy in the presence of the king during the time of his blood-letting'.[7] In sickness or health, day or night, the royal harpers might be summoned, as Thomas 'of the king's chamber' must often have been called to calm the troubled mind of Henry VI.[8] Thomas de Chabham's tolerance of the *joculatores* who sing of heroes or the lives of the saints is qualified by the important and usually-omitted words, 'to console the sick and the unfortunate'.[9]

At very much lower social levels – those of the yeoman-farmer and the inn where English remained the dominant language – it is at least arguable that harper-minstrels of the old tradition retained their position and popularity throughout that whole period when French was the only language spoken at court and in the households of the nobility. Many of these men must have played a double role.

It is perhaps significant that some of the earliest-surviving examples of the English romances are addressed precisely to such an audience:

> Herkneth to me, gode men,
> Wives, maidnes, and alle men,
> Of a tale that ich you wile telle..

announces the poet-performer of *Havelok the Dane* (c.1275), adding a few lines later,

> At the beginning of ure tale,
> Fill me a cuppe of full good ale.

The anonymous authors of the English lays were indebted to the French poets of the new romance literature – men such as Beroul and Chrétien de Troyes – for much of their subject matter and for some of the verse forms in which their lays were composed; but recent critics of the genre stress the distinctiveness and originality of the native contribution.[10]

Turning back for a moment from the extant texts of the romances to the records of the harpers' performances – usually in monasteries where such records are most likely to have been kept – it is interesting to find that in the few instances where an indication is given of their subject matter, its provenance is English or Latin, rather than French. The earliest I have found, from 1338, has a *joculator* named Herbert performing for Adam de Orleton, bishop of Winchester, in his Cathedral Priory, the 'Song of Colbrond' and a 'geste of Queen Emma acquitted by Ordeal of Fire'.[11] These are legends local to Winchester. Colbrond was a Danish champion defeated by the Christian hero, Guy 'earl of Warwick', in a meadow outside the city wall. (The enormous sword he is reputed to have used is still on display in Warwick Castle.) Emma is an historical person, the mother of Edward the Confessor, who was required to walk scatheless through a fire, nine ploughshares in length, to prove her innocence of treason – also at Winchester. Though the ordeal of Queen Emma is paralleled in a unique manuscript of *Athelston* (c.1375), the text of Herbert's geste about her has not survived; but there are several extant versions, in both French and English, of the Guy of Warwick legend, the latest of which is entitled *Guy and Colbrond*. The earliest English version of about 1300 would obviously have been available for Herbert's use – if, indeed, he was not the author of it – as would its Anglo-Norman original of 1132–42; the story was immensely popular.[12]

At Bicester Priory in 1432 (*temp.* Henry VI), the Treasurer rewarded six minstrels from Buckingham for singing in the refectory on the feast of Epiphany a legend of 'The Seven Sleepers'.[13] (These were sixth-century Christians believed to have been walled-up in a cave at Ephesus during the persecution of Decius, who woke up from a miraculous sleep two hundred years later to find their city Christian.) Again, no text has survived.

The harpers' debt to their Celtic past is made explicit in the *Lay Le Freine* (c.1330):

> We redeth oft and findeth y-write –
> And this clerkes wele it wite –   *scholars well know*
> Layes that ben in harping...
> In Breteyne bi hold time
> This layes were wrought, so seith this rime.
> When kinges might our y-here   *anywhere/hear*
> Of ani mervailes that ther were,
> Thai token an harp in gle and game,
> And maked a lay and gaf it name.

The same lines appear in two versions of *Sir Orfeo* (c.1300), which suggests that such openings were interchangeable at the discretion of the individual performer and may, indeed, have been personal to him. If he was performing in a monastery, an opening prayer might be advisable, if not *de rigueur*, such as the one now attached to *Athelston*:

Lord that is of mightis most,
Fadir and Sone and Holy Gost,
Bring us out of sinne
And lene us grace so for to wirke   *grant*
To love bothe God and Holy Kirke
That we may hevene winne.
Lystnes, lordingis...

Sir Orfeo combines classical myth with an element of Celtic mystery. Though 'His fader was comen of King Pluto / And his moder of King Juno', he is a king 'In Inglond' whose capital is, at the same time, at Winchester and in Thrace. Two later versions have the lines already quoted from *Lay Le Freine*, but the earliest has a page missing from the manuscript and goes straight to its story.

Orfeo was a king,
In Inglond an heighe lording,
A stalworth man and hardy bo;   *both*
Large and curteis he was also.   *generous*

The performers of these metrical romances who appear in the records are described as *joculatores, mimi, lusores* (players), minstrels and harpers. Those who assisted at the installation of the abbot of St Augustine's, Canterbury, in 1309, 'accompanied their songs with a harp'. References to harping, playing, singing and 'telling' mingle indiscriminately in both records and texts. At Maxtoke Priory in 1441, six minstrels from the household of Lord Clinton of Maxtoke Castle 'sing, harp and play' in the monks' refectory during dinner. [14] *King Horn* (c.1225) begins:

Alle beon he blithe
That to my song lithe!   *listen*
A song ich shall you singe
Of Murry the Kinge.

Although the narrator switches, shortly afterwards, to 'telling' and 'talking', the tale ends, as it begins, on a musical note,

For thus him endeth hornes song.

As the author of *Kyng Alisaunder* (c.1300) informs us,

Mery it is in halle to here the harpe,
The mynstrales synge, the jogelours carpe.

And in *Sir Cleges,*

> An harpor sange a gest be mouth. *by mouth*

It is clear that harpers were not the only performers of *gestes*: there were also those described as *gestours* and 'rhymers'; at York in 1449, there is mention of a *fabulator* (story-teller). Though some of these would certainly have played a harp, others may have accompanied themselves on viols or croudes and other instruments or, like the *seggers* and *disours* (both words meaning literally 'sayers'), dispensed with instruments altogether.

The period in which the English romances are thought to have been composed extends from about 1200 to 1450; the harper records begin with William le Harpur in the reign of Henry I (1100–1135), increase markedly in the reign of Edward I, and continue into the fifteenth century and beyond. The assimilation of English by the French *trouvères* imported by Queen Maud and Eleanor of Aquitaine, and of French by the native English harpers, and their gradual coalescence into a single body of bilingual harper-minstrels, cannot be traced in detail, but is part of a general process affecting all the middle ranks of English society in the thirteenth and fourteenth centuries. Can there be any real doubt that the performers in both cases – the performers of the English romances and those mentioned in the harper records – belong to the same class of people?

We have already encountered some of these men at the courts of Henry III and Edward I. But what of the rest? Where did they come from and what sort of people were they?

In the first place, it is important to understand that the small groups of harpers gathered about the person of the king – on whom we have concentrated all our attention so far – though constituting a tiny, privileged elite within an elite (the king's minstrels), were not closed off from the rest of medieval society. Not only was the household itself peripatetic and, to that extent, more widely available to outside scrutiny than it has since become; but the minstrels themselves, including the harpers, are seen to be continually on the move in and out of the revolving constellation of the court – like wandering stars.

Take, for example, Hugh de Naunton, one of Edward I's harpers. He joins the household (with two horses and a groom) at Kennington on May 20, 1305; remains on duty for just under four weeks, then takes a week off. He is back at work for six weeks until August 20, when he disappears for two whole months, rejoining at Westminster on October 31. Between the end of January and May, 1306, he is away for almost four months. Of his first year's service, only four months in total were actually spent at court.[15] Though there are exceptions, the pattern is not untypical. The question remains: what was Hugh doing with himself for the other eight months of the year? It is possible that he simply returned home to live the kind of life enjoyed by other prosperous citizens or members of the minor landed gentry; but, from a professional point of view, would performers receiving a generous daily wage so choose to put themselves out of employment for often lengthy periods unless there was an alternative and richer source of income awaiting them elsewhere? Or were they given their marching orders from time to time in accordance with some pre-arranged schedule? But the question of choice becomes largely hypothetical after Edward's death and the accession of his son in 1307 when, as we have already noted, the pressures of administrative and financial reform of the household began to take effect. The Ordinance of 1315 to remove 'unnecessary members' of the king's household is alleged to have resulted in an immediate saving of £10 in daily expenses. In a contrary move, Edward III insists that his favourite minstrels are to receive their 7½d. per day whether they are *within or without* the household; but the general tendency is all the other way and, by 1478, the string-men among the thirteen minstrels of Edward IV are instructed to be at their stations on festival days but to 'avoyde the next day after the festes be don'. (Even his trumpeters and pipers will be encountered later on extensive tours.) The six trumpeters belonging to the riding household of George, duke of Clarence, in 1469 are to be on duty at feasts and 'other tymes' only 'if they be commaunded'. [16]

But what of those others – the many minstrels who were *not* in royal employment? From almost as far back as the time of the Conquest, we have seen the royal establishment of minstrels duplicated on a somewhat smaller scale by those of magnates and, as the years go by, there comes into existence equivalent layers at lower and lower levels of the armigerous class; so that, by the reign of Edward I, there is hardly a country manor visited by Bishop Swinfield of Hereford which does not boast at least a harper in residence. Of the one hundred and nineteen minstrels (including twenty-six harpers) named as appearing at the Pentecost feast at Westminster in 1306, thirty serve the king, one the queen; the Prince of Wales contributes fourteen and other royal children, five; two come from Bishop Bek, one from the Abbot of Abingdon; twelve are from the households of earls, five from those of countesses, twenty-two from barons and knights, three from 'ladies', eight from separate establishments of the king's officers, and six are visitors from abroad. [17] Thus, in summary, fifty minstrels are from the several royal establishments; fifty-three from those of earls, knights and ladies; none are 'wanderers'. But this is only a sampling – and still from the upper end of the spectrum.

If we turn from the minstrels' home bases and look instead to one of the places where they are known to have supplemented their income by touring, a more comprehensive picture emerges. Between 1278 and 1395, literally hundreds of visits by minstrels to Durham Abbey and its manors are recorded – mainly at those times of the year (the great feasts) when the monks are *ad ludem* (on holiday). The majority of entries refer in a general way to *histriones* and are not, therefore, of any help to us; but of those who are personally named or otherwise identified as belonging to named households or towns, thirty-two are of the royal household, eight of the King of Scotland, forty-six are of 'lords', twelve of bishops, eight are town minstrels, and only about a dozen apparently unattached. (Among the latter, there is Robert le Taburer (1299), a 'certain harper called Rygeway' (1357), a Barry and several Thomas Harpours who may have been resident (1362–81), Peter Crouder (1360), a lute-player who accompanies his wife's singing (1361), an *histrio* and *jestour* called Jawdewyne (1362), Bartholomew Wright, wrestler (1369), a rotour of Scotland (1394), and several blind harpers.) [18]

If, as Widsith pointed out, the 'maker's wierd is to be a wanderer', it becomes increasingly apparent, that, for the most part if not 'always',

> they meet with someone, in the south lands or the north,
> who understands their art, an open-handed man
> who would not have his fame fail among the guard...

and that if they did not, they had little chance of picking up any sort of a decent living. Certainly, if we are looking for the performers and possible authors of the English romances, it is among the mass of liveried minstrels that we are most likely to find them.

The advantages for all concerned of this extensive use of patronage are not hard to see: for the patron, the prestige of having a minstrel or minstrels to extol his or her fame without the necessity of having to pay them a regular wage throughout the year; for the minstrel, the protection of a well-known name to serve as a stamp of approval and passport of admittance to monasteries, castles, guildhalls and manors; the more powerful the name, the surer he could be of a welcome and the larger the reward he might expect. Lord Percy, earl of Northumberland, has even a scale of rewards written into the household ordinances of his castles in Yorkshire and, though late in date (1512 to 1534), they are wholly medieval in their logic: 6s. 8d. for the king's 'jugler' or bearward if they come yearly; 3s. 4d. for an earl's minstrels if they come yearly but, if they come only once in every two or three years, 6s. 8d.; if, however, the earl in question is his special friend or kinsman, they are to receive 6s. 8d. whether their visits are yearly or less often than that. [19] No smaller fry get a look-in! A much earlier economy measure of the reign of Edward II is interesting in this respect. After an injunction to lords to limit the number of courses served at their tables, it goes on to forbid minstrels to visit the houses of great lords 'beyond the number of *three or four a day*, unless requested to do so by the lord, or go to the houses of smaller people at all unless requested', and then to be content with whatever reward (*curtasie*) is offered them, without asking for more. [20] But that 'three or four a day' which is allowed, when multiplied by the considerable number of such houses throughout the length and breadth of the country and the days of the year, adds up to a prodigious total. And these, be it noted, are assumed to be *liveried* minstrels, as the punishments prescribed for infringement of the regulations make clear; for the first offence, they are to be deprived of their 'minstrelsie', i.e. liveried status.

The minstrels travelled singly, sometimes in pairs, or, in the case of those attached to 'great lords', in groups of three, four and more. Exceptionally, there were nine minstrels of the lord of Salisbury at York in 1447.[21] In this, as in other respects, these touring minstrels were blazing a trail for the companies of Tudor and Elizabethan players, who were also to find shelter under the nominal patronage of the great.

One interesting exception to all this are the blind minstrels (mainly harpers), several of whom have already been mentioned as performing for the monks of Durham; exceptional in that many of these appear not to have been 'attached'. Durham has a 'William Blyndharpour of Newcastle' who makes two appearances in 1357, and is probably to be identified with the 'William ye kakeharpour' who was present for a feast of St Cuthbert in 1362. On the same occasion, we find a blind minstrel from France with his young brother, probably his guide. At Christmas 1376, a blind harper called Roger is rewarded. The Chamberlains of York, in 1447, record the visit of a blind minstrel 'from the south', and another with the intriguing title, 'Minstrel of God (ministrallus dei) – perhaps a Franciscan.[22] At the Pentecost feast of 1306 at Westminster, there is the strangely-named 'Perle in the eghe' with his companion and guide; 'Pearl in the eye' being a colloquial term, still current, for cataract.[23] There may have been an element of charity in the reception of such people at Durham Abbey, but they would hardly have been included in the prestigious Westminster programme (where 'Pearl' and his partner receive half-a-mark from the Prince) if they were not, as performers, of a high standard.

But even these blind harpers were sometimes successful in obtaining regular patrons, and several are known to have risen as high as the royal service. Nicholas le Blund – for whom Dr Bullock-Davies gives a detailed itinerary in 1299–1300 – was a 'King's harper' to Edward I, and is found in company with another of Edward's harpers, Adam de Clitheroe, at Ipswich in 1297, though neither of them were able to secure a place in the programme for the wedding feast. Nicholas was also present at Carlaverock.[24] ('Blund' is a dialect word meaning blind, related to the verb 'blunder', originally to disturb sediment, to make turbid, muddy.) William Dodmore was to serve Richard II and Henry IV in the same capacity; in 1392, he was granted £10 a year from the 'fee farm' of the city of London for 'good service and especially because he is blind'.[25] (I give some further records of these and other blind harpers and minstrels in Appendix C.)

For the rest, moving as they do from the courts of kings and their magnates to monasteries, from monasteries to manor-houses and guildhalls, and from there to the ale-house postulated in *Havelok*, it is clear that the performers would – as a basic necessity of their calling – be required to have command of at least two languages (French and English), and a bilingual repertoire to match; in addition, most would have had a smattering of Latin. Even within the monasteries, there may well have been a need to switch languages. At St Swithin's, Winchester, in 1374, six minstrels and four harpers helped to celebrate an anniversary by performing in the hall of the Priory during the monks' dinner, and gave a repeat performance for the Prior at supper.[26] At Maxtoke, the six minstrels who sang, harped and played for the monks at dinner in 1441 were afterwards entertained by the Sub-Prior in his painted chamber, the Chamberlain providing 'eight massy tapers' to light their table.[27]

There is no evidence that I know of to support the idea that the majority of harpers were illiterate – as they are so often assumed to have been. On the contrary, there are as many references to reading and writing in those romances which have the strongest claim to minstrel authorship as there are to harping and singing.[28] We have seen that among the king's minstrels were men who corresponded with the monarch in person, and engaged in property deals and other business. Some, including William le Sautreour, psaltery-player to three queens (Eleanor of Castile, Margaret of France and Isabella), and John Harding, watchman and wait to Edward II and III, possessed personal seals which are still in existence.[29] Nicholas, de Vere's harper, acted as his attorney when his patron was abroad – and he is not the only harper to have dabbled in the law.[30] Grammar schools attached to abbeys and cathedrals had been in existence since the twelfth century, and not all the boys who attended them can have gone on to become monks or priests.

It would seem that the whole question of the minstrel authorship of the English romances may need to be re-considered, along with the precise nature of that 'oral tradition' of which (I have claimed) the minstrels, especially harpers, were the natural inheritors and guardians. It may be found that, as with the popular, 'improvised' drama we glanced at in chapter two, the oral character of many of the romances has more to do with the original conditions of their performance – the extent to which it remained open to adaptation in response to the varying demands of particular audiences and occasions – than with the literacy or illiteracy of its performers. Whether literate or not, it would be absurd to suppose that any minstrel could improvise several thousand lines of rhyming couplets, or the more complicated 'tail-rhyme' stanzas, off the top of his head – and then remember them all afterwards. There is an important distinction to be made here between poetry intended for performance, and extemporary techniques of composition, which – however employed among the *guslars* of Jugoslavia[31] – are foreign to our western cultural tradition. Whether literate or illiterate, the harper would need to prepare his material. I see no reason to doubt that when, in *Havelok*, the performer asks his audience to

Say a pater-noster stille
For him that haueth the rym maked,
And therefore fele nihtes waked.

– he is talking about anyone else but himself!

It is true that by the fifteenth century, references to harping, talking and singing, as well as to the books from which the stories are usually said to derive, are becoming literary conventions, not to say clichés, and were being used by clerkly authors who probably would have been hard put to it to tell one end of a harp from the other. The signs by which minstrel authorship can best be judged will have to do rather with the poem's length, its likely effectiveness when performed in holding an audience, the quality and pacing of its story-telling; criteria of a kind wholly different to those applicable to a text intended to be read at leisure – or even read aloud in instalments. The most difficult challenge that the harper-poet was to encounter was probably that of the mixed audience of the manor-hall; of that I shall have something more to say in a moment.

First, we must take notice of the historical fact that, from the beginning of the fourteenth century, the harper as court-entertainer entered on a steady decline in popularity, from which he was never to recover. Though Edward II continued to employ some harpers of his father's later years (William de Morley – a king of heralds known as *Roi du North* – and Hugh de Naunton) and three of his own former retinue as Prince of Wales (Elias Garsington, Robert Clough and Henry Newsom, [32]) they appear to have had no later successors of any importance. The eclipse continues and intensifies through the long reign of Edward III, and neither he nor Henry V (in spite of being himself a skilled player of the instrument) take any harpers with them on their expeditions to France. (The chroniclers of these later campaigns are clerks writing to be read, not minstrels composing for performance.) Only Richard II's harper, the blind William Dodmore, achieved any later prominence at court.

Though the personal tastes of these monarchs may have had something to do with it, there is, of course, a deeper and more fundamental reason for the change: the spread of literacy and rapidly-widening distribution of books, which anticipated the invention of the printing-press that was to accelerate and complete the process.

When ordinary, moderately-educated men and women could read stories from a book – aloud to the assembled household or privately for their own pleasure – the harper as story-teller was well on his way to becoming redundant; when poets like Geoffrey Chaucer came to declaim their verses to the court of Richard II, the harper was directly supplanted in what had been his most prestigious sphere of influence. This was not the only change; there was also a shift of sensibility away from the archaic matter of Troy and Rome, and the fabulous adventures of Arthur and his knights, which the harper had made his own. 'The artificial music of the minstrels' – so the French court poet, Eustache Deschamps, informs us in 1391 – 'could be learnt by *le plus rude homme du monde* but *musique naturelle* was primarily inspired by a loving will to give praise to ladies'.[33] The velvet-covered volume of love-poems that Froissart presents in person to Richard is, after being dipped into with pleasure and anticipation, carried away to the king's private chamber.[34] William Dodmore will sleep undisturbed.

Even as musician, the harper's pre-eminence was threatened by newly-imported, more exotic instruments such as the lute. On all fronts, he was becoming old-fashioned. Fortunately for him, there were those – then and for many years to come – who would prefer the old fashions to the new.

Ironically, the harpers and heralds were among the first to commit their words to writing for commercial exploitation, and thus to encourage the very movement that ultimately was to undermine their position. The earliest 'biography' in the French language (that of William Marshal) was written in verse by a thirteenth-century English *trouvère* called Jean; some of the texts of the romances themselves are believed to have been copied for cash sale in a London scriptorium.[35]

Chandos Herald, in the introduction to his *Life of the Black Prince* (c. 1376–87), gives us the performers' point of view on the upheaval that was taking place in the minstrel profession. 'In days gone by', he tells us, 'those who made fine poems were regarded as authors or in some sort recorders, who set down their knowledge of good deeds, remembered such things in their heart, and were hosts to honour'. But now, 'people prefer chatterers, false liars, jongleurs or jesters who will pull faces and imitate a monkey to make them laugh, to someone who can tell true stories. Such people are not welcome at court nowadays; but whatever people think of them they should not give up writing poems about good deeds, if they know how to, but should write them in a book, so that when they are dead there is an honest record'.[36] (Note the distinction here between 'setting down' their knowledge of good deeds which are remembered in the heart, and writing them in a book.)

Speaking, as he does, on behalf of the herald-harpers – authors of such epics as *The Song of Carlaverock* – Chandos Herald's reference to true stories is important; it is doubtful if he would have had much time for the minstrel-romancers. Chaucer has a poor opinion of the harpers of his time in general. While justly giving their profession pride of place among minstrel specialities in his *Hous of Fame* (c. 1380), no contemporary harper is considered worthy of a place beside Orpheus, Arion, Chiron (who learnt the art from Apollo himself) or the Breton bard Glasgerion – but only on a lower level, where the

> smale harpers with her glees
> Seten under hem in sees,
> And gone on hem upward to gape,

And countrefete hem as an ape,
Or as craft countrefeteth kinde. [37]   *art imitates nature*

But I must not exaggerate the extent or speed of the changes that were taking place; in this, as in other respects, the situation at court was far from being a necessarily true reflection of what was happening in the country at large. As Chaucer himself admits,

The mynstralcye, the service at the feeste,
The grete yiftes to the meeste and leeste...   *gifts, most*
Ne who moost felyngly speketh of love;
What haukes sitten on the perche above,
What houndes liggen on the floor adoun –
Of al this make I now no mencioun. [38]

As I said earlier, a major problem that must have confronted the harper-poet was the mixed audience typical of the country manor hall.

The answer to this was found to lie in exciting narratives of multi-layered meaning, in which indications of character, emotion and mood are so economically conveyed as never to impede the onward thrust of the action.

In *Sir Orfeo* – to give just one example – when the bereaved harper-king is enduring a self-imposed exile in a mysterious Celtic waste-land, he sees his queen, whose name is Herodis, riding by in a company of the dead and resolves to go in search of her. (For ease of reading, I draw here on Professor Tolkien's modernised version.)

He rose and thither made his way,
and to a lady came with speed,
and looked at her, and took good heed,
and saw as sure as once in life
'twas Heurodis, his queen and wife.
Intent he gazed, and so did she,
but no word spake; no word said he.
For hardship that she saw him bear,
who had been royal, and high, and fair,
then from her eyes the tears there fell.
The other ladies marked it well,
and away they made her swiftly ride;
no longer might she near him bide. [39]

The silent, yearning look between Orfeo and his queen says all that needs to be said of their love for each other; at the same time, it acts as a trigger, propelling the story forward as the king sets out in pursuit of her.

In 1412 (the last full year of Henry IV), we find an unnamed, unknown harper at work, in just such a situation as I have postulated, at the Suffolk home of Dame Alice de Bryene, widow of Sir Guy de Bryene, the son of one of Edward III's Garter knights. (Perhaps the harper was an old retainer sent over from one of the great magnate houses of Suffolk – from Nayland or Clare – to provide the kind of old-fashioned entertainment that Dame Alice would most have appreciated.)

It is Christmas Day, a Sunday, and the harper is seated at table along with the Lady herself, her scrivener, bailiff and harvest reeve, and sixteen others of the household. The only guest is a certain Agnes Whyte; a fairly intimate household occasion. (The menu for the day – a quarter of beef, a quarter of bacon, one young pig, a capon and a cony, 'wine from what remained, ale from stock' – is meticulously recorded in Dame Alice's household book; she is nothing if not a careful provider.) The harper is still there on Boxing Day, and throughout the week, as the guests gradually increase to twenty-six, taking in various neighbouring gentry who come and go in succession, and (on the Saturday, a fast day) two friars. But the big occasion comes on the Sunday following, New Year's Day, when the guests at table swell to thirty-six, and 'Thomas Malcher with three hundred tenants and other strangers' crowd in to enjoy the harper's performance; 314 white and 40 black loaves are consumed with two pigs, two swans, two joints of meat, 24 capons and 17 conies from the pantry, and a quantity of other meat brought in for the occasion; the wine is still 'from what remained, ale from stock'. [40]

One begins to appreciate in very concrete terms how the harper would have needed to vary his choice of repertoire to take account of changing numbers, presence of clergy etc., and the particular challenge of New Year's Day with its 'full house', including Dame Alice, her guests and household servants, down to the farm workers and poor tenants of her estate – a complete cross-section of medieval, rural society.

If I had to choose a single occasion that would stand for medieval minstrelsy at its most characteristic and best, I would choose this one; our nameless harper holding his audience with a *geste* at Acton Hall in Suffolk, on New Year's Day, 1412.

8

Minstrels and the Hundred Years' War

After the deposition and murder of Edward II, followed by a period of misgovernment by his murderer Mortimer in collusion with his former queen, Isabella, the seizure of power by the young Edward III marks a new beginning in the fortunes of the English monarchy. But it was a revival that, in the event, could only be maintained by successful military adventures overseas: the assertion of a dubious claim by the new king on the crown of France in right of his adulterous mother.

The great victories of Crécy and Poitiers – in which the king's eldest son, the Black Prince, played a leading role – accumulated royal capital, which was then steadily dissipated in the remaining forty years of Edward's over-long reign, ending as it did in senility and political corruption.

A passage from the Chronicle of the Hainaulter, Jean Froissart, captures the early mood of optimism and will also serve to indicate the role of minstrels in time of war.

A Spanish fleet, gathered at Sluys after a trading mission to Flanders, was preparing to make its way back through the Channel. In retaliation for attacks on English shipping, Edward decided to intercept it, and mustered the English fleet off Winchelsea. The year was 1350. (Froissart could not have been there in person, but he may have obtained this eye-witness account from one of his chief informants, Chandos Herald.)

King Edward had already drawn up his fleet and decided how he wished to fight the battle... He stood in the bows of his own ship, wearing a black velvet jerkin and a black beaverskin cap which greatly suited him. On that day, I was told by some who were with him, he was in a gayer mood than he had ever been seen before. He told his minstrels to strike up a dance tune which Sir John Chandos, who was there beside him, had recently brought back from Germany. And out of sheer high spirits he made Sir John sing with the minstrels, to his own vast amusement... While the King was enjoying this gaiety and his knights were cheerful at seeing him so cheerful, the look-out shouted: 'Ship ahoy! And she looks like a Spaniard.' The minstrels stopped playing, and the man was asked if he saw more than one. In a moment he answered: 'Yes, there are two, now three, now four'. And then, seeing the huge fleet, he shouted: 'There are so many, God help me, I can't count them!' The King and his men realised it must be the Spanish. The trumpets were sounded and the ships drew close together so as to be in battle order and more safely positioned... It was already late, somewhere about four o'clock'. The King therefore had wine served to himself and all his knights. Then he and the others put on their battle helmets.

A bloody and costly sea-fight ensued, but the English counted it a victory. Fourteen Spanish ships were sunk though others escaped and sailed on.

When the English had no one left to fight, they sounded the retreat on their trumpets and set course towards England. [1]

If, as I suggested earlier, the royal court constituted at all times a standing staff for military or naval operations, capable of rapid expansion to meet the exigencies of war, it must now be said that in war it remained a court, and the minstrels' function as entertainers of the king and his courtiers – now his commanders – was as important as ever. The piper and fiddler remained at his side, or instantly summonable. At the same time, the trumpeters are seen to have performed a special, somewhat separate function as signallers.

The trumpets referred to here and in other chronicles of the time are said to derive, partly from the Roman *tuba*, and partly from Arab instruments that the Christian armies had encountered in Spain and the Holy Land. The S-shaped bend of some instruments seen in fifteenth-century manuscript paintings dates from about 1400. (See, for example, the instrument shown L of the illustration on p.117.)

The long trumpet retained something of the exclusiveness it had enjoyed in the Orient, and was reserved to the minstrels of kings and their greater nobles. A painted banner with the royal or seigniorial arms was often hung from it. Such instruments were naturally expensive, especially if made of silver. In 1346, the Black Prince paid 19 marks (£12 13s. 4d.) for two of them. [2] In peace or war, trumpets heralded the presence of the king; in battle, their signalled messages carried his personal authority and, in theory at least, were to be instantly obeyed. We have seen them used to muster the fleet off Winchelsea and order its withdrawal. In a campaign-diary from Crécy in 1346, there is mention of 'the dawn trumpet-call' – clearly a form of *reveille*; and at Poitiers, when the French were in retreat and elements of the English army had pursued them to the gates of the nearby city, they were recalled by the same imperative summons. [3] A shorter form of trumpet, known in England as a clarion, is also mentioned in the chronicles; this was sometimes made of wood. (See p.117, R.)

As trumpets were reserved for the king and his commanders (later, for the cavalry), horns and cornetts were used by the foot soldiers, archers and others. The cornett (not the modern brass instrument) was a development of the horn, in which holes were pierced to give a diatonic scale. Originally of animal horn – 'bugle' derives from the name of a now-extinct species of wild ox – cornetts were now also being made from hollowed-out pieces of wood, fitted with a leather sheath; they might be curved or straight. [4]

In a description of the battle of Otterburn (Chevy Chase) between the Scots and the English in 1388, Froissart tells us that it was the Scottish custom 'for all the foot-soldiers to carry horns slung from their necks like a huntsman's. When they all blow them together, some high, some full, some on a middle note, and the others at their own choice, they make such a noise, with the big drums that they also have, that the sound carries at least four miles by day, and six at night. It gives them a tremendous thrill and strikes terror into their enemies'. [5] There were Scots troops under William Douglas present on the French side at Poitiers where, in Geoffrey le Baker's account, 'the trumpets sounded and clarions, warhorns and drums replied, until the sounds echoed along the Poitevin woods, until the hills seemed to roar to the valleys and the clouds of thunder'. [6]

We are fortunate to have a contemporary record of the exact composition and numbers of Edward's minstrels between 1344 and 1347 – for the Crécy campaign. [7] There were five trumpeters, five pipers, two clarioners, three waits, a fiddler, taborer, citoler and a nakerer, with 'retinue' of three mounted archers and three foot archers, making twenty-five in all. (It is not clear if the retinue were also minstrels, as their inclusion in the total suggests, or a 'guard detachment'.) They received 20s. a year in time of peace and 12d. a day in time of war. The latter rate puts them on a par with the royal chaplains, esquires and sergeants of arms, and is a useful indication of their standing. (Knights receive 2s. a day, and the king's archers, hobilers and craftsmen, 6d.) It is doubtful still if they ever played together as an ensemble – except, as off Winchelsea, in twos or threes to accompany singing or dancing. At a period when nearly everyone – from the shepherd boy on his hillside to the young noble in castle or manor – learnt to play at least one instrument as a normal part of his upbringing, minstrels in general were required to be specialists and virtuosi; the royal minstrels – whether in war or peace – were representative of the finest instrumental musicians of their day.

The names of some of Edward's minstrels between 1344 and 1347 have survived, along with a few biographical details. By comparison with a list of royal servants in the Close Roll of 1341, owed wages for their service in 'parts beyond the sea' (presumably Flanders), and assuming the same men are still serving, the king's trumpeters can be named as Roger Trumpor, Nicholas Trumpor, Peter de Bayon, Robert Barber and Giles Trumpor; Giles was rewarded with a place in Wycombe in April 1344. [8] The pipers will have included Godescale Piper, Libekyn Piper and his son, Hanekin. Libekyn is first mentioned in 1342, and continues in the king's service until about 1347. Hanekin Fitz Libekyn (as he is always named) partners his father in the early years. Later, he was appointed 'Marshal of the Minstrels', and appears as such in an account of a Garter ceremony in 1358. In 1360, he is granted 7½d. daily whether he is 'within the household or without'. In 1363, we catch a glimpse of him in his garden in the London parish of St Katherine, Aldgate, where he is neighbour to Thomas Hok, butcher, John Baudre, fishmonger, and a lady with the fragrant name of Maud Lavender. Hanekin, 'pyper of the king', is still receiving wages in 1370.[9] ('Piper', as I have said, was used of players of many different wind instruments.) In 1352, the Black Prince bought four pipes, silver-gilt and enamelled (perhaps flutes) for his own minstrels, as well as pouches to keep them in.[10]

The Harding family served Edward II and his son as waits (*vigiles* or watchmen) for over sixty years. John Harding (whose personal seal shows crossed shawms) first appears in the records in 1311 under Edward II, and continues in royal service until at least the twelfth year of Edward III (1338). He is partnered by William (probably his son) from the first year of Edward III, and William outlives the new king – a rare achievement. He retired to the convent of Dunstable in the year of Edward's death, and is last mentioned in the first year of Richard II (1377). Both John and William are also described as pipers.[11] These two families, the Pipers and Hardings, are a good example of the way in which royal minstrels constituted something of a self-perpetuating oligarchy among minstrels in general. Apart from the occasional recruitment of distinguished players from abroad and apprentices from among the king's boy choristers, they rarely had need to go outside their own family circles to recruit new members; this is one of the difficulties of tracing their individual histories.

Thomas Citoler was another survivor from Edward II's reign, as was also Ivo Vala who slightly preceded him. The citole is now known to have been a form of short lute, plucked with a plectrum; not, as previously believed, a gittern.[12]

Edward III's tabrett or taborer was a man called Lambert de Stokerode, who was also known as Lambekin the Taborer. In 1344, he and his wife Alice were granted a messuage in the parish of St Mary, Fenchurch, though they did not remain there long because in 1349 it passed to one of the king's yeomen. By 1360, Lambert was in receipt of a life annuity of 100s. and, like his colleague Hanekin Piper and several others, was getting an additonal 7½d. daily, 'to wit for the time he shall be without the household as when he shall stay within'. This uniquely generous arrangement meant that he and his fellows could go off on tour when they were not required at court and still be assured of their daily wage. Along with Hanekin, he was still receiving wages in 1370.[13]

Of course, these were not the only minstrels present at Crécy – merely those in personal attendance on the king. The fourteen earls, seventy-eight banerets (commanders entitled to display a personal banner), and many of the 1,066 knights enumerated in the payroll would have brought their own minstrels with them, and these performed a similar function in relation to their lords and their varied following of squires, men-at-arms, archers etc. as the king's minstrels did for him and his household battalion. The same was true of the French. Hence that great volume of sound as the two great armies advanced upon each other. And over all, there would have been the majestic blasts of the trumpet and the higher-pitched calls of clarion and cornett.

The character of the Black Prince as it shines through the predictable hyperbole of the chronicles and Chandos Herald's 'Life', though it does nothing to redeem the naked brutality and carnage of the Hundred Years' War, may help us to an understanding of why and how men thought about it as they did. Like William Marshal before him, he was everything that a medieval knight was supposed to be but so rarely was in reality and, as a military commander, phenomenally successful into the bargain. Even his defeated enemies could find no bad word to say of him, and Froissart's report of the one alleged blot on his posthumous reputation – the 'massacre' at Limoges – has been shown to be largely false. It is hard not to warm to a man who apologises for his victories and serves his defeated royal opponent of France (the captured King John) on bended knee. Though invariably short of cash in spite of the rich booty that came his way, he was famous – as a good knight should be – for his generosity to his followers. Fortunately, some of his *Registers* – the accounts kept by his stewards of day-to-day expenditure – survive, and enable us to come a little closer to the many minstrels who took part in his campaigns and who were recipients of his wages and gifts; the two are always clearly distinguished.

His first encounters with minstrels pre-date the *Registers*. The eight-year-old prince, when ill with some childish ailment, is visited by his mother's violist, Richard Merlin, and the Welshman's playing is rewarded by the gift of a coat. In the following year, he is entertained by a minstrel with a small (portative) organ, and by John, the 'fool of Eltham'. [14]

Though often pictured in the hands of angels, the portative organ was also a popular secular instrument used by minstrels. Eltham was one of the royal manors; John was still in place five years later with his 'master', which suggests that he was a simpleton.

The earliest relevant entries in the *Registers* date from the years between Crécy and Poitiers (1346–55), when the Prince was in England. In 1348, a destrier or war-horse called Morel de Burgherssh, presumably captured in the course of a joust, was given to a minstrel at a tournament in Bury St Edmunds. (This may have been in conscious imitation of the Prince's exemplar in chivalry, William Marshal. When, at a party following a tournament, Marshal was serenaded by a minstrel with a new song, of which the refrain was 'Marshal, give me a good horse', William had immediately ridden out, engaged the first knight he met in combat, captured his horse and, returning to the party, presented it to the minstrel.[15]) It has to be remembered that such animals were of immense value; in modern terms, little short of that of a thoroughbred racehorse.

The Prince employed some dozen minstrels in his household at this period. As we might expect of a man who was already an international figure, they were a cosmopolitan group. Four pipers had been sent to him by the Count of Eu, Constable of France, who had been captured at Caen and later ransomed for twenty thousand marks. They seem to have arrived, however, without their instruments, and it is for them that the Prince purchased the silver-gilt and enamelled pipes already mentioned. The English clerks had great difficulty with their names; I shall take the most usual spellings and call them Jakelyn, Ulyn, Yevelyn and Countz. Hankyn the piper – not to be confused with Hankin Fitz Libekyn,the king's minstrel – was probably English. On the same day on which the pipes were bought, the Prince also acquired a bagpipe, a cornemeuse (a type of bagpipe with single drone), and a tabor which, like the pipes, was silver-gilt and enamelled. The taborer's name was John Cokard.[16]

Many entries relate to the purchase of equipment and transport in preparation for the 'Great Raid' of 1355, which was to culminate in Poitiers and the taking of Calais. In 1352, horses were bought for the use of the French pipers. Two German minstels called Hans and Soz were supplied with three cart-horses and saddles (the third perhaps for a servant with their instruments), three-quarters of a rayed cloth for making robes for themselves, and two habergeons – a type of hauberk or jacket of chain mail – leaving little doubt of their expected involvement in the action or close proximity to it. (For the later Gascon campaign, Jakelyn Piper received a 'ketilhat'.) A whole list of minstrels, craftsmen and other servants of the Prince's 'riding household', some twenty-seven in all including a Thomas Wafrer, are allotted a cart-horse each, though a group of Burgundian minstrels had to make do with two horses between the four of them.[17]

The Prince's trumpeters were Ralph Dexcestre (Ralph of Exeter) and John Martyn. It was for them that the two trumpets were bought. At the same time (1346), the Prince paid four shillings for the tube (*canoun*) of a latten trumpet; latten being a mixed metal similar to brass. The tube would have been of the type with mouthpiece attached that was made at this time to slide in and out of the main bore of an ordinary trumpet, thus extending its musical range to become what was known as a Slide Trumpet, a precursor of the sackbut and trombone.[18]

For the expedition to Gascony in 1363, the Prince was accompanied from England by six minstrels only, dressed, like Hans and Soz, entirely in ray – a broadly-striped cloth similar to that worn today by the Papal Swiss Guards.

The rates of pay of these men are not stated but were probably commensurate to those received by the king's minstrels: 20s. a year in peace, 7½d. or a shilling a day on campaign. Payment of wages, as for the army generally, was usually in arrears. On the other hand, unlike the footmen and archers, minstrels were often rewarded with generous largesse. In 1361, the pipers Jakelyn and Ulyn received the very considerable sum of £26 13s. 4d. 'as a gift from the prince to clear their debts for a time'.[19] Equipment – instruments and horses – was replaced as necessary; in 1358, Jakelyn got £6 13s. 4d. towards the cost of a new pipe, and Ulyn 66s. 8d. for a riding hackney.[20]

An example of the care and concern the Prince had for his minstrels and former minstrels appears in his efforts on behalf of a trumpeter called Gilbert Stakford. On the Prince's departure from England to take up his new command as ruler of Aquitaine in 1363, Gilbert had been left behind through incapacity of some kind – perhaps he had been wounded in the Poitiers campaign. In 1365, the Prince wrote from Bordeaux to his permanent officials of the Duchy of Cornwall, enclosing a letter which Gilbert is to deliver personally to the Prior of St Michael's Mount, with a request to admit him to his house and provide him with sustenance on account of his good service. The Prior is to specify by letters patent precisely what Gilbert is to receive while in his care. The Steward of Cornwall is meanwhile to use 'all the influence he can to secure that the letters take effect according to the prince's desire'. Whatever the immediate result of this high-powered correspondence, it seems that Gilbert recovered sufficiently to be of future service to the Prince's son, Richard II, and, over twenty years later, was awarded a pension of 6d. a day 'for service to the king's father and to the king'.[21]

When we look more closely at what was happening at court during Edward III's reign, we notice that a significant change in the whole nature of court entertainment was taking place. Gone were those long sessions in the interludes of feasts, when performers of every conceivable speciality took their turn before the king and his guests as they had done before Edward I at Ipswich; now the king himself is leading the dance in an extraordinary series of plays and disguisings, tournaments and elaborate ceremonies.

As early as 1343, Edward had conceived the idea of reviving the Arthurian Round Table, but before the project which included a huge amphitheatre to house the table could be completed, he abandoned it, to found the Order of the Garter.

Though there was doubtless a solemn, even sincerely religious, aspect to the new order and to the tournaments and other ceremonies that surrounded it, it is clear from the records that these also provided a welcome opportunity for a good deal of light-hearted dressing-up and make-believe drama. For the Jousts at Windsor in 1344, Edward is equipped with three 'harnesses' (suits), two of which are of white velvet worked with blue *Garters* and diapered throughout with wodewoses (wild men), and the third of cerulean velvet. On one occasion, the king and his Garter knights gallop through the city of London dressed as Moors. For the 'King's Plays' of Christmas 1348 at Otford, fifty-three vizards (masks) are ordered: twelve of 'men's heads having above them a lion's head, twelve of men's heads surmounted by elephants' heads, twelve of men's heads with bats' wings, twelve of heads of wodewoses, seventeen of virgins' heads'; for the Plays at Epiphany in the same year, kept at Merton, order is made for a 'Harness of white buckram for the King, tinseled with silver, and the tunic and shield worked with the King's motto,

> Hay hay the wythe Swan,
> By Godes soule I am thy man',

and of thirteen masks of dragons' heads and thirteen men's heads with diadems. [22]

Towards the end of the fourteenth century we first begin to hear the expression, 'minstrels' table'; in 1379, a clarioner called John Buckingham is indentured to join *la table des ministralx* of the Black Prince's younger brother, John of Gaunt. [23] Though becoming static, the minstrels are still involved in the festivities; but their role is now restricted to that of court musicians and accompanists only, in which capacity they are provided, in 1344–5, with 'sixteen tunics with as many hoods – lined, furred and buttoned before'. [24] As the harper-poets are displaced by the new breed of courtly writers, minstrel entertainers of the old traditon – singers and dancers like Vassall and Matilda Makejoy – give way to the gifted amateur; the masked players of interludes – Griscote, Visage and Magote – to the masquerades of the king and his courtiers. Sir John Chandos is himself required to sing the new song his minstrels have brought back with them from Germany; and when, in 1363, King John of France returns voluntarily to his captivity in England, it is the young Lord de Coucy, one of his hostages, who takes the prize for singing and dancing when his turn comes round. [25]

There can be little doubt that in all this Edward was indulging his personal tastes; but there is more to it than that. Riding the crest of a surge of nationalistic fervour fanned, and in part created, by the victories in France, royalty itself is seen to be moving into a new position of dominance in the national life and consciousness, which now finds appropriate expression in visual and mimetic symbols. However, the fact that minstrels are displaced to a subsidiary role in court entertainment does not preclude their continuing to serve the king in a more personal and private way in his inner chamber. For paradoxically, while it is true that the monarch is now taking a more public, ceremonial role as personification and symbol of the more aggressive nation-state that is coming into being, he is also and at the same time separating himself from even the greatest of his subjects; and when, at the end of the day, he retreats into his private apartments, he is able to enjoy a private life there of a kind that was quite unknown to even the most powerful of his predecessors – to Henry II or Edward I. As the door of his solar or privy chamber closes behind him, it will become our special task to distinguish and trace those few individual minstrels who are privileged to share his intimacy, serving him in the way they have always done and which now, as ever, defines their true identity – as his 'little servants'.

The distinction I make here between chamber minstrels and court musicians will become clearer and more explicit in the records as we proceed; but that the conditions in which it was to operate were already in place is suggested by a writ of 1351, referring to the movements of 'the king with his household, and at other times with his private household (*secreta familia*)'.[26] It is the first of several crucial changes and divisions affecting the minstrel profession in the fourteenth and fifteenth centuries which, in the end, were to result in its destruction.

Meanwhile, the former association of minstrels and heralds continues; Andrew Norreys, a King of heralds, is also listed as a minstrel and, in 1360, William Volaunt is named as 'King of the Heralds and Minstrels';[27] but as the heralds become more active in diplomatic errands abroad, the day-to-day organisation of the minstrels at court – their rotas of attendance, payment etc. – now falls to the newly-created 'Marshals', of whom Hanekin Fitz Libekyn appears to have been the first.[28]

It should also be said that if the changes in the nature of court entertainment now taking place resulted – for the majority of minstrels – in some restriction of their former versatility and accustomed access to the person of the king, such losses were compensated to some extent by new opportunities opening up to them as musicians. The process throughout is one of increasing specialisation.

In France, this was the period of the influential *Ars Nova*, of which the most notable exponent was the composer, Guillaume de Machaut (c.1330–77), a clerk who for twenty years had been secretary to the blind King of Bohemia, who died bravely at Crécy. It is to Machaut that we owe the first cohesive setting of the Ordinary of the Mass (Kyrie, Gloria, Credo etc.). The absence of text in certain passages, and often unsingable character of the middle registers, indicate that instrumental collaboration (supplied by minstrels) was required for their performance. The role of instruments in the new music generally, though important, was never spelled out, and much was left, as before, to the improvisational skills of the performers.[29] (The possible involvement of minstrels in the music of the Chapel Royal will be looked at below.)

It is in this period also that we first hear of 'minstrel schools (*escoles*)'; schools, not in the sense of places of learning (though they existed too), but of large assemblies – conferences, as we should call them now. These were held, probably annually, in various Flemish towns, and at Beauvais in France, during the third week of Lent – the week before Laetare Sunday. The earliest known was at Bruges in 1318, and the latest at Damme in 1447.[30] On these occasions, minstrels of every European nationality could meet with each other, learn new tunes and techniques or purchase instruments. There is a record from 1335 of Edward granting permission to two of his bagpipers, Barbor (or Barberus) and Morlan (John de Morleyns, a specialist on the cornemeuse) to visit one such gathering.[31] In 1358–9, a minstrel called Walter Hert is rewarded on returning to court from a *scola Menstralcie* in London – but this was probably a school of the more obviously instructional kind.[32]

The Black Prince having died prematurely in 1376, it was his son Richard who succeeded Edward III when his fifty-year reign finally came to an end in the following year. Though he was ultimately successful in his policy of achieving peace with France, Richard had also to contend from the start with bitter domestic strife on his own doorstep. The Peasants' Revolt – a reaction to the political corruption and economic instability of the latter part of Edward's reign – was followed by a relentless struggle for power between the king and his earls, which was to end – disastrously for Richard – in the usurpation of Henry Bolinbroke.

I have little to add to what has already been said in the last chapter of the court of Richard II, where – with the solitary exception of Richard's blind harper, William Dodmore – the minstrels remain in the shadows as musicians and accompanists only. In 1387, a man called John Caumz, described as *Rex Ministrallorum nostrorum* (King of our minstrels), is given a safe-conduct to travel abroad. Could he have been, like his predecessor, William Volaunt, a King of *heralds* and minstrels?[33]

Richard himself – for all that has been written about him – remains an enigmatic figure, seemingly trapped in a self-image of grandeur unsustainable in the political circumstances of his time, and so doomed to tragedy. Only Dodmore appears to have been admitted to the secret world, shared by Richard with his beloved Anne of Bohemia, that must have lain behind the public mask of kingship; and Dodmore's voice is silent. (That the harper had influence with the king is proven by his intervention in quite a serious case of burglary and robbery, in which he was successful in obtaining a pardon for the accused man.[34])

We must shift the focus of our attention now to Edward III's younger son, John of Gaunt, who outlived his brother to become the elder statesman and power behind the throne during the reign of his nephew, and posthumously – through his son, Henry Bolinbroke, the usurper – founder of the Lancastrian line of kings. (The nineteen-year-old Gaunt had married Blanche, daughter of the earl of Lancaster, and, through her, inherited the earldom with its vast estates, especially in the north; he had been created

Duke by his father.) At his Palace of the Savoy in London, and at Kenilworth Castle, Gaunt maintained a considerable household establishment, including his own chapel with its singers and clerks.

His *Registers* (like those of his brother) yield valuable information about the minstrels he employed. In 1373, his clarioner is a man called James Sauthe (or Sanche), and his pipers are named as Smelltes, Hans Gough, Henry Hultescrane and a companion, Roger. In about 1375–6, the pipers are joined by Hankyn Frysh – possibly the same Hankyn we have already met with in the company of the Black Prince. John Buckingham, a former minstrel of Edward III's, joins the duke's 'table' in 1379, and John Gibson in 1381. (In 1384, Buckingham was to be in trouble for marrying an orphaned heiress without permission of her legal guardians.) Standing a little apart from these are a certain John Tyas, described simply as 'one of our minstrels' or 'our good friend John Tyas' – of whom I shall have more to say a little later – and John Cliff of Coventry, the duke's nakerer. In 1381, John receives a splendid gift from the duke of a silver *escucon* with a collar for a minstrel, a pair of nakers, two more collars and a belt (*ceyntoure*), and two drum sticks, also of silver. [35]

In his multiple identities as duke of Lancaster, earl of Derby, Lincoln and Leicester, the great man enjoyed the services of a number of heralds – one for each of his titles. Leicester Herald was a man called Henry Grene who, like John Tyas, we are to meet again.

The most prominent of all the Lancastrian minstrels is a piper called William Byngeley; we shall try to follow through the events of the next few years in his company. He first comes into view as one of the minstrels who accompanied Henry of Bolinbroke when, in 1390 and again in 1392, he set out on 'crusade' to Prussia, where the Teutonic Order of Knights was engaged in territorial warfare with their pagan Lithuanian neighbours to the east. The twenty-four year-old Bolinbroke (who had now succeeded to one of his father's titles as earl of Derby) travelled in state with two heralds (Lancaster and Derby), two trumpeters (John Brothir and Robert Crakyll), a group of pipers including Byngeley, William Algood and William of York, together with John, his father's nakerer, now dignified by the title of Master John. One feels that the older man must have put in a special plea to go with the expedition. The name of another piper and musician of later importance, John Aleyn, first occurs in 1392 when, in fact, Henry found that his services were no longer required by the German knights, and decided instead on a voyage to the Holy Land. Aleyn was one of those sent home by Henry before he embarked on this longer, rather different journey. [36]

Henry Bolinbroke has been described as a 'passionate devotee' of music. [37] We catch a charming glimpse of him at home in Monmouth in 1386, with his first wife, Mary de Bohun; Henry playing a recorder to Mary's singing. In 1395–6, he rewards a man for presenting a harp to their ten-year-old son, Henry (the future Henry V), for which additional strings are bought.[38]

If Bolinbroke's motive for his journeys abroad had been to stay out of mounting political troubles at home, it was shown to have been justified when, five years later, back from the Holy Land, he became involved in the bitter quarrel with Mowbray, which led to the famous Coventry Joust of 1398 when Richard banished them both. On the death of John of Gaunt in the following year, the king – intimidated by the might of the house of Lancaster and greedy for its possessions – made the fatal mistake of forbidding Henry to enter on his inheritance, and extending his banishment to lifelong exile. In an attempt to mollify the reaction of shock and alarm which this unprecedented interference with the laws of inheritance created among the nobility and property-owning classes generally, Richard granted pensions to a long list of Lancastrian dependents in England, but some thirty of Henry's and his father's old retainers were simply transferred to the royal service; among these were Henry Grene, the Leicester Herald, William Byngeley and his fellow piper of the Prussian expedition, William of York, and a nakerer called Claus who had been on the old duke's payroll since 1389.[39] When, in April 1399, Richard set sail 'with trumpets sounding' for Ireland to deal with an insurrection there, he took Grene, Byngeley and York with him, along with his devoted Dodmore.[40] Leaving England at such a time was another mistake, as Richard was to discover just a few weeks later when news reached him of Bolinbroke's invasion. Returning in haste to Conway in Wales (presumably bringing the minstrels with him), the king, outmanoeuvred and finally tricked by Henry into compliance, soon found himself a prisoner in the Tower of London.

For Byngeley and his fellow-Lancastrians, Bolinbroke's usurpation of the throne achieved both a speedy return to their true allegiance and the means of rapid advancement. At a knighting ceremony in the Tower on 22 November, prior to their lord's Coronation as Henry IV, Henry Grene appears as 'King of the Heralds', entrusted with the payment of largesse to the other heralds, English and foreign, who were present,[41] and Byngeley takes the place previously occupied by Dodmore as the king's most favoured 'chamber minstrel', his yeoman and personal servant as well as musician.

A succession of gifts, additional to wages, are seen to come his way. In 1401, a quantity of cloth ordered from a London tailor by John Holland, Richard's half-brother – executed for his part in the magnates' revolt of the previous year – is delivered by the king's order to Byngeley and his fellow-minstrel, Claus Nakerer. In 1402, he shares a grant of £21 5s. 8d. in fines and sequestrations with another yeoman of the chamber, John Grene – perhaps a relation of Henry's. He may even have been a little over-zealous in his loyalty. In the same year, there is a warrant to set free a Norwich draper who had been imprisoned on Byngeley's charge that he had claimed to have 'seen the face of the late king deceased and that the said king is yet alive'. In 1405, he is given 'protection' to accompany the king to Wales, where Owen Glendower had raised the principality in rebellion and, in September of that year, is rewarded with the fees of the office of Bailiff of Flint. [42] Later entries suggest that William's extramural activities extended to an involvement in piracy against ships of the Hanse merchants, requiring (in 1410) a pardon from the king for all felonies and breaches of prison short of murder and rape, and the consequent withdrawal of some, at least, of his fees and privileges. [43] But in November 1412, within a few months of his death, Henry, ill and exhausted as he then was, is sufficiently mindful of his old retainer to order the Treasurer to provide him with £2 6s. 8d. for 'apparel for his person'. [44]

What happened to William Dodmore is equally instructive. Minstrels and other retainers who found themselves on the losing side in the dynastic upheavals of the age were not unduly prejudiced by the fact of their former allegiance. Henry, as usurper, may even have had a personal interest in retaining the former royal harper's services. At all events, he lost no time in confirming Richard's previous grant to him of £10 a year. But the relationship between minstrel and master, being essentially a personal one, rarely survived such changes for long, and it is no surprise to find that in 1408 Dodmore is with the king's son, Thomas, in Ireland. There, it would seem, he remained. [45]

The revolution of 1399 left the royal power, though it remained undiminished in constitutional form, significantly weakened in relation to that of the magnates, at whose sufferance Henry IV had struggled to retain and consolidate his uneasy tenure of the throne. Henry V was able to restore something of the old glory; and the way he chose to do it – by reviving Edward's claim to France, thus renewing the Hundred Years' War – though ultimately disastrous, was brilliantly successful in the short term.

He took fifteen minstrels with him to France in 1415, and at their head appears the familiar name of John Cliff – almost certainly a son or grandson of Master John, Gaunt's nakerer. Earlier that year (in February), John Cliff II, had been granted a pardon for 'all treasons, murders, rapes' etc. 'before 8 December last', indicating an involvement in the recent Lollard rising of Sir John Oldcastle; but in the present atmosphere of war fever and national emergency all that was to be put behind and forgotten. [46] The Agincourt Roll gives fourteen other names: Thomas Noreys, John Panell and John Payte were trumpeters; Richard Geffrey, John Brown and William Maisham, pipers; Cornuce Snayth was a fiddler; the instruments played by the remaining seven – as of John Cliff himself – are unknown. Two trumpeters, William Bradstrete and Thomas Chaterton, and Thomas and John Wilde were to join the expedition later. [47]

Their pay remained at the former rate 'in time of war' of a shilling a day, but when or whether they ever received it is open to doubt. In 1433, the executor of the will of John Cliff's widow, Joan, was still claiming £33 6s. from the Treasury owed to the estate in back-pay for John's service in France. As security for the debt, John had been given a silver lantern, a tabernacle (used to reserve the Blessed Sacrament), two silver ewers and 'divers relicks', amounting in value (at 40s. per pound weight) to £53. These and a miscellany of other precious articles were delivered to the Treasurer and Chamberlains 'to the King's use' for a settlement of £10 – less than a third of John's entitlement and some eighteen years late – far *too* late to be of any benefit either to him or to his widow. [48] However, the king did have the grace to remember his minstrels on his deathbed in 1422, when he gave a verbal instruction that they were to receive a life annuity of £5; and this appears to have been respected well enough in the years that followed. But of the fifteen minstrels listed in the Agincourt Roll, only eight survived long enough to receive it. The names of John Cliff, the trumpeter Noreys, the piper Brown, and of three others, William Baldewyn, John Michel and William Haliday, simply disappear from the records prior to 1423. They may have been killed in action or – like so many of Henry's invading army – succumbed to dysentery and camp fever outside the walls of Harfleur. [49]

The functions of these men in the Agincourt and later campaigns of Henry V remain very much as they had been a century earlier; part military, part court musicians.

There is an important development, though, in the second of the minstrels' functions; they are now seen to be playing together as an ensemble. Before I give the evidence for this, I need to say a little more about Henry himself.

Like his father before him, Henry V not only appreciated listening to music, but was something of a performer in his own right. There was nothing very unusual about his learning the harp as a boy. The 'Black Book' of Edward IV ordains that 'henxmen' of the royal household are to be taught 'herping, to pype, sing and daunce', among other things; [50] such skills were regarded, as they always had been, as essential to anyone with a claim to gentility. But even while on campaign in France, Henry appears to have continued playing. In 1420, new harps were purchased to be sent into France for his use and that of his young French queen, Catherine. Was he teaching *her* to play? In the following year, a further instrument complete with travelling case and some dozens of replacement strings were bought from a London harpmaker called John Bore. [51] Henry V must surely be the only commander of an English army in the field – at any rate, since Alfred – to have packed a harp in his kitbag! This brings us back to the minstrels' ensemble-playing.

Again in 1420, during the four-and-a-half months' siege of Melun, special accommodation was arranged for Henry to entertain Catherine near to his tents, but far enough from the town to avoid the danger of stray arrows. There 'six or eight English clarions and divers other instruments played melodiously for a good hour at sunset and at the daybreak'.[52] To judge by the number of instruments mentioned, it would seem that virtually the whole of the king's company of minstrels was involved in this dawn and evening serenade, and that the nature of the ensemble was predominantly brass and woodwind.

Henry's treatment of a French cornet-player named Oraces, and of some of his fellow soldiers, shows a less attractive side of his character. At Meaux in 1421–2, some of the defenders brought an ass on to the walls of the besieged town, and made it bray by beating it, calling out that 'this was King Henry and that they (the English) should come and help him'. When, in due course, the time came for the French to surrender, Oraces, who may have supplemented the ass's bleating on his instrument, was specifically exempted from Henry's mercy, and later executed in Paris. (At Louviers, some French gunners who had the misfortune to fire at the king with a stone shot and narrowly miss him were similarly treated; one biographer insists that eight of them were crucified!).[53] There was a priggish, vindictive side to Henry's character – connected perhaps with his obsessive belief in the God-given nature of his mission to conquer France – which made him totally intolerant of mockery.

Henry V's love of music also found expression in his encouragement of the music of the Chapel Royal, which accompanied him to France and remained with him on all his campaigns there. In 1419–20 (about the time of the truce with Burgundy and the Treaty of Troyes), an *organista* called Walter Wodehall from St Paul's, along with five others, were appointed by the King's Council to proceed abroad to serve the king in his chapel. These men were not 'organists' as Devon has it – not even Henry could have made use of *six* – but singers of polyphony; a month later, they were joined by a chaplain and four additional singers. Then in January 1420, John Pyamour, a clerk of the Chapel and a composer, was commissioned to recruit choirboys in England to take them over to the king in Normandy.[54]

The only existing evidence as to the nature of the liturgical music of the period is that provided by the famous Old Hall manuscript, a collection of Mass settings and motets, the earliest section of which contains the work of some nineteen English composers, and is believed to have been compiled during the lifetime of Henry V; the dates of composition are necessarily earlier and some may belong to the reign of Henry's father. Few of the composers named have as yet been positively identified.[55]

I am not competent to judge to what extent, if any, the music as written would require or accommodate instrumental accompaniment. In view of Philippe Mézières' recommendation to Charles VI of France in 1389 that he should cause his minstrels to 'sound sweetly at the elevation of the Host',[56] and the known participation of minstrels in coronations and other royal ceremonies, it would seem strange if Henry's minstrels were never called upon to contribute their special skills to the celebration of the liturgy in his Chapel – especially on feast-days. But more than that; the occurrence among the Old Hall composers of several names already familiar to us as minstrel retainers of John of Gaunt and Henry Bolinbroke (both of whom are known to have given particular encouragement to the music of their chapels), suggests that these men may also have made a contribution as composers to its current repertoire.

One of the most important of the Old Hall composers, John Alanus, has been tentatively identified with the John Aleyn who took part in Bolinbroke's Prussian expedition of 1392 who, as 'Jean Alain', was rewarded by the Duke of Orleans among other Lancastrian minstrels in 1396. [57] If, as seems likely, he was also the John Aleyn who became a Minor Canon of St Paul's in 1421 and died in 1437, he was following exactly in the footsteps of Rahere in an earlier age. (On the other hand, it is possible that we have here one of those father/son combinations we have found to be so common among the minstrels; the composer signs himself in the last stanza of his Old Hall motet as 'J Alanus minimus'. [58]) A further possible identification arises between the John Tyas we met with at the 'minstrels' table' of John of Gaunt, and the Old Hall composer, John Tyes; the slight variation in spelling of the name seems hardly significant in view of its unusualness. There appears to be no evidence to suggest that the sharp distinction between chapel singers and minstrels that becomes apparent in the fifteenth century applied in the fourteenth; minstrels were often skilled singers as well as instrumentalists, and practised in polyphony.

Much scholarly argument has revolved around the identity of another of the Old Hall composers whose name is given as 'Le Roy Henry'. Henry IV, Henry V and Henry VI have all had their supporters, though Henry VI is now excluded because of the earlier dating of the manuscript – or, rather, that of its first layer. That either Henry IV or Henry V had the leisure, inclination or ability to compose the settings of the *Gloria* and *Sanctus* attributed to him is improbable, if not impossible. What seems to me more likely is that the Roy Henry in question was a King of Minstrels or Heralds (perhaps both) in the service of John of Gaunt or Henry IV, in company with Aleyn and Tyas. Bearing in mind the long association of heralds and minstrels and the proven musical ability of heralds such as Le Roy Capenny and Le Roy Druet, the most likely candidate would seem to be Henry Grene, the Leicester Herald of John of Gaunt, promoted 'King of Heralds' by Henry IV in 1399; though Henry Hultescrane, another minstrel of Gaunt's, might also be considered. If it still appears improbable that minstrels composed chapel music, we might bear in mind that John Dunstaple, the greatest church composer of the fifteenth century, is now believed to have been a lay musician in the service of Henry V's brother, the Duke of Bedford, who, on Henry's death in 1422, was appointed Regent of France. [59]

Finally, contrary to what one might expect of a man so apparently lacking in humour and averse to mockery, Henry V also included in his entourage while on campaign in France – in addition to the musicians of his household and of the Chapel Royal – a fool, long after court fools had gone out of fashion. The evidence of Rymer can hardly be doubted. In the first year of Henry's invasion, we are given the complete wardrobe (*apparatu*) supplied to William '*Stulto Regis*' (the King's fool) for himself and his servants – the most detailed list of its kind to survive from any reign: some sixty yards of cloth of various kinds – scarlet, long-cloth, single-coloured, blanket, woven linen of Flanders – twelve pairs of shoes, two pairs of over-boots, two pairs of black hose and, most remarkably, over a hundred and fifty skins of fur, including the royal ermine. [60]

S-bend trumpet and clarion c.1450.
Lambeth Palace Library MS 6,
f.233 (detail).

9

Minstrels of the Towns

The time is overdue for us to leave the world of the court and to look more closely at those other minstrels resident in towns, whose presence we have so far only noted in passing.

In doing so, we are immediately confronted with a problem. If, as I have maintained throughout, the essential and definitive characteristic of the minstrel lies, not so much in his combination of musical and other performing skills, as in his relation as a special kind of servant to king, magnate or knight, how are we to define those others who had no such regular patron, and were obliged to pick up a living wherever and however they could on the strength of their particular talents? Were such people 'minstrels' at all in the true meaning of the word?

The difficulty is more than semantic; it raised very real problems in its time, both for the unattached minstrels themselves, and for the authorities who had to deal with them at local and national level; and nowhere is this more apparent than in the field of law and order. A liveried minstrel in trouble with the law would – like any other retainer – be reported to his patron (who, in a certain sense, was responsible for him), and appropriate action taken. If unjustly accused, the minstrel could look to his lord for protection and, if necessary, the lord might appeal to the king on his behalf; if guilty of some minor offence, it would usually be left to the lord to punish him; only in the case of the most serious crimes was the ultimate sanction applied, whereby the minstrel was stripped of his 'minstrelsy' and abandoned to the rigours of the law. The unattached minstrel in similar trouble enjoyed no such cushioning; whatever the circumstances of his alleged wrong-doing, he was on his own from the start, though he too might appeal to the king and, as we shall see, sometimes did so with success. From the point of view of the authorities, he was the more difficult to deal with because responsible to no one but himself.

The distinction between the two types of minstrel – liveried and un-liveried, licensed and unlicensed – emerges clearly enough from the restrictive regulations of Edward II already quoted (pp. 94–95). Those who offend by crowding in upon great houses in excess of three or four a day, unless specifically invited, or visit the houses of 'meaner men' without an invitation, or, when invited, press for rewards beyond what is freely offered, are, for the first offence, to lose their 'Minstrelsie', and for the second, to forswear their craft 'and never to be receaved for a Minstrel in any house'. [1] The liveried minstrel is still regarded here as the norm, but a minstrel who has lost his 'minstrelsy', in the sense of liveried status and the protection that this gives, is not thereby automatically barred from continuing to practise his craft, if he can do so, though obviously that is already much more difficult for him. (The two meanings of 'minstrel', as previously set out in chapter one – as 'little servant' and as one who practises a craft or 'mystery' – are neatly exemplified here, and shown to have been concurrent.)

For the unattached minstrel, the advantages enjoyed by his more fortunate colleagues – both in terms of regular employment and the degree of acceptance and extramural patronage which a livery obtained – were such as to constitute a standing temptation to deception – and worse. Thus, in 1324, one David le Harpour and five others who, 'asserting themselves to be of the king's household and following it at a distance, committed divers larcenies and felonies at Winchester and elsewhere in the county of Southampton without the verge', were committed for trial to the Marshalsea. [2] In 1341, Edward III appointed a commission of 'oyer and terminer' to investigate and punish crimes alleged of members of his household and of his *secreta familia*, as well as by 'others *asserting* that they are of those households'. [3]

By the reign of Henry VI, the rewards available to the liveried minstrel were so rich that,

Whereas many rude husbandmen and artificers of England, feigning to be minstrels and some of them wearing the king's livery and so feigning to be king's minstrels, collect in certain parts of the realm great exactions of money of the king's lieges by virtue of their livery and art, and though they be unskilled therein and use divers arts on working days and receive sufficient money thence, they fare from place to place on festivals and take the profits, wherefrom the king's minstrels and others, skilled in the art and using no other labours or misteries, should live:- the king has appointed William Langton, Walter Haliday, William Maysham, Thomas Radeclyf, Robert Marshall, William Wykes and John Clyf, king's minstrels, to enquire throughout the realm, except the county of Cheshire, touching all such and to punish them, to hold the same inquisition themselves or by deputies during good behaviour. [4]

The problem here is thrown back to the minstrels themselves – from whom the original complaint had surely come. William Langton, Walter Haliday and William Maysham were veterans of Agincourt; John Clyf (III) was the probable son of John Cliff (II), the former marshal; Clyf, Radeclyf and Wykes are known to have been chamber minstrels of Henry VI. (The date was 1449.) The powers they are given are sweeping: to enquire where they will (with the significant exception of Cheshire), to punish and to delegate. But the abuses aimed at here go beyond the comparatively simple matter of deception to take in the larger problem presented by part-timers who, while earning a sufficient income by 'divers other arts' on working days, are robbing the professionals of their due rewards on holidays – an interesting anticipation of the present-day concerns of the entertainment unions. However, in the absence of any recognised union membership, the problem of definition remains. Here, a minstrel is someone 'skilled in the art' who uses 'no other labours or misteries'; in other words, a full-time professional, irrespective of whether or not he wears a livery. As to what 'skilled in the art' really means, that is left to the judgement of Langton and his fellow commissioners. To what extent their powers were ever applied, or to what effect if they were, is impossible to say for want of any further evidence.

The fact that the only occasions on which unattached minstrels feature in the State records is in connection with serious crime of one kind or another may give a false impression; we know from other sources that very many such minstrels – probably the vast majority – led perfectly peaceful and hard-working lives in London and provincial cities and towns without attracting publicity of any kind. It should also be borne in mind that, in the medieval context, an unattached minstrel – especially if he was itinerant – made an ideal scapegoat for corrupt judges and the hard core of lawless ruffians who (then as now) preyed on society. It is good to see the well-intentioned, but often ineffectual, Henry VI coming to their rescue on more than one occasion.

In 1451, a certain William Luter of Selby, Yorkshire, described as 'luter and mynstrell', is pardoned of 'the felony and murder whereof he was indicted by the procurement of his enemies before certain justices of the peace in the county, to wit, of having with William Smythbarne of Selby, co. York, "souter", on Tuesday called "Fastyngang even" at Selby by night about the eleventh hour, 28 Henry VI, slain Richard Humfray with two "carlelhaxes" worth 10d. each, though William Luter is no wise guilty; and of any consequent outlawries.'[5] Similarly, in 1437, William Hore of Hunden, Suffolk, 'mynstrell', along with Richard Albryght of Hadenham, co. Cambridge, 'mynstrell', and William Hoby of Ware, 'mynstrell', are reported as having been 'maliciously indicted' for the murder of a tallow-chandler named Stephen Cook, between eight and nine at night, in the London parish of St Benet's, Gracechurch; but the king, 'considering the good service they have done him in France and in his good town of Cales, and especially their innocence in the present matter', pardons all three of them.[6] This looks like an itinerant band of French-war veterans falsely accused of a mugging as a cover for the real culprits. (On the other hand, of course, Henry, who was inclined to be over-free with his pardons, may have been naively taken in by the minstrels' protestations of innocence and of former loyal service; there would undoubtedly have been some bad hats among such itinerant bands.)

What is quite clear is that, from all points of view, there was every incentive for those minstrels who were unable to find personal patrons to regularise their profession in alternative ways. Sometimes, these were imposed from above; sometimes they appear to have come from the minstrels' own initiatives; most commonly perhaps, they were the result of a meeting of different but mutually-concordant interests.

The traditional origin of the earliest of such attempts at regularisation – the founding of the Chester 'guild' by Earl Ranulph (Randle Blundevill) in the reign of King John – has already been narrated in chapter five. Though often described as a guild, it was, in fact, no such thing, but a simple jurisdiction conferred by authority of Ranulph on the man who had raised the minstrel army which had come to his relief at Rhuddlan. This was his Constable, Roger ('Hell') Lacy. How Lacy's son-in-law, Dutton, came into the picture – whether he was himself present at Rhuddlan or not – remains unclear. All we know is that the jurisdiction over minstrels and whores was passed by Lacy to Dutton, and thus came to be exercised by him and his heirs as an hereditary privilege down the years.[7]

Nothing is known from contemporary or near contemporary sources of the original form of the jurisdiction but, by the fifteenth century, it is functioning as a 'Minstrels' Court', presided over by the current Dutton heir with the aid of a jury of minstrels or – if the heir was still a minor as happened in 1478 – by the Bishop-Abbot of St Werburgh's with the Mayor of Chester and one Peter Dutton the elder, acting on behalf of the Prince of Wales, who was then earl of Chester.[8] The Court meets annually on the feast of St John Baptist (Midsummer Day), when complaints are heard of any minstrel who has brought his craft into disrepute by drunkenness or other bad behaviour in the preceding year, and licenses are issued or renewed for the year to come; only minstrels so licenced were allowed to practise in the city or throughout the county of Cheshire. It is a *real court*, established originally by Palatine authority of the Earl of Chester, and now approved and sustained by that of the Prince of Wales and of the king himself – not just a guild or association with official blessing. (It is nowhere included in the Chester records as one of the city's many craft guilds.) That this was so is shown by the specific exemption of Cheshire from the jurisdiction of Henry VI's Minstrel Commission of 1449, and from later Poor Law legislation (including the famous Elizabethan Statute against 'Rogues, Vagabonds and Sturdy Beggars') down to the reign of George III. Its practical success is attested by its long survival.

An anarchic, potentially disruptive element in society is thus harnessed, apparently at a single stroke of genius (or desperation), to an immediately useful purpose in the relief of Rhuddlan, and thereafter develops – doubtless over a period of time – into a largely self-regulating body affording, at the same time, protection to its members and a safe-guard for society. Most interestingly, from our point of view, it reaches down from the more respectable exponents of the minstrel art – the men of standing in city and county who would have served on its juries – to the humblest level of fairground entertainers and street musicians – *tota joculatorum scena*. As for the Commissioners of 1449, the only qualification for acceptance is professionalism.

An eye-witness account of the ceremonies surrounding the annual meeting of the Court, though late in date (1642), is worth looking at, both for its own interest, and because the ceremonies it describes are likely to have followed – at least to some extent – earlier usages. The day begins with a reading of a royal proclamation in the streets of Chester in the presence of Dutton's successor, who is mounted and has a Banner displayed before him, and the assembled minstrels. The proclamation announces Dutton's credentials as 'Protecter of all & euery musicions and Minstrells whosoeuer, either resident or resortinge within or to ye County Pallatine of Chester', and charges them to approach and attend. They are further instructed to 'Drawe forthe their sundry Instruments' to play before their Protector, and to accompany him 'playing vpon their severall Instruments vnto the Courthouse, And there to make their severall apparances.... and from thence in like good order, playinge vpon their said sundry Instruments, to his Lodginge, & not to departe without Licence' etc. The reading of the proclamation over – I have given only the gist of it – the minstrels set out in procession, playing as instructed, first to St John's church for a short service, and then to the Courthouse. What a glorious noise they must have made! At the Courthouse, the Steward of the Court 'calleth the suitors one by one' – presumably new applicants for a license – and a jury is impanelled. Those who had served as jurors at the previous Court wear long linen towels over their shoulders in the manner of a scarf, though it is not made clear whether this disqualifies them from serving again. The Steward then gives the jury their charge, which is to declare and present any instances of treason against the king, or 'scandalous words tending to the prejudice of the heire of Dutton', or profanation of the Sabbath (an obviously recent insertion), or 'whether any of them hath beene drunke, or the like'.

Dutton, along with the gentlemen friends who have accompanied him so far, now withdrew to eat the dinner which had been provided for them, leaving the Court to get on with its real business. But unfortunately, our eye-witness goes with them, so we learn nothing more about it; except that when the business was concluded, one of the minstrels made a formal presentation to Dutton of a 'lance' – a pole from which the previously-mentioned banner was hung – and that a new lance was presented each year, though the banner was preserved. We also learn that the renewal fee for licenses – originally 4½d. for minstrels and 4d. for whores – now stood (in 1642) at 2s. 2d. for minstrels; the whores, it would seem, having fallen by the wayside in the intervening years. [9]

Reading between the lines of this account, it is apparent that Dutton's role in the proceedings of the Chester Court had, by then, become largely ceremonial and formal, and that practical matters of organisation and discipline were left to the jury of minstrels, with the Steward (one of Dutton's household officers) holding a watching brief; but from a legal and constitutional point of view, Dutton's continuing participation – whatever its extent – was all important. While falling short of personal patronage, it still provided the essential element of feudal allegiance to a structure in which the otherwise unattached Chester minstrels could hold up their heads as recognised members of medieval society, with rights and responsibilities like everyone else. The only surprising thing about it is that similar structures were not more widely adopted elsewhere.

The only other Minstrels' Court I have come across is that of Tutbury in Staffordshire, which claimed a similar jurisdiction over minstrels in the counties of Stafford and Derby – possibly extending into the Midland shires of Nottingham, Leicester and Warwick. In the fourteenth century this was Lancaster country, and the earliest record we have of it is a charter of John of Gaunt's, dating from 1380. I give a seventeenth-century translation of the original French, which is in John of Gaunt's *Register*. [10]

JOHN By the Grace of God King of Castile and Leon, Duke of Lancaster, to all them who shall see or hear these our Letters greeting. Know ye we have ordained constituted and assigned to our wellbeloved the King of the Minstrells in our Honor of Tutbury, who is, or for the time shall be, to apprehend and arrest all the Minstrells in our said Honor and Franchise, that refuse to doe the Services and Minstrelsy as appertain to them to doe from ancient times at Tutbury aforesaid, yearly on the days of the Assumption of our Lady: giving and granting to the said King of the Minstrells for the time being, full power and commandment to make them reasonably to justify, and to constrain them to doe their Services, and Minstrelsies, in manner as belongeth to them, and as it hath been there, and of ancient times accustomed. In witness of which thing, we have caused these our Letters to be made Patents. Given under our privy Seal at our Castle of Tutbury the 22 day of August in the 4th year of the raigne of the most sweet King Richard the second.

It seems fairly clear from this that Gaunt was lending his authority to an existing institution, rather than founding a new one, as has sometimes been claimed. (It is interesting though that both the Chester and Tutbury courts are seen to have Palatinate authority behind them.)

If the Chester court was imposed from above – however willingly received – Tutbury has more the look of a self-generating body, though, like any other medieval institution, whatever authority it exercised was derived from above – originally from the Duke of Lancaster, ultimately from the king. Certainly, its structure was more democratic, with an elected 'King of Minstrels' as its central figure, rather than a feudal lord whose personal allegiance lay elsewhere; but this may also have been its weakness. Though Gaunt's charter was confirmed by an *Inspeximus* of Henry VI in 1443, the Court's jurisdiction was not exempted from sub-sequent, State legislation relating to minstrels, as was that of Chester, and it was thus reduced to citing the example of Chester in a feeble attempt to claim its privileges by virtue of a certain similarity of aims. On the other hand, in a set of official regulations emanating from the Duchy in 1630 (*temp*. Charles I), it is still referred to as 'his Majesty's Court, called the Minstrels' Court', which suggests that its authority was real enough so far as it went. It was certainly something more than a guild. [11]

For the rest of our knowledge, we are again reliant on the testimony of antiquarians, drawing partly on old documents which may or may not still exist, and partly on personal observation of its later proceedings; it survived in an attenuated form into the nineteenth century. (One feature of its early history not dependant on retrospective evidence is an associ-ation with the foresters, recalling my earlier account, in chapter five, of the minstrelsy of the chase, and suggestions of a possible link between hunt-ing and fooling. The source for this is a report by the antiquarian Blount of a document in the fifteenth-century 'Tutbury Cowcher'; as the passage is too long to quote here and difficult to paraphrase, I give it in full in Appendix B.)

There are eye-witness accounts of the Court's proceedings from 1680 onwards, from which it appears that two juries were chosen out of the 'sufficientest' of the assembled minstrels, one of Staffordshire men, one of men of Derbyshire. The twenty-four jurors then retired to elect three Stewards from among themselves, a fourth being chosen by 'him that keeps the Court and the deputy Steward' – presumably officers of the Duchy. Two of the Stewards are to be of Staffordshire, two of Derbyshire. The King is chosen from the four men who had served as Stewards of the Court in the preceding year, again alternating between men of the two counties.

The 'King' presides over the sessions of the Court, sitting with the Duke's Steward on one side and his Bailiff on the other. The charges to the Jury – as reported in 1784 – have to do with whether any of the minstrels have 'abused or disparaged their honourable profession by drunkenness' and other bad behaviour, such as profaning the Sabbath and brawling, or by 'playing for any mean or disgraceful reward'; whether they have been 'decent in apparel and skilful in their art, and respectful to their supreme, the king of the minstrels'; whether those elected to office have done their duties in the preceding year; whether 'those that owe suit and service to this court' have duly appeared; and, lastly, whether any minstrels not enrolled with the Court have presumed to execute their art within the Honour; any who have so offended to be presented and judged.[12]

If the Tutbury Court was (as earlier records suggest) at least as ancient in origin as Chester's claimed to be, it survived even longer. Its later history – though lying outside the scope of my survey – would make a fascinating study in the continuity and lasting-power of popular institutions and customs. It survived the Reformation, the Puritan Revolution, the break-up of minstrelsy itself, even the physical destruction of Tutbury Castle in the Civil War; as late as 1817, a remnant of local musicians was still meeting annually to elect a King in a house they had built for themselves among the castle ruins.

Another and very different way in which those minstrels who lacked the status and regular income enjoyed by their liveried colleagues sought to improve their situation was by obtaining an appointment as a town 'wait'.

These were minstrels employed by borough and city chamberlains to act as a kind of musical watch – very much on the pattern of the royal watchmen of Edward I, described in chapter six. Both probably derive from the ancient custom of stationing a watchman on the battlements of castles, throughout the night, to sound the hours and act as a look-out for nocturnal attackers. Three of Edward's watchmen were regularly stationed at Windsor, and used 'de Windsor' as a surname.[13] Watchmen (*vigiles*) of Norwich are mentioned by name in the Domesday Book of 1087 and their duties again appear to be connected with a castle.[14] It would have been a short step from using such castle watchmen to having them patrol the walls and streets of the town. Because of the paucity of civic records surviving from the thirteenth and fourteenth centuries, it is impossible to put an exact date on this development, or say where it began. (Though 'waits' was the usual term, it was by no means invariable; they are as frequently described as minstrels or, later, musicians and, in Latin documents, as *ministralli, mimi* or *lusores*.)

During most of the middle ages, the waits were usually three or four in number. At Norwich, there were three in 1426, four by 1437, and only in 1553 was a fifth appointed. At Coventry in 1423 (the earliest mention), Mathew Ellerton, Thomas Sendell, William Howton and John Trumpere, Minstrels, were appointed and were to receive 'as other haue had Afore them'.[15] They were to stay four in number to as late as 1615. At Ipswich, there were still only three in 1539, but in 1587,

John Betts and 4 more of his company shall be musitians to this Towne, and shall goe about the Towne every night, beginning about 2 of the Clock in the morning, and shall be at the Bayliffs order at other times, and for this shall have 4 li (£4) with convenient liveries, besides to receive the benevolence of the inhabitants of this Towne as John Marten formerly used. [16]

Their basic pay averaged a pound a year, but this made up only a part – and probably the least significant part – of their income. Like other liveried minstrels, their richest rewards came from the additional largesse which they picked up from playing on special occasions; for the waits, these included weddings, funerals, dinners, civic processions, receptions and ceremonies of all kinds; the demand for their services appears to have been constant throughout the year (except, of course, in Lent), and virtually insatiable.

At Beverley, the waits belonged to a Minstrels' Guild, which included in its membership 'all or the more part of the mynstralls playing of any musical instruments and thereby occupying there honest lyvinge inhabiting dwelling or serving any man or woman of hounoure or worshipe of citie or towne corporate or otherwise between the rivers of Trent and Twede', and which met annually on the rogation days of Lent to choose an Alderman. [17] In the reign of Henry VI, when St Mary's church was built, the waits were wealthy enough to have their portraits carved as patrons on one of the pillars of the church; five in number, they appear to be playing bass and treble recorders, lute, fiddle, tabor and pipe. Between 1495 and 1540, five of the Coventry waits achieved sufficient financial standing to gain admission to the prestigious *Corpus Christi* guild. [18]

The instruments used by the waits were chosen, in the first instance, for the penetrative quality of the sounds they produced, and that is why a type of shawm came to be particularly associated with them, and to be named a wait or wayte-pipe after them. (An idea of its likely effectiveness in this respect can be gained from the somewhat similar sound of the bagpipes, as heard from the battlements of Edinburgh Castle during the annual Tattoo.) But like Male Bouche, the watchman of *Roman de la Rose*, most waits were able to play a variety of instruments, appropriate to different occasions. For night-time patrols, a combination of two or three shawms and a slide-trumpet was common. At Norwich, as early as 1346, a trumpeter called John Sturmyn is mentioned. At Coventry in 1439, it is laid down that the 'Trumpet schall haue the rule off the whaytes, And off hem be Cheffe'. [19] But for use indoors, at dinners and 'drinkings', viols, recorders and flutes were considered more suitable. At Ipswich, for a *Corpus Christi* feast in 1470, 'If ffidlers doe comme to the Dinner, their wages shall be gathered at the Dinner'; at Newcastle in 1592, there is an extra reward for Robert Askew, one of the waits, 'for plainge of his flute'. [20]

The instruments themselves were sometimes, as at Coventry, provided by the city; sometimes, as at Chester – where, in 1590, Alice Williams, widow of a wait, disputed ownership of hautboys, recorders, cornetts and violins with her husband's former colleagues [21] – they were expected to provide their own. Everywhere, the waits received colourful liveries and metal escutcheons – shields or badges impressed with the town or city arms that were suspended from the neck on chains; sometimes collars as well. (The Beverley minstrels are seen to be wearing both. Two beautiful examples of escutcheons, complete with their chains, survive in Norwich from the sixteenth century; the links of the chains are alternating lions and castles.) At Coventry, where the waits seem to have been treated with exceptional generosity, they were even provided with houses by the *Corpus Christi* and Trinity guilds. [22]

As the danger of sudden attack on castles and fortified towns receded in the later middle ages, and the waits' original functions as look-outs and security patrol were taken over by the official Watch, the musical side of their activities grew in importance. It is clear from the Beverley Statutes quoted above that, as minstrels, the waits were accounted very much on a par with those serving men and women of 'honoure or worshipe', and it seems unlikely that the waits of Coventry, York or Chester, for example, would have wished to change places with any of their liveried colleagues, bar those of the king himself or his greater magnates. In these circumstances, we might expect to find their nocturnal music-making gradually dropped in favour of the daytime and evening engagements for which they were so much in demand. But that is not at all what happened; their nightime duties continue to be insisted upon to a surprisingly late date.

That there was a tendency in that direction is suggested by an order of 1539 from Chester, in which the waits are sharply ticked-off because, having been given a certain leeway as regards hours and times, they have got into slack ways, 'to goo & not goo when it pleased best theym selffes wherby good ordre hath not beyn obserued ner the Citie by theym serued as they ought to be'. In future, therefore, it is laid down

> that from hensforth euery sonday monday tuysday thursday and saturday the said waites shall goo Aboute and play in the evenyng in suche circuite placys and Owres as hath beyn accustomed in tymes past And euery monday thursday & saturday in the mornyng they shall goo and play in lyke maner And this rule and ordre to be kept contynually heraftur except that speciall sickenes or extreme weddur lett theym or ellz that Appon some other their resonable sute to be moved vnto the Mair and his bretheryn they obteyne lycence for A ceason as case shall require. [23]

At Coventry, an undated, probably sixteenth-century, document informs us that the waits are to play on Mondays, Tuesdays, Wednesdays and Thursdays, for a period of six weeks, in each of the first three quarters of the year – from the first week of 'Cleane Lent' to Easter, May 1 to Midsummer Day (June 24), and Lammas to Michaelmas – beginning at two o'clock in the morning. During the final quarter, they are to play on five days from All Hallows till Christmas, beginning at twelve midnight and continuing till four in the morning. The city is divided into four quarters which, presumably, they visit in turn, spending six weeks in each. [24]

A strenuous schedule during six months of the year (including, suprisingly, part of Lent), but one which left plenty of time for another of the waits' activities which, curiously, has received little attention in any previous accounts of the waits that I have seen: their touring. Like the royal minstrels and those attached to lesser households, it would seem from the records that they were almost as frequently 'on the road' as at home, and that their badges of office as waits were as efficacious a passport to monasteries, and to towns other than their own, as those of their liveried colleagues. In this way, they were able to establish a reputation for themselves as musicians and entertainers far beyond their immediate locality and, for the most part, their employers appear to have been content with the prestige that this brought them.

During the reign of Henry VI, minstrels from Coventry visited Abingdon (a distance of 50 miles) for a feast kept there by the Fraternity of Holy Cross, together with seven others from Maidenhead, receiving an especially generous fee of 2s. 4d. each, besides 'diet and horse-meat'. In 1432, a reward of a shilling was paid to *'duobus mimis de Coventry'* at Maxtoke Priory (8 miles), when the consecration of a new Prior was celebrated, and at least three other visits to Maxtoke by *mimi* and *lusores* (players) from Coventry are recorded by Warton. [25] We cannot be sure, of course, that all these refer to waits and not to some other free-lance minstrels resident in the city – of whom I shall have more to say in a moment; we do know that by 1467 the touring of the Coventry waits had become so extensive that the City Fathers found it necessary to order 'that the waytes of this Cite that nowe be & hereafter to be shall not pass this Cite but to abbottes & priours within x (ten) mylees of the Cite'. [26]

Monasteries, however, were not the waits' only ports of call and, as the years go by, the Coventry Fathers are themselves seen to act as hosts to an increasing flow of visiting waits, not only from neighbouring Midland cities and towns like Derby, Leicester, Newark, Nottingham and Worcester, but also from much further afield: Cambridge, Chester, Gloucester, Halifax, Hertford, Kendal, Leek, Lincoln, Newcastle-under-Lyme, Newmarket, Pontefract, Preston, Ripon, Shrewsbury, Southam and Westminster. But with this list, we are reaching forward into the seventeenth century and out of our period.

A more exact measure of the extent of minstrel touring, and the waits' participation in it, can be gained from York in a three-year period, 1446–9, when the Chamberlains operated what seems to have been virtually an open-door policy. Excluding performances by the York waits, and one or two named individuals who were probably also resident, a total of 268 visits by minstrels are recorded, ranging from individuals to groups of four, five and more; the total of performers involved exceeds 400. Of the 268 visits, 190 are by liveried retainers of the King (4 visits) and of other lords, knights and esquires, sixty-one are unspecified (of whom about a dozen have the look of itinerants), and seventeen are by town minstrels; the last are mainly in groups of three or four, and almost certainly waits, though only one group (from Nottingham) is specifically named as such in the Latin record. They come from Allerton, Beverley, Donington, Durham, Knaresborough, Lincoln, London, Newcastle-upon-Tyne (a man called Harding), Nottingham,Pocklington and Wakefield. [27] It seems probable that every town of any size had waits, amounting to a substantial body of people.

The waits of Norwich established such a high reputation as musicians in the fifteenth century that, in 1475, they were invited to accompany Edward IV to France, when deputies were appointed to take their place for the installation of a new Mayor. Later, they were to go with Sir Francis Drake to Lisbon. The waits were the English equivalent of the German *stadtpfeifer*; many of the Bach family were town musicians in Thuringia. Orlando Gibbons' father was a city wait in Oxford, later in Cambridge.

It would be unfortunate and wrong to leave an impression that the waits were the *only* minstrels of any consequence to be resident in towns. There were a great many others who, because they did not enjoy an official position, or work regularly for important people, or tour, except, perhaps, on a very limited scale to neighbouring fairs etc., are more difficult to trace as individuals, but who, nevertheless, can be seen to pick up a sufficient, if modest living in their own localities.

In the larger cities and towns, these were numerous enough to form guilds, as at Beverley and York, and thus associate themselves with their more influential, liveried colleagues. Among guilds responding to the edict of 1398, which required all such bodies to submit evidence of their history and status for royal approval, is a Guild of Minstrels and other entertainers in Lincoln, and one attached to an unnamed Carmelite foundation in London, founded in 1350, which provided payment of 14d. per week to those of its members incapacitated by illness or old age. [28]

Other craft guilds provided the substance of their livelihood. There is hardly a gathering of any one of the numerous Coventry guilds which does not record payment to a minstrel; sometimes the waits are specified, or the names of individuals we know to be waits; but these could not possibly have satisfied all the demand, and more usually the reference is to an otherwise unknown minstrel, sometimes to '*our* minstrel'.

> Carpenters, 1450: Item paid to Robert harper for Midsomer
> nyght and peter nyght xiiijd.
> Smiths, St Loy's Day annual dinner, 1453: Item paid to a luter
> viijd.

Carpenters, for Midsummer and St Peter's Nights, 1458:
> Item to owre Mynstrels on bothe nyghtys xxd.

for White Friars' Dinner, 1465:
> Item to mynstrelles cook & turnebroche vd. [29]

Many such entries are repeated annually, and there were over forty craft guilds like those of the Carpenters and Smiths in Coventry.

The Cordwainers and Shoemakers of Chester were especially generous in their patronage of minstrels – as can only be shown in context. Here are some typically bibulous pages from their accounts of 1548–50:

1548–9	Item geyuen to a menstrell on mertens even (St Martin's eve)	vjd.
	Item geyuen to a menstrell on oure month dey	viijd.
	Item geyuen to a menstrel on corpos creste dey	viijd.
	Item spend in peter tounges hause	vjd.
	Item spend on gotedes mondey ouer oure shoute	iijs.iiijd.
	(A 'shoute' was a collection for 'drink money'.)	
	Item payd to a menstrell ye thorsdaye affter	iiijd.
1549–50	Item peyde to the menstreles on martenes dey	xijd.
	Item spente on menstreles at wyllyam acokes drenking	xijd.
	Item peyd ffor a pottel of wyene	vjd.
	Item peyde to the wyettes of shorresbere (waits of Shrewsbury)	xijd.
	Item peyd to the menstreles that dey wye toke in wyllyam lineker (reception of a new guild brother)	xijd.
		[30]

The names of the performers surface occasionally as at Chester in 1575. Here we have the Cordwainers again (St Martin's day was their annual feast).

In primis payde the Whetemen (waits) on martens day	vijd.
Item payde peter cally the same day	vijd.
Item payde Shurlocke the menstrell	iiijd.
Item payde thomas fidler the same day	iiijd.
	[31]

The Smiths, Cutlers and Plumbers of Chester sum it up effectively in 1557 when, after listing a further series of payments to minstrels, they insert the following,

> Memorandum the Company neuer mett at Tauarne or any howse without musick. [32]

The payments the minstrels receive are modest indeed compared to those we have become used to at court; at a time when the daily wage of craftsmen was reckoned in pence, not shillings, the scale of living such employment afforded was strictly of the bread-and-butter kind – at the opposite extreme from the cakes and ale enjoyed by royal retainers. In both economic and social terms, the gap between the two was immense – as great as it is today between international virtuosi and Hollywood stars and the working musicians and actors who scrape a living in regional pubs and theatres; but in serving local community needs, the town minstrel (like his modern counterparts) might establish a modest niche for himself and a degree of social acceptance, as the phrase 'our minstrel' testifies. In the case of an exceptionally talented individual, there might even be some competition for his services, and in 1453, the Coventry Carpenters made sure of their harper, Robert Crudworth – he has already been mentioned as 'Robert harper' in 1450 – by making him a brother of their guild. He was to be followed by two other minstrels, William Barnbroke and William Metcalf. Barnbroke, with his wife Alice, was admitted in 1454. From 1471, their house (perhaps a tavern) became a popular meeting place for the carpenters, where they could do their business in a convivial atmosphere. Metcalf was also married; he and his wife Johanna were enrolled as brother and sister of the guild in 1463.[33] In the following century (1533), the Coventry Weavers were to enrol a minstrel called William Blakbowrn;[34] none of these men were waits. Even down to village level, the Guild of St Peter at Bardwell, Suffolk, found it worth their while to pay a minstrel 1s. 4d. a year as a retainer.[35]

Where, as in Coventry, York, Chester, Beverley, Wakefield, Ipswich, Norwich and many other towns, large and small, the guilds were involved in the production of plays – especially the 'mystery cycles' at *Corpus Christi* or Whitsun – the local minstrels were especially in demand, and these were undoubtedly the busiest times of their year. At York, by 1561, the Minstrels' Guild was itself responsible for one of the plays, a Herod play which formed an introduction to *The Three Kings*; and we cannot exclude the possibility that individual minstrels with acting skills played other parts in other plays for a professional fee – which would explain some wide disparities in the amounts of the players' rewards.[36] But aside from that, the purely musical element in the plays – for which a good deal of evidence exists, both in stage directions of the extant texts and in guild records – was of immense importance. I can only touch upon it here. For the Chester play of *Christ Among the Doctors*, the Smiths are instructed in the Bans (preliminary announcements) of 1608,

> Yow Smythes, honeste men, yea & of honeste arte,
> How Criste amonge the Doctors in ye temple did dispute,
> To sett out your playe comelye, hit shalbe youre parte
> Gett mynstrelles to that Shewe, pype, Tabrett and fflute.[37]

And in earlier records of the same play and guild (from 1560), we see them doing just that. It is not clear how many minstrels were involved – whether two or three – but in either case their joint fee of 3s. 4d. compares favourably enough with those received by most of the actors: Dame Anne 10d., Our Lady 10d., First Doctor 16d., Second and Third Doctors, a shilling each, Little God (the boy Jesus) 16d., Angel 6d. Only Simeon (which part J M Salter suggests was taken by a professional) does substantially better with 3s. 4d. However, that is not the whole story; a bill for liquid refreshment had also to be taken into account: 'payd for drinke for ther breckfast before they play & after they had don when th(ey) were vnbowninge them (undressing themselves) 3s.' – a large amount by any standard. (It seems that they appeared on the pageant in costume.) And there were payments for additional music: 'payd to Sir Io (John) Genson (probably a monk of St Werburgh's) for songes, a shilling; to the 5 boyes for singing, 2s. 6d.; to William loker (luter) for plleyinge, 16d.'[38] For the Mercers' play at Coventry in 1562 – a *Last Judgement* – the all-important trumpeter gets 4s. (the largest individual payment), the 'Syngyng men', 2s., and the player of the regals (a kind of small organ), 16d.[39]

The York *Judgement* ends like this:

> JESUS: Now is fulfilled all my forethought,
>   For ended is all earthly thing.
>   All wordly wights that I have wrought,
>   After their works have now woning: *abode*
>   They that would sin and ceased nought,
>   Of sorrows sere now shall they sing;
>   And they that mended them while they might,
>   Shall build and bide in my blessing.

> *And thus he makes an end, with the melody of angels crossing from place to place.*[40]

At the end of a long day, in the evening light, it must have been a deeply impressive moment. When the final reckoning is made, the contribution of the town minstrels to the *Corpus Christi* drama should not be forgotten.

10

On the Road

.amn apo'r·xrr·q·l·ff nō mīlh ɑ ꝛꝛꝛ́fúm
pbſtūm·ff·cyꝗinb·cꝛ·mꝛ·l·nꝰnō·�10́ꝰ·ꝗꝛꝛis
tꝛ·pꝛꝛꝺ́ꝛꝺ́u
uꝰ·mꝛllis·

King's messenger. British Library, MS Royal 10 E iv, f.302v.

It is a paradox that, at a time when society in general was static, rooted to the land – when a man was named in his native place by his occupation, and away from it by the town or 'vill' of his birth – the roads of England should present a picture of such evident bustle and movement.

One explanation put forward for this is that whereas the great majority of people stayed in the place where they were born and rarely, if ever, moved away from it, there was another smaller, but complementary, body of people – the wayfarers – who spent their lives in almost ceaseless travel between the various centres of population, and thus served to keep channels of communication open. But this is far too simple a view.

The closer we look, the more movement we shall see. At the level of basic human necessities, there is a constant flow of agricultural produce from country to town, carried in horse-drawn carts and by pack-animals, which snarl up the centres of cities and towns and damage their unmetalled streets, leaving an indescribable tide of filth behind them; crafted goods, bought at market and fair, return in the opposite direction and by the same means. Livestock is transported 'on hoof', or shepherded – sometimes for considerable distances – between summer and winter pasture. Merchants travel both to buy and to sell, taking their goods with them; raw materials – wool, for example, for the clothing industry – are purchased in person from the rural producers by city entrepreneurs. The revolutions of the agricultural and liturgical year bring an endless succession of feasts and fairs to town and village alike, which act as a magnet to their surrounding populations. The great cathedrals, abbeys and minsters are built by bands of travelling masons. Bishops or their archdeacons journey along country lanes in periodic visitation of their vast dioceses; itinerant justices make regular circuits of the towns. Feudal levies – the only means open to early medieval kings of raising an army – produce all-too-frequent, if short-lived, migrations of a fixed proportion of the entire male population, drawn from every level of society. Though professionally vowed to stability, even the Black monks were – if Langland and Chaucer are to be believed – as frequently on their travels as others of the clergy. Friars – black, white and grey – are tirelessly peripatetic, moving from one foundation to another, pausing only to preach at Town Crosses and in village churchyards. The extraordinarily lengthy journeys undertaken by quite humble pilgrims in the cause of religious devotion argue, perhaps, a degree of restless curiosity, as lying beneath or alongside the desire for spiritual advancement, as the motivation for such journeys. What seems to have been admired in hermits as evidence of outstanding sanctity was not so much their isolation – which, in many instances, appears more token than real – but their exceptional stability.

The higher up in society we go, the more normal and necessary travel becomes. The knight is by definition a man who goes to war on a horse, accompanied on foot by his squires and retainers; the apotheosis of chivalry is the longest journey of all, a crusade. The great estates of the nobles were not contained – as their titles suggest – within a single county, but scattered by accident of inheritance or matrimonial gain throughout the whole of England, if not further afield; their lives involved a ceaseless round of visits to widely-separated castles and manors. The king with his large, ever-increasing household (also the centre of government) is, as we have seen, almost constantly in motion until as late as the Tudors.

The minstrels' part in this moving picture has already been touched on in earlier chapters. They too were professionally mobile – either in company with their patrons or in touring on their own behalf, with the passport of acceptance that a livery gave them; even the town waits are seen to have been part of the minstrel circus. But the important point about this touring – so often overlooked – is that, for the most part, it was not of the wandering, wayfaring kind, any more than that of most other medieval travellers; but undertaken for reasons of economic necessity – to earn a living, to survive and prosper – and usually with a planned itinerary and destination.

In March 1368, four minstrels of Sir John Chandos – James Pountoyse, Peter Man, and Paul and Anselm Tabourner – set out for Gascony from

134

Dover with '2 yeomen, 4 hackneys, their girdles, buckles and other gear, 20s. each for their expenses, and a letter of exchange for 200 marks';[1] we do not need to know the precise purpose of their expedition to see that it had been carefully planned and prepared for. Such journeys, undertaken by liveried minstrels on behalf of their patrons, were not necessarily connected with minstrelsy at all in the usual sense. At the Lincolnshire port of Boston, for example, in 1358, a minstrel of Bartholomew de Burgherssh called Concius Piper is found arranging with his foreign kinsman, Hermann Vyncorp, for the export of 200 quarters of wheat to Durdraght, armed with a license obtained for them by the Black Prince.[2]

The royal messengers are a special case in point, for they too are often accounted minstrels. (The illumination at the head of the chapter is from the early fourteenth century.) The York lists of 1447 and 1449 (referred to in the last chapter) are headed *Haraldi nuncij ministralli*: 'To heralds, messengers and minstrels', though messengers are nowhere distinguished as such among the names that follow. (The same expression occurs frequently in the Durham Abbey Accounts.) Does this mean that the messengers – like the heralds – shared some of the minstrels' skills as performers? Simond le Messager, who was closely associated with Edward I's Queen Eleanor, and remained in royal service for over twenty-seven years, is included among the minstrels rewarded at the Pentecost feast of 1306.[3] There are even some messengers with the name of 'Fool' or its equivalents. A man called Robert le Sot, 'a messenger from our faithful and beloved W Bisset', is rewarded with a mark by Henry III in 1242, and less happily, one named as 'Thomas Fool, messager' is hanged for his felonies by Edward III in 1351.[4] Edward I had a messenger called John de Arches who is also designated as the king's 'wobode' (woodwose?).[5] Conversely, minstrels were often rewarded as messengers, as was Alan the trumpeter in 1301 for 'carrying the king's letters' and, in 1316–7, 'a certain minstrel of the Count of Savoy, coming to the lord King (Edward II) with the permission of his master and returning to him with letters of the lord King'.[6] The probability is that such overlappings of function originated from the undifferentiated character of the royal household – especially prior to the Ordinance of 1318 – in which, as Professor Tout put it, 'every royal officer was jack of all trades'.

It is clear that, in the matter of travel, liveried minstrels, whether of the king and his lords or of cities and towns – however much latitude they might be given at certain seasons and often for considerable periods – were acting under orders. Even when, like Coppinus Caleye, 'king's minstrel' to Edward II, they are allowed to make a pilgrimage, their leave of absence is of limited duration; Coppinus is given three months for his journey to 'Santiago' (the shrine of St James at Compostela) and back; his safe conduct, dated 19 March, is valid only to Midsummer.[7]

But what of the rest, the many unliveried minstrels, some of whom we have encountered in towns, others 'on the road', visiting Durham and

Minstrel with bells. Oxford,
Bodleian Library MS 264, f.188v.

York? To what extent were these unattached minstrels true itinerants in
the mould of Shakespeare's Autolycus, or that of the pedlars, ballad-mon-
gers and quack doctors who wandered as fancy took them from fair to
fair, scratching a living from credulous villagers and the more purposeful
travellers they met on the way? Most of the town minstrels and those
owing allegiance to one of the Minstrel courts must again be excluded.
However precarious their livelihood, they had a local base, and their
guild membership or court licence gave them identity and status, however lowly. To judge by the records from Durham and York already
quoted, the true itinerants would seem to have been a minority and, with
the special exception of the blind harpers, mainly of the kind previously
described as belonging to John of Salisbury's *tota joculatorum scena*: acrobats, tumblers, an occasional crouder or luter accompanying his wife's
singing, a rotour of Scotland (Durham); the odd Frenchman or Spaniard,
'Adam with the Bells', and *ludentes* (players) with 'Joly Wat and Malkyn'
(York). This sounds like the title of a comic interlude, but could equally
well refer to performing animals.

If such evidence as this is held to be too meagre or selective on which to
base any firm conclusions, there is another source of information from
which we can draw. As kings and other important people travel about the
country, they meet with a great variety of minstrels and other performers
who take the opportunity of showing off their skills for a reward; usually,
it would seem, on the spot – in the road or wherever else they might be. It
is only rarely that their names are recorded but we are usually told what
they do, and (always) the amount of their reward.

Though records of this kind are by no means uniformly available, by
taking those that are in sequence, we should still arrive at a fair cross-

136

section of minstrel activity at the popular level over a considerable period of time. The arbitrary nature both of the meetings, and of the survival of the manuscripts in which they are preserved, can only add to their value as evidence. One very relevant point that we shall need to keep in mind, however, has to do with which of the two parties who are meeting each other are truly itinerant; in many instances, it will be found that, of the two, only the patron is mobile, and the minstrels to be rewarded are lying in wait for him or otherwise *in situ*.

Harpers usually travel singly, if at all, but Edward I met no less than five Scottish harpers on the sands between Durie and Sandford in 1303–4; we may reasonably suspect an 'ambush'. Their performances were rewarded with a shilling each, distributed by one of the king's bodyguards.[8] Walter Lund, a 'harper of Chichester', was discovered by the king in the crypt of Chichester Cathedral, playing 'in front of the tomb of the Blessed Richard' – a former diocesan bishop – and received half a mark in 1296–7. Three years later, when Edward visited Carlisle, a harper of the town called Ricard, was rewarded for 'coming before the King and making his minstrelsy'. In 1303, Edward was given a musical send-off from Perth by 'divers vielle-players, timpanists and other minstrels' – perhaps the town or castle waits – and in the same year, again in Scotland, rewarded seven women who met him on the road and sang for him 'in the way in which they were wont to do in the time of the Lord Alexander, lately King of the Scots'.[9] These last received three shillings between them and are unlikely to have been professional minstrels at all but, more probably, a group of weavers and spinners singing one of their work-songs. (We should not forget that always, in the background of minstrelsy, there is this more widespread musical tradition of the folk, in which it is rooted; the same will be found to be true of the drama.) At Watford, Herts, in 1305, an unspecified minstrel named Alkin was given no less than 100s. in cash 'for himself and his wife'.[10]

Edward II seems to have encountered some true wayfarers in 1312–3 on one of his visits to the Fen country. Returning through Surfleet, he was entertained by William le Saltor (acrobat) and his companions, 'making their vaults', and they were rewarded, like the Scottish women, with three shillings between them; the date was July 8th.[11] Were they in town for a summer fair?

Eleanor of Woodstock must be one of the least-known of royal princesses. She was the third child and eldest daughter of the murdered Edward II. In May 1332, in the fifth year of the reign of her brother Edward III, when still a month short of her fourteenth birthday, she was to be married to Reginald, count of Gelderland. We find her, on the last day of April, before the Cross at the north door of St Paul's, about to set out on a pre-marital pilgrimage to Canterbury, rewarding 'divers vielle-players' of London with a shilling. At that time of year, the pilgrim way would have been as crowded and lively as it was later to be for Chaucer. 'A certain minstrel called baggepiper' received a shilling from her into his own hand. Was he leading a company of pilgrims, like Chaucer's Miller in his white coat and blue hood, who, with his bagpipe, 'brought us out of towne'? Arriving at Canterbury on May 4, Eleanor discovered, as her grandfather had done thirty-six years before, 'divers minstrels' making their minstrelsies in the crypt of the Cathedral 'before the statue of the Blessed Virgin', and rewarded them with two shillings. It was, appropriately enough, the feast of St Monica, mother of the great Augustine, author of the *Confessions*. Within a few days, she was in Flanders, accompanied by two minstrels of her own from Hoyland in Yorkshire. There, at Bruges, she rewarded thirteen minstrels for 'dancing and making their minstrelsy' before her. Was this at her wedding feast? Whether it was or not, she was soon back in England because, by May 23, a violist named Ricard was personally receiving a shilling from her at Rosedale in Yorkshire. [12]

No one was busier or more peripatetic in the service of Edward IV than Sir John Howard of Stoke by Nayland. In 1461, he had become the first Yorkist Sheriff of Norfolk and, in the same year, was appointed to the prestigious office of King's Carver and made Constable of Norwich and Colchester castles. In 1463, he took part in the siege of Alnwick, and went on to become Deputy Commander of the Channel Fleet. In 1467–8, he sat as MP for Suffolk. He has a harper and a bearward at home in Stoke, but the only minstrel to accompany him on his travels is a taberet.

We first pick him up – by means of the careful accounts kept by his Steward – in Suffolk in 1463, when the minstrels of Polstead village are rewarded with 2s. and Robert of Dunwich, trumpeter, with a shilling. Later that year we find him on the road to York. At a tavern in Lincoln, a priest who sang a song 'afor my mastyr that nyte' is given fourpence, there is eightpence for the Lincoln waits (who must have turned out to greet him), and a penny for a harper there. [13]

In April 1464, back home in Suffolk, three minstrels of 'my lord of Suffolke' are rewarded with 3s. 4d. On St George's eve (April 22), six minstrels of 'my lord of Warwykes' are given 6s. 8d., on April 26 the 'Kyngys trompetys' also get 6s. 8d., as do 'my lord of Norffolkes trumpetys' on April 29. [14] A feast of brass! (It is not clear if these visiting ensembles are in company with their lords, or touring independently.)

In May, he is in Newmarket where a harper of the town is rewarded with twopence; in June, at Stamford, Lincs., where minstrels receive fourpence and a new cord is provided for his drummer's tabor at a cost of twopence. On June 3, a Cambridge minstrel merits only a penny. In July he is in London where Clarencieux Herald collects 3s. 4d. and the taborer is given 2s. 4d. to buy himself new hose. In September, four of the king's minstrels on tour receive the usual 6s. 8d. [15]

It is an irony that the most informative of all the surviving 'privy purse' accounts of English kings bearing on the matter of minstrelsy should belong to the austere Henry VII. The person we shall meet with here – to whom a woman at York cried out from the crowd, 'King Henry! King Henry! Our Lord preserve that sweet and well favoured face!' – is hardly recognisable as the miserly accountant of the White Tower of some later histories. If the records are to be believed, no other king took so much genuine pleasure in the traditional recreations of the people of England, or was so assiduous and generous in his patronage of them; one could compile an itinerary from such entries as these: [16]

1492	July 31	To the shamews of Madeston (shawms, i.e. waits, of Maidstone) in rewarde, 6s. 8d.
	August 1	At Canterbury. To the children for singing in the gardyn, 3s. 4d.
	September 24	To the mynstrels of Sandwych in rewarde, 10s.
	October 2	To the mynstrels that pleyed in the Swan (a ship), 13s. 4d.
	18	(but relating to the journey from Windsor to Sandwich) To the waytes of Canterbury, 10s. To the waytes of Dover, 6s. 8d.
1493	April 30	To the waytes of Coventre in reward, 10s.
	May 13	To the waytes of Northampton in rewarde, 13s. 4d.
	16	To Pudesey piper on the bagepipe, 6s. 8d.

He has a soft spot for the minstrelsy of children. Their rewards are in pounds, not shillings.

1492	March 1	to the childe that playeth on the records (recorders), £1.
1493	August 5	To the young damoysell that daunceth, £30.
1497	January 7	To a litelle mayden that daunceth, £12.
1504	January 1	To litell Mayden the tumbler, £1.

or simply –

| 1492 | February 10 | To a litell feloo of Shaftesbury, £1. |

– who apparently does nothing!

Fools make a strong come-back in this reign. Some of them are clearly court-fools.

| 1492 | February 12 | To Peche the fole in rewarde, 6s. 8d. |
| | June 10 | To a Spaynarde that pleyed the fole, £2. |

– who later joins the establishment.

	October 2	To Dego the Spanishe fole in rewarde, 6s. 8d.
1493	November 3	To John Flee for Dikks the foules rayment, £1 1s.
1494	January 6	For clothing mad for Dick the fole, £1 15s. 7d.
	June 1	To Peche for the disguising, in rewarde, £26 14s.
1495	January 1	To Scot the fole for a rewarde, 6s. 8d.
	December 17	To Dix the foles master for his moneths wages 10s.

Dick was not, it would seem, wholly competent.

| 1500 | December 1 | To Thomas Blakall the Kinges foule, 6s. 8d. |

And Henry has no objection apparently to a fool being named after himself, as duke of Lancaster.

| 1492 | June 18 | To the folysshe Duke of Lancaster, 3s. 4d. |

Other fools are met with on his progresses.

1494	June 10	To one that joculed before the King, 10s.
1498	August 11	To my Lorde of Oxon Joculer, 6s. 8d.
	20	To a fole at Master Knyvett's, 3s. 4d.

But many of the entries relate to altogether humbler performers, including tumblers and acrobats – even tight-rope walkers. It is difficult to do justice to the rich variety of minstrelsy attested by these entries. I shall let the following speak for themselves.

Taborer and woman as hobby-horse. Oxford,
Bodleian Library, MS Douce 118, f.34r.

1494	January 2	For playing of the Mourice daunce, £2.
	April 29	To one that tumbled before the King (no amount stated).
	November 14	To a Spaynyard that tumbled, £2.
1495	February 13	To hym that pleyeth upon the bagpipe,10s.
	July 9	To a tumbler opon the rope in rewarde, 3s. 4d.
	27	To one that leped at Chestre, 6s. 8d.
	August 2	To the women that songe before the King and the Quene, in rewarde, 6s. 8d.
	November 2	To a woman that singeth with a fidell, 2s.
1496	August 25	To a preste (priest) that wrestelled at Cecet' (Cirencester), 6s. 8d.
1497	January 6	To Hugh Vaughan (a gentleman usher) for two harpers, 13s. 4d.
	April 3	To a Walshe rymer in rewarde, 13s. 4d.
	December 18	To blynde Cunnyngham, 13s. 4d.
1498	March 10	To one that tumblet at Eltham, £1.
	April 1	To Arnolde pleyer at recorders, £1
	18	To one that bloweth on a horne, 8s. 4d.
	September 8	To a piper at Huntingdon, 2s.
1499	June 6	To the Maygame at Grenewich, 4s.
		To the pleyers with marvels (miracle players or conjurors?), £4.
1500	January 1	To the trumpettes that blowe when the King come over the water, 3s. 4d.
1501	March 25	To a berward in reward, 6s. 8d.
	June 25	To a Spanyarde that pleyed on the corde, £10.
1502	February 4	To the grete woman of Flaunders, £2. (Her name was Anne, a 'giantess', and a favourite of the Queen's.) To one Lewes for a mores daunce, £1 13s. 4d.
1503	January 13	To Laurence, master of the tumblers (leader of a troupe), £5.
1504	January 1	To Vonecorps the tumbler in rewarde, £1.
1505	October 4	To Watt the luter that pleyed the fole, 13s. 4d.

11

Parting of the Ways, the final Phase: Henry VI to Henry VIII

With the return of the acrobats, tumblers and other popular entertainers of the streets in the previous chapter, we may seem to have come full circle in our survey; but that is not quite true. We have still to take in some important developments in the fifteenth and early sixteenth centuries, and to say a word or two more about the royal minstrels of Henry VI and Edward IV.

But the process of dissolution in the concept of minstrelsy is by now well advanced, and it may give a useful focus to our discussion of the final phase of minstrel history if we can see it in the light of that process: as a logical outcome of tendencies towards specialism and division that had been implicit in minstrelsy from the beginning, and which we can trace as actually taking effect from as early as the reign of Edward III.

As individuals, the minstrels did not, of course, suddenly die, disappear or simply fade away. Indeed, the fifteenth century appears to show significant increase in both the number of minstrels and their popularity among all sections of the population. This may be an effect of the abundance and greater availability of records from that period; but I do not think so. The question, rather, is whether these were any longer *minstrels* in the full sense of that word as previously defined; and, if not, of when it ceased to be valid, and why.

The cohesive elements in minstrelsy were twofold: the idea of the minstrel being a 'little servant' of the king or (by extension) of one of his lords or knights, and the principle of versatility which (as we have seen) is closely connected with the originally undifferentiated character of the royal household. As minstrels moved out on a surge of popularity from royal and magnate households to invade every corner of medieval life and society, and the royal household itself changed in character to become departmentalised in all its functions and offices, the minstrel found it more and more difficult to maintain his essential identity. The wonder is that he managed to do so for as long as he did.

The first loss that he suffered – and perhaps the most serious – was the loss of his role as poet and storyteller, which becomes apparent in the decline in status of the harper. Though individuals maintain a token presence at court and in noble and knightly households where the old ways are still honoured – mainly perhaps as tutors to the young, who are still expected to learn the harp as a form of class differentiation as middle-class children were once put to the piano – the majority end up in the fifteenth century as little better than street musicians, receiving a penny from the likes of Sir John Howard. This, of course, is a negative way of looking at things: the harper's loss was the poet's gain. (Or was it? One could argue that when the poet lost his function as performer, he lost an essential component of his own identity.)

The second loss was in the differentiation at court between court musicians and chamber minstrels. The minstrel's loss is here undoubtedly music's gain. The third loss, the third parting of the ways, is in the separation of the minstrel's histrionic from his musical and other abilities, which results in the emergence of the Players; this we shall go on to examine a little later in the chapter.

When Henry V, the warrior king, died at the height of his fame and achievement at the early age of thirty-five, the only child of his marriage to Princess Kate of France, Henry of Windsor, was a nine months-old baby. However, as his most recent biographer puts it, 'fifteenth-century kings were expected to grow up fast'.[1] Too fast! Crowned King of England at eight and King of France at ten, six years later (1437) he was to be invested with the full powers and responsibilities of his dual sovereignty. But even before the mental instability he had probably inherited from his Valois mother first showed itself in 1453, when he was in his early thirties, it was plain to most of his subjects that the man in charge of their destinies was more than a bit of a fool – well-intentioned but vain and capricious, as inept in diplomacy as in the arts of war. Two qualities – perhaps the only two – that he *did* inherit from his father were his piety and his love of music.

The twelve minstrels of Henry V who survived his French campaigns continued to serve at court during the minority of his son. I have said earlier (in treating of the reign of Edward III) that the royal minstrels were something of an oligarchy among minstrels generally. This was never more marked than in Henry VI's reign. As the veterans grew older, they were joined and eventually replaced by their offspring; but the seniors proved, for the most part, exceptionally long-lived; nor was there any more talk of retirement to monasteries. The trumpeter John Panell was still serving with his son William (also a trumpeter) in 1451, together with his old comrades William Bradstrete and Thomas Chaterton; they had been joined only by William Godyere and Nicholas Gildesburgh. Among the pipers and other minstrels, William Maisham and the two surviving Halidays, Walter and Thomas, were also still at work in 1451, and had been joined by John Cliff III, the son of their former marshal; only three new names have appeared in the meantime: Thomas Radcliff, Robert Marshall and William Wykes.[2]

That this was an oligarchy jealous of its privileges has been seen in the setting-up of the Minstrel Commision of 1449, when seven of the twelve (not the trumpeters) were granted extraordinary powers to restrain and punish 'amateurs', who had been muscling in on their rewards by means of deception of various kinds.

But by 1455, the Agincourt veterans were thinning out rapidly (as was only to be expected forty years on), and a group of four – Walter Haliday, Robert Marshall, William Wykes and John Cliff – are commissioned by the king 'to take boys elegant in their natural members and instructed in the art of minstrelsy and to put them in the king's service at the king's wages, to supply the place of certain of the king's minstrels deceased'.[3] (Some strange interpretations have been put on this quite straightforward instruction; good-looking boys – not children – who are already skilled in the instrumental arts and therefore, presumably, sons or apprentices of other competent minstrels of the time, are to be recruited to fill the gaps in the ranks that are now appearing.)

It is in this reign that the distinction first postulated in an earlier phase of the Hundred Years' War – that between court musicians and chamber minstrels – now becomes explicit in the records. Though all twelve of the current establishment receive the same basic pay of £5 a year from the Exchequer, and 4½d. a day from the Wardrobe when on duty at court, four of them – Thomas Radcliff (or Ratcliff), William Wykes, John Cliff and a wait called Thomas More – are now designated to 'entend (wait) upon the Kyng', the others as 'comyng at the principall fests in the yere'.[4] In other words, only the four who are named are permanently employed in the household; the others 'come and go', but for most of the year are engaged in touring – which is doubtless why the activities of provincial amateurs are of such concern to them.

One of the paradoxes of the whole period is that, for all his personal piety and simplicity, Henry's household establishment grew larger and more extravagant than in any previous reign, and the drain which this made on the Exchequer, as well as the resentment caused by the behaviour of its over-privileged members, was a significant factor in the political situation which eventually deteriorated into the Wars of the Roses; while the extrovert Edward IV, who took a positive delight in ceremony and display, was a much better financial manager and was able, in the end, not only to pay off the accumulated debts of his predecessor's extravagance, but to leave behind him a sizeable, personal fortune – the first English monarch since Henry II to have done so.

Poor Henry VI was finally reduced – at the time of his brief resumption of power in 1470 – to being paraded through the streets of London with his hand being held all the way by the Archbishop of York and a paltry following of his few remaining supporters, which, as the London chronicler put it, 'was more lyker a play than the shewyng of a prynce to wynne mennys hertys, ffor by this mean he lost many & wan noon or Rygth ffewe, and evyr he was shewid In a long blew goune of velvet as thowth he hadd noo moo to chaunge with'. [5]

Though Edward IV's minstrel establishment rose, in fact, to sixteen and stayed at that through most of his reign, the economy measures spelt out in the 'Black Book' of 1478 ensured that while a suitably impressive show could be made on major feasts and other special occasions, the household was no longer burdened with the payment of regular wages to any but a handful of men; the others 'avoyde the next day after the festes be don'. [6]

When Edward's queen, Elizabeth Woodville, was crowned in Westminster Abbey on May 26, 1465, Walter Haliday, Marshal of the King's Minstrels, is granted £20 for 'largesse and reward for the attendance of the kings and all the mynstralls to the nombre of C (100) persons', but most of these – as at the wedding of Henry II three hundred years' earlier – are 'attendant on certain lords' who are there as a matter of duty. [7]

A subsidiary parting of the ways now becomes apparent, which was to prove permanent. The eight trumpeters were divided off from the other minstrels under their own marshal (Richard Paten) to form a separate corps of trumpets and drums, which still exists. [8] At the Coronation of Richard III, over twenty of them are named. [9]

We thus see the creation of two separate ensembles: a brass ensemble of trumpets, sackbuts and drums (the 'Kyngys trompetys'), and another of wind and string instruments; only the latter are to be described in future as the 'Kyngys menstralys'. (We have encountered both groups on tour in 1464, rewarded by Sir John Howard.)

The formation of the State Trumpeters was paralleled in 1469 by the foundation of a Guild (later College) of Royal Minstrels, but unlike the former, it was largely self-regulating.

Licence for Walter Haliday, marshal, John Cliff, Robert Marshall, Thomas Grene, Thomas Calthorn, William Cliff (son of John Cliff III?), William Cristean and William Eynesham, the king's minstrels, to establish, continue and augment a fraternity or perpetual gild, which the brethren and sisters of the fraternity of minstrels of the realm erected in times past (?), that they may pray for the good estate of the king and his consort Elizabeth, queen of England, and for their souls after death and the soul of the king's father Richard, late duke of York, in the chapel of St Mary within the cathedral church of St Paul, London, and the king's free chapel of St Antony in the same city. They shall admit other persons, men and women, to the fraternity, and shall form one body and perpetual community, and shall elect from themselves a marshal to remain in office for life and two wardens yearly for the governance of the fraternity, and shall make ordinances for the governance of the fraternity, and shall have the supervision of the art of minstrels, except in the county of Cheshire, and shall nominate the king's minstrels, subject to the royal assent. [10]

The general supervision over minstrels – again with the exemption of Cheshire – proved as nominal and ineffective as previous legislation to the same end, but so far as the royal minstrels were concerned, they are here granted a remarkable degree of control and independence in the running of their own affairs.

But where, if anywhere, does this leave our original concept of the minstrel as a little servant of the king? What has happened to the chamber minstrels? Or is the William Cristean mentioned above as a founder-member of the Guild, but who is also, rather mysteriously described elsewhere as 'one of the king's dumb minstrels', a sole survivor? [11]

I must leave these questions in the air for a time while we retrace our steps a little to pursue that other line of development by which the minstrels became Players.

There is an anecdote of Henry VI as a young boy being entertained by a group of French dancing girls with bared breasts and turning his back on them with the words, 'Fie, fie, for shame, forsooth ye be to blame!' [12] The incident was put forward after Henry's death by a former chaplain as evidence of his sanctity; it is just as likely to express the natural embarrassment of a pious and innocent seven or eight year-old confronted for the first time by a *Folies Bergères* display at close quarters!

Sincerely pious Henry certainly was; but he took as much pleasure in plays and interludes as any other boy of his age. At Christmas 1426 (spent, as usual, at Eltham), he enjoyed the interludes of 'Jack Travail and his companions', and of four boy-players sent by his great-uncle, Exeter. Jack's troupe must have gone down particularly well because they were back again the following Christmas with more of what are described in the record as 'Jeuues & Entreludes'. The same entry goes on to mention a further reward to 'autres Jeweis de Abyndon, feisantz autres Entreludes'. [13] (As Jews were still officially banned from England at this date, I suspect a mis-spelling or mis-transcription by Rymer of *Jeuues* – as above – or *jouers*, 'players'; 'players of Abingdon'.) In 1429, a 'miracle-play' of St Clotilda was acted before the young king in Windsor Castle. [14]

We are all so conditioned by our early schooling to believe that professional players came on the scene only in the Tudor period that we may find it difficult to accept the implications of this earlier evidence; the fact is, of course, that minstrels had been acting occasionally in plays since the thirteenth century – and probably much earlier. (See, for example, the *Interludium de Clerico et Puella*, the records of 'Griscote, Visage and Magote', and *miracula* acted for Edward I's Queen Margaret cited in chapter six – not to mention the singing and dancing *mimi* of chapter two.) The increasing incidence of such performances, and the emergence of companies of full-time player-minstrels early in the fifteenth century, may well have been a reaction to the decline in popularity of the harper-poets – the minstrel as story-teller. As that particular function was taken over by the literary poets, the minstrels had greater recourse to this other, still more immediate way of telling a story – the dramatic interlude. The matter is somewhat obscured by a simultaneous adoption of the interlude-form by choir and grammar-school boys, and by some town and village players who may or may not have been fully professional; also by a misunderstanding of the term *miracula* as implying a connection with the religious drama of the towns (the 'mystery' cycles), whereas, though ostensibly religious in subject-matter, they were the popular entertainments of their day, generally disapproved of by the Church. But the evidence for the performance and touring of interludes by minstrels is altogether too widespread to be ignored.

As early as 1384–5, players (*ludentes*) were visiting King's Lynn in Norfolk, and were rewarded by the Mayor for their May-day performances of a *Corpus Christi* miracle-play (perhaps the Croxton *Play of the Sacrament*, which is extant), and another on the subject of St Thomas Martyr. [15] The 'players of the city of York' are first mentioned in 1446, the 'players of London' (as visiting York) in 1447. [16] 'Player' – as we shall see below – is an elusive term, but there can be no doubt at all about the four *interludentes* who are rewarded in company with a harper called J Meike at Winchester College in 1466; and little doubt either about the '*lusores* of the town of Winton', who visit the College in 1467 with *apparatu* (perhaps costumes or props) and receive the large reward of 5s. 8d. [17]

It is perhaps a little strange that some of the earliest recorded groups of these specialist players should belong to towns, rather than to titled individuals; but the lords were not far behind. In 1482, Sir John Howard rewards 'my Lord of Essex men, plaiers' and four 'pleyers of my lord of Gloucestres' [18] – the future Richard III. It is not known if Richard retained his company on becoming king. Henry VII employed four such players, described unequivocally as 'lusores regis, alias in lingua Anglicana, les playars of the Kyngs enterluds'. Their leader was a man called John English; they received a regular salary of five marks a year, and, when not required at court, went on tour like other minstrels. [19]

I said earlier that 'player' was an elusive term. By that, I meant that it retains the same ambiguity as 'minstrel'; it can apply equally well to a player of music as to a player of interludes – or, for that matter, to a player of tennis or a player of dice. (The verb, 'to play', is used in all these and several other contexts in the *Privy Purse Expenses of Henry VII*, cited in the previous chapter; Wace's minstrels of 1155 not only play a large variety of instruments and tell 'tales and fables', but also 'ask for dice and tables', i.e. backgammon.) We may complain about the vagueness and ambiguity of these terms but, in truth, they point to something very important and very specific: to the concept of *play* itself which lies at the heart of medieval entertainment, including its drama, and is the very air that minstrels and players breathe in common. It is also the most precious legacy that minstrels were to leave to the future.

The same ambiguity of definition and the same virtuosity were later to be characteristic of the Elizabethan player and his theatre. As M C Bradbrook explains,

> The theatre of the Elizabethans, in its social atmosphere, was less like the modern theatre than it was like a funfair. Indeed, George Gascoigne terms the performances at Belsavage Inn 'worthy jests' of 'Belsavage fair . Merriment, jigs and toys followed the performance: songs, dumb shows, fights, clowns' acts were interlaced.
>
> When Leicester's Men visited the court of Denmark in 1586 they were described as singers and dancers; Robert Browne of Worcester's Men, who toured the continent for thirty years with other English actors, jumped and performed activities.

Can anyone doubt that these men were true successors – in spirit and fact – of our medieval minstrels? The Puritan Gosson, whom Bradbrook goes on to quote, makes it even clearer:

> For the eye, beside the beauty of the houses and the Stages, he (the Devil) sendeth in gearish apparel, masks, vaulting, tumbling, dancing of jigs, galliards, moriscoes, hobby-horses; shewing of juggling casts, nothing forgot, that might serve to set out the matter with pomp, or ravish the beholders with variety of pleasure. [20]

His description takes us back to John of Salisbury and his *tota joculatorum scena*, to the hurly-burly of St Werburgh's and Rahere's Bartle-my Fair.

The description of Elizabethan players as 'singers and dancers', and the fact that others – like Shakespeare's fellow, Augustine Phillips – were famed for their instrumental skills, introduces a note of caution into our analysis of the process of dissolution and specialisation to which minstrelsy generally became subject in the fifteenth century. The new terms that were coming into use to distinguish the emergent specialties – player, musician, jester, clown – do not tell the whole story; and individual minstrels maintained their old versatility in often surprising ways.

Alexander Mason, who succeeded John Cliff III as Edward IV's 'Marshal of the Minstrels' in 1482 and went on to serve Richard III and Henry VII in the same capacity, is invariably described as 'geyster'; and whether this means an old-style *gestour* (teller of *gestes*) or a new-style 'jester', it is not what we would expect of a royal minstrel at this date – least of all, a *marshal* of minstrels. [21] John A Wodde, court singer and player of the virginals to Henry VIII, emerges as John Heywood, playwright, whose early farces such as *The Four P's* are said to mark the transition from medieval interlude to Elizabethan comedy. (Heywood married a niece of Sir Thomas More and was to have John Donne as a grandson; he appears to have had a connection with the singing-school at St Paul's and to have written plays for the boys, which were performed at court. He became a kind of court buffoon to Queen Mary and is reputed to have been one of the few people who could make that lady's stern features relax into laughter. But he had also a serious side and became a voluntary exile for his Catholic faith at the accession of Elizabeth. He died in Flanders in about 1580.)[22] At first sight, none of the minstrels look more settled in their chosen specialty than the town waits; yet, in 1576, the whole company of the famed Norwich waits applied to the City Court for leave to 'playe commodies and upon interlutes and souch other places (plays) and tragedes which shall seme to them mete' – and obtained it.[23] These examples do not gainsay the general tendency, but make it clear that the new categories into which the mass of minstrels divided were not so rigid then as they have since become; that within each category a large degree of virtuosity was allowed for, if not expected; and that individual minstrels remained capable of changing rôles to the last. (That instrumental virtuosity was still a valued attribute in minstrels of the wholly musical kind until as late as the middle of the sixteenth century is attested by a letter of 1545 from Thomas Chamberlain, Governor of the English merchants in Antwerp, to Sir William Paget, one of Henry VIII's principal secretaries in London, on the subject of some minstrels Chamberlain is recruiting for Paget in Antwerp. He has found 'five musicians who can all play upon five or six sorts of instruments'; others in the town are Italians who play on the viols only 'and are no musicians'. 'Now is the worst time to get minstrels', he adds – the date is 18 December – 'for between this and Shrovetide is their harvest'.[24])

Meanwhile, certain solo performers – men originally described as artificial fools or 'disours' – were on the way to becoming the jesters familiar to us from Shakespeare's plays.

My enumeration of court fools from King John's William Picol onwards has given little indication of what they actually did. The first clear, if brief, description of a solo performance by such a fool belongs to the reign of Edward IV (1469); it relates to a man called Woodhouse, who is described as a 'Sage dyzour (wise 'sayer') beyng in good ffavour of the kyngys grace ffor his manerly Raylyng & honest dysportys which he offtyn excercysid in the Court'.

His 'act' on this occasion had a sharp political bite; so much so that – to make sense of it – I must briefly explain the political circumstances. In 1464 – five years earlier – Edward had secretly married Elizabeth Woodville, whose Coronation we have already noted. Elizabeth was the first English queen not of royal blood; and the marriage caused endless resentment among Edward's nobles; the fact that she was also a widow with two children by a previous marriage did nothing to assuage their outraged feelings; her family name was Rivers. In the course of a particularly hot and dry summer, Woodhouse appears before the king at court dressed unseasonably in long, high leggings with a pike in his hands. 'Why are you dressed like that?', the king obligingly demands. 'Upon my faith, sir', says he, 'I have passed through many countries of your realm and in places the Rivers have been so high that I could scarcely have passed through if I hadn't been able to search their depth with this long staff .

The reference is obvious, but what did it mean? Was he warning the king, reassuring or insulting him? Had he been put up to it by the disaffected nobles, or was he poking fun at their exaggerated fears and jealousies, or simply making a rude joke? The London Chronicler, who reports the incident, has nothing to say of the king's reaction, except that he knew what it meant, adding darkly that it was an 'Ill prenosticacion'. [25]

Another solo performer who may have been known to Edward IV was a buffoon called Scogan; but he was one of those semi-legendary characters who – like Robin Hood – attract good stories from a variety of sources, early and late, and end up belonging more to popular myth than to history. There is the old chestnut of his being banished, and returning with earth in his shoes, so that, when challenged, he could reply that he was still standing on foreign soil; another of his being hopelessly in debt to the king, and deciding to stage his own death and funeral. He arranged for his cortège to intercept the king (allegedly Edward) while out walking. The king naturally enquires whose funeral it is; then, on being told that it is Scogan's, Edward is moved to pity and, as a relief to the dead man's family, cancels his debt. Thereupon Scogan leaps up from his coffin, announcing that the king's mercy has brought him new life. Shakespeare, perhaps, had the best idea in placing him in the earlier time of Henry IV, when Shallow could report of having seen Falstaff, in his salad days, 'break Skogan's head at the court-gate'! But, in doing so, he was probably confusing him (as Holinshed had done) with Henry Scogan, a serious poet and friend of Chaucer's, who became court poet to Henry IV and wrote a ballad for Prince Hal and his brothers. Under the same misapprehension, Ben Jonson introduces Scogan into his Twelfth-night masque of *The Fortunate Isles* (1624) as,

> a fine gentleman, and a Master of Arts,
> Of Henry the fourth's times, that made disguises
> For the Kings sonnes, and writ in ballad-royall
> Daintily well...
> In rime! fine tinckling rime! and flowand verse!
> With now & then some sense! & he was paid for it,

150

Regarded, and rewarded: which few Poets
Are now adaies.

– and subsequently brings him on stage, though he has little of any interest to say for himself. [26]

Another fool rewarded for a 'disguising' was Peche, one of several fools (natural and artificial) employed by Henry VII; but as I have learnt little else about him, I pass on to the last and best-loved of all the later medieval fools, Will Somers, the fool of Henry VIII. Though he too (like Scogan) was to gather apocryphal stories of impossible date, he has a much firmer foothold in history, and there are references to clothes being bought for him in contemporary wardrobe accounts. [27] There is even a portrait of him in company with his royal master. This dates from about 1540, and is said to be the last portrait made of Henry. It is a strange and unusual picture in several ways. (See below.)

It is from a Psalter made for the king's personal use – and that he did use it is clear from the annotations in his own hand contained in the manuscript. The picture illustrates Psalm 52 (53 in the later, Authorised Version) which begins:

The fool has said in his heart,
'There is no God!'

– traditionally used to illustrate professional fools. There is an element of impersonation, then, in Will's pose; he is seen to be turning away from the king (representing David, the psalmist) in an attitude of rejection and with an uncharacteristically disagreeable expression; but in other respects, the picture is strikingly realistic.

Henry, who did play the Welsh harp and was a most accomplished musician, is rapt in his music; but the face and figure are of a man prematurely aged by recent events. Will too has the hollow-eyed look and stoop described by those who had known him, and the clothes he is wearing correspond well enough to those recorded as having been made for him a few years earlier. If Robert Armin's account of him is to be believed, Will was a most lovable character and a true eccentric.

His relationship to the king was close and familiar; and he seems always to have been ready to use it to the advantage of those worse off than himself; 'one not meanly esteemed by the king for his merriment: his mellody was of a higher straine, and he lookt as the noone broade waking'. The dialogues that Armin reports as having taken place between the two can only have been invented reconstructions, yet have an authentic ring to them.

Henry VIII with Will Somers. British Library, MS Royal 2 A xvi, f.63v.

The king being on a time extreame melancholy, and full of passion, all that Will could doe will not make him merry. Ah! sayes hee, this must haue, must haue a good showre to clense it; and with that goes behinde the arras. Harry, saies he, Ile goe behind the arras, and study three questions, and come againe; see, therefore, you lay aside this melancholy muse, and study to answere me. I, quoth the king: they will be wise ones, no doubt. At last out comes William with his wit, as the foole of the play does, with an anticke looke to please the beholders.

There follows a typically-Tudor riddling session in which Will asks his three questions, the last of which is this:

Now tell me, saies Will, if you can, what it is that, being borne without life, head, lippe, or eye, yet doth runne roaring through the world till it dye. This is a wonder, quoth the king, and no question; I know it not. Why, quoth Will, it is a fart. At this the king laught hartely, and was exceeding merry, and bids Will aske any reasinable thing, and he would graunt it. Thanks, Harry, saies he; now against I want, I know where to find it, for yet I neede nothing, but one day I shall, for euery man sees his latter end, but knows not his beginning. The king understoode his meaning, and so pleasantly departed for that season, and Will laid him downe among the spaniels to sleepe. [28]

Finally, I take up the question of that remnant of the minstrels – the chamber minstrels – in their quintessential function as 'little servants of the king'. To what extent did they survive the fifteenth century?

Edward IV was one of the most secretive of kings as regards the details of his private life. If he had any chamber minstrels, we do not know who they were – or even how many he had. The record is equally blank for the short reign of Richard III. A man called Bartram Brewer is named as 'minstrel of the chamber' to Henry VII. At the old king's funeral in 1509, he is joined by two others under the same description, John Buntance and a luter called Giles, [29] but that is virtually all we know about them.

Henry VIII was, as I have already mentioned, an accomplished musician – a competent performer on harp, organ, virginals, lute and recorders, and a fairly prolific composer of songs, motets and, it is said, of two masses. During his reign, the 'King's Music' was greatly expanded; and, by 1538, he was paying regular wages to thirteen trumpets (at 16d. a day), six sackbuts, two luters, two rebecs, two tabrets, two viols, two 'dromslades' (players of a large bass drum), a harper, a virginals-player (John Heywood), a wait and trumpeter called Andrew Newman, and at least five others described simply as 'minstrels'; thirty-seven musicians in all; [30] and these included some of the finest European virtuosi of their day. But Henry, though generally regarded as among the first and most powerful of Renaissance rulers, was also in many ways the last of the medieval kings; and his musicians included a small but very significant group of chamber minstrels, whose position at court was wholly in line with the minstrels' original function as the king's most intimate companions and comforters of his leisure hours.

Thanks to the survival and publication of his Privy Purse Expenses for the period, November 1529 to December 1532, we are privileged to enter the private world of Henry's inner chamber. Though these are the years of the 'Great Matter' of the Divorce and the impending separation of the English church from Rome, few echoes of such momentous, public events penetrate here.

A succession of minstrels is seen to enter, perform and depart with their rewards. The king's harper is a man named as 'blind More' – William More, yet another of those blind harpers who have become so familiar at court and elsewhere. More's 'two fellawes' are Thomas Bowman and Timothy Evans; Timothy is a rebec-player. They get 40s. between the three of them as a New Year's gift, 20s. each for their liveries, and another 2s. each for badges. Peti John (Little John) is a senior minstrel of Henry's who has been with him since 1503–4, when he was still Prince of Wales. Nowell de Lusala (or Sale) is usually in debt;he receives advances against his wages of 45s. in 1530, and £13 6s. 8d. in the following year; he is a taborer, like Peter. In April '32, Peter Tabret is married and receives a wedding gift of £3 6s. 8d. He and John Bolenger, a sackbut-player, work together in September '30 and receive a joint reward of £4. Mark Anthony is the king's principal sackbut, and a man called Arthur his lutanist. All these men are close to the king; but none so close as those who are specifically described as 'of the Privy Chamber', and who are referred to simply as 'Mark, Philip (or Philip's boy) and the two Guilliams'. Along with Sexton, the king's fool at this time, these five are the dominant, recurring names in the accounts, and there is hardly a page which does not have a reference to them, collectively or singly. They are sometimes linked with 'Maister Weston' or 'Yonge maister Weston'. (Sexton, also known as Patch, has been acquired by the king as a gift – in a last, despairing gesture of farewell – from the departing Wolsey; Will Somers has not yet come on the scene.) [31]

By comparison with other records and lists of wages, we can learn the full names and identities of this inner group. Mark can only have been the virginals-player, Mark Smeaton, also described as an 'incomparable dancer'. From his being given money to buy lute-strings on several occasions, Philip's identity is never in doubt. He is Philip Van Welders, an outstandingly-gifted musician from the Netherlands, who is thought to have had a more general responsibility for the music of the inner chamber and for its instruments. [32] Henry Van Wilder, his son, is mentioned in later accounts; he may be the 'Philip's boy' who often appears to deputise for Philip. The two Guilliams, most frequently mentioned together, appear singly as 'Little Guilliam' and 'Great' or 'Grande Guilliam'. Their full names were Guilliam de Trosshis (or Trosshes) and Guilliam Dufayt. In March, 1531, Little Guilliam fell ill and was looked after by Peti John, all his expenses being met by the king. At the same time, a rebec was bought for Great Guilliam; but, in later records, both Guilliams are described as flautists – in which capacity they went on to serve both Edward VI and Elizabeth; the probability is that, as true minstrels, they were at least as versatile as the king himself. Sir Francis Weston, one of the chamber knights, is known to have played the lute. [33]

Here then is this small group of minstrels – playing virginals, lutes, rebec and flute – constantly at Henry's side. To judge by the use of their first names and the way that every one of their personal needs is met from the Privy Purse, they might even be children: endless supplies of hose, 'Milan hats'; their diet and surgeon's fees paid when they are ill; shirts, shoes, laundry, even their offerings in church when they make their Easter Rites (Confession and Communion); all are provided by an indulgent king, in addition to regular wages and rewards. It is possible, indeed, that some of them, including the two Guilliams, *were* children – or little more than children. There are references to 'Philippe and his fellows yong mynstrels' in documents dating from 1538. [34] And yet, within fifty years, with the accession of a boy king, his early death, and the succeeding reigns of Mary and Elizabeth, though music continued to flourish, the concept of minstrelsy in its full and proper meaning was dead. And within only three years, Mark Smeaton, along with 'Yonge maister Weston' and several other of Henry's most intimate companions, were to be executed for their alleged (and improbable) adultery with Anne Boleyn. (Only Mark confessed, and that was under threat of torture and the false inducement of a pardon.)

It would be hard not to see in this violent dissolution of the group the end of an era. No doubt, there were other musicians – professional and amateur – to take their place, but it can never have been quite the same again.

Appendices

Appendix A

Royal Harpers and Fools

A check-list of harpers and fools to the Kings and Queens of England, as recorded in the State Papers. (Fools are classified as 'natural' or 'artificial' on a basis of probability only. See Index of Minstrels or notes at foot of page for further information and sources.)

	HARPERS	FOOLS	
		Natural	*Artificial*
WILLIAM I		(?) Goles	
WILLIAM II (Rufus)		Robert ('Horny')	Rahere (*scurra*)
HENRY I/MATILDA	William le Harpur		
HENRY II	Henry, *citharista*		Roland le Pettour Roger Follus, otter-hunter
JOHN	Alexander le Harpur Roger, *citharista*		William Picol Ralph Stultus, huntsman John le Fol, huntsman
HENRY III	Richard le Harpur		→John le Fol, huntsman John de Blavia, *scurra* (Sir) Fortunatus de Luca, *scurra* Jacominus
EDWARD I	Walter de Stertone Le Roy Capenny (James de Cowpen) Nicholas le Blund William de Morley John de Newenton Hugh de la Rose Adam de Clitheroe Hugh de Naunton		Thomas le Fol

HARPERS	FOOLS	
	Natural	*Artificial*

	HARPERS	FOOLS Natural	FOOLS Artificial
ELEANOR OF CASTILE		Robert Fatuus	
MARGARET OF FRANCE	Walter de Wenlok[1]		
EDWARD II	→William de Morley (*Roi du North*) →Hugh de Naunton Robert de Clough Henry Newsom Elias de Garsington John de Trentham	Robert Buffard Robert II (son of Dulcia Witherstaf) John del Cuphous[2]	
ISABELLA OF FRANCE		Michael[3]	
EDWARD III	→John de Trentham	John of Eltham	
PHILIPPA OF HAINAULT		Robert le Fol[4]	
RICHARD II	John Hilton[5] William Dodmore		
HENRY IV	→William Dodmore		
JOAN OF NAVARRE	John Harper[6]		
HENRY V	William Corff[7]	William	
HENRY VI	(?) Thomas Harper		
MARGARET OF ANJOU	John Turges[8]		

1 Bullock-Davies, *Register*, p. 67.
2 CCW, 1244–1326, p. 570.
3 *Household Book of Queen Isabella*, p. 103.
4 CCR, *Edward III*, 1360–64, p. 280; 1364–68, pp. 48–9; Bullock-Davies, *Register*, p. 53.
5 CPR, *Richard II*, 1388–92, p. 493.
6 Rastall, pp. 26–7.
7 Rastall, p. 28
8 CPR, *Henry VI*, 1446–52, p. 512; Rastall, p. 31.

	HARPERS	FOOLS	
		Natural	*Artificial*
EDWARD V RICHARD III	Walter[9]		
HENRY VII	James Hide[10]	Dick	Thomas Blakall Peche (or Pache)
ELIZABETH OF YORK		William[11]	
HENRY VIII	William More	Sexton ('Patch')	Will Somers Thomas Jester[12]
EDWARD VI	Bernardo[13]		
MARY	→William More[14] Edward Lake[15]	Jane	
ELIZABETH	→William More[16]		Richard Tarleton

[9] Rastall, pp. 33–4; Lafontaine, p. 1.
[10] Rastall, p. 37; *Excerpta Historica*, p. 89.
[11] *Privy Purse Expenses of Elizabeth of York*, pp. 6, 24, 26, 61.
[12] *Privy Purse Expenses of Henry VIII*, pp. 126, 204.
[13] Lafontaine, p. 8.
[14] Lafontaine, pp. 9, 10.
[15] Lafontaine, p. 12.
[16] Lafontaine, p. 16.

Appendix B

Hunting and Minstrelsy

The foresters of Nedewoode join with the Tutbury minstrels for their annual gathering on the feast of Our Lady's Assumption (15 August), as reported by T. Blount, *Fragmenta Antiquitatis*, ed. Beckwith, London, 1815, pp.529-32, drawing on 'the Coucher-book of the honour of Tutbury, Cap. de Libertatibus'.

The prior of Tutburye, shall have yearly, one oure Ladydey, the Assumption, a bukke (buck) delivered him of seyssone by the wood-master and kepers of Nedewoode: and the wood-master and kepers of Nedewoode shale, every yere, mete at a lodgge in Nedewoode, called Birkeley Lodgge, by one of the cloke att afternone one Seynt Laurence Dey (10 August); at which dey and place a wode-moote shall be kept, and every keper makinge deffalte shall loose xiid. to the kinge, and there the wood-master and kepers shall chose II of the kepers yearly as itt cometh to their turne, to be stewards for to prepare the dyner at Tutburye Castell one oure Ladyedey, the Assumption, for the wood-master, and kepers, and officers within the chase, and there they shall appoint in lykewyse where the bukke shall be kylled for the prior against the saide Ladye-deye; and also where the bukke shall be kylde for the keper's dyner against the same day; and on the saide feaste of Assumption the wood-master or his lyvetenant, and the kepers and their deputies, shall be at Tutburye, and every man one horsebake, and soo ryde in order two and two together from the Yate, called the Lydeat, goinge into the common felde unto the highe crose in the towne; and the keper in whose office the Seynte Marye bukke was kylled, shall beire the bukk's heede garnished aboute with a rye of pease; and the bukk's heede must be cabaged with the hole face and yeers being one the sengill of the bukke, with two peces of fatte one either side of the sengill must be fastened uppon the broo-anklers of the same heed, and every keper must have a grene boghe in each hand; and every keper that is absent that day, beinge nodder sikke nor in the king's service, shall lose xiid. and soo the kepers shall ride two and two together tyll they come to the saide crosse in the towne; and all the minstrells shall goe afore them one foote two and two together; and the wood-master, or in his absence his lyvetenant, shall ride hindermast after all the kepers; and at the said crosse in the towne the foremast keper shall blow a seeke, and all the other kepers shall answere hyme in blowinge the same, and when they come to the cornell against the Yue-hall, the formast keper shall blowe a recheate, and all the other kepers shall answere hyme in blowinge of the same; and so they shall ride tyll they come into the church-yorde, and then light and goo into the churche in like arrey, and all the minstrels shall pley one their instruments duringe the offeringe tyme, and the wood-master, or in his absence his livetenant, shall offer up the bukk's head mayd in silver, and every keper shall offer a peny, and as soone as the bukk's head is offered uppe, all the kepers shall blowe a morte, three tymes; and then all the kepers goo into a chappell, and shall there have one of the monks redye to sey them masse; and when masse is done, all the kepers goo in like arreye uppe to the castell to dynner; and when dynner is done the stewards goo to the prior of Tutburye, and he shall give them yearly xxxs. towards the charges of ther dinner; and if the dynner come to more, the kepers shall beir it amongst them; and one the morrow after the Assumption there is a court kept of the minstrells, at which court the wood-master or his lyvetenant shall be; and shall oversee that every minstrell dwellinge within the honor and makinge defaute shall be amercyed; whiche amercement the kinge of the minstrels shall have; and after the courte done, the pryor shall deliver the minstrels a bull, or xviiis. of money; and shall turne hyme loose amongs them and if he escape from them over Dove-river, the bull is the priour's owne agene; and if the minstrels can take the bull ore he gett over Dove, then the bull is their owne.

Appendix C

Some Records of Blind Harpers and Other Blind Minstrels

Names marked with an asterisk are mentioned in text; see Index of Minstrels.

1296–1303	Nicholas le Blund*, harper to Edward I	Bullock-Davies, *Register*, pp.11–13
1306	'Pearl in the Eye' and companion* perform at Pentecost feast at Westminster, receiving half-a-mark from the Prince	Bullock-Davies, *MM*, pp.145–6
1357	Rewarded at Durham Abbey: William Blyndharpour of Newcastle* (two visits)	Chambers, II, pp. 240–3
1362	William ye kakeharpour* A blind *istrio* from France with his young brother*	
1376	Roger Harpour, blind*	
1392–1408	William Dodmore*, harper to Richard II and Henry IV	CCR, *Richard II*, 1389–92, p. 458; CPR, 1391–96, p.13; CPR, 1396–99, pp.104–5, 525; CPR, *Henry IV*, 1399–1401, p.141; CCR, 1402–05, p. 57; CPR, 1405–08, p. 462

Reign of Henry VI (1423–61)	A blind minstrel (*mimus cecus*) is rewarded with 2d. by the Prior of Maxtoke	Warton, I, p. 90
	Rewarded by the City Chamberlains of York:	REED: *York*, I, pp. 66–76; II, pp. 744–54
1446	A blind minstrel (*ministrallus cecus*), 4d	
1447	A blind minstrel from southern parts (*partibus Australibus*)*, 4d	
	A blind minstrel called the 'Minstrel of God'*, 6d	
	A blind minstrel, 2d	
1449	A blind minstrel, 6d	
	A blind minstrel, 4d	
1497	'Blinde Cunnyngham'*, rewarded by Henry VII with 13s. 4d	*Excerpta Historica*, p.115
1530–61	'Blynde More' (William More, harper)* and his two fellows are rewarded by Henry VIII in 1530 with 40s. More went on to serve both Mary and Elizabeth as harper	*Privy Purse Expenses of Henry VIII*, pp.16, 187; see Appendix A for further references
1531	A 'blynde woman being a harper' is rewarded by Henry VIII with 7s. 6d. (This is the only woman harper I have come across.)	*Privy Purse Expenses of Henry VIII*, p.168

Notes

All works cited are listed in the Bibliography. Citations are by author or, for anonymous works and records, abbreviated title. When more than one work by the same author is cited, abreviated title is also given.

Chapter 1: Who Were the Minstrels?

1 The derivation from *ministrellus* is generally accepted; but see Wright, 'Misconceptions', pp. 35–7.
2 Welsford, p.114.
3 Waddell, p.186, n. 3; p. 200, n.1.
4 John of Salisbury, *Policraticus*, tr. Dickinson, p.16.
5 John of Salisbury, *Policraticus*, tr. Pike, pp. 33, 37.
6 Axton, p.18.
7 John of Salisbury, *Policraticus*, tr. Pike, p. 38.
8 Page, pp. 77–91.
9 John of Salisbury, *Policraticus*, tr. Pike, pp. 33–4 and n. 95.
10 See below, Chapter 6, p. 69–70, for the distinctions set out in de Chabham's Penitentiary of c. 1220. De Chabham may have had some influence on the great Dominican theologian, Thomas Aquinas, who was later to declare (c.1265) that 'the profession of an *histrio* is by no means in itself unlawful. It was ordained for the reasonable solace of humanity, and the *histrio* who exercises it at a fitting time and in a fitting manner is not on that account to be regarded as a sinner'; cited by Chambers, I, p. 58.
11 Wilkins, p.126.
12 Chambers, I, p. 67.
13 Wilkins, p.126.

Chapter 2: Tota Joculatorum Scena

1 Beare, pp.149–50.
2 Nicoll, p. 85.
3 Nicoll, pp. 84–5.
4 Chambers, I, pp. 70–1.
5 Axton, pp. 21–2. The liturgical drama also had its animal performers, notably the Ass.
6 Chambers, I, p. 71, n. 6.

7 Nicoll, p. 37.
8 This is not to claim that the mimes' performances are necessarily thought up on the spur of the moment. On the contrary, a part of their content – sometimes a substantial part – might be carefully rehearsed and polished over a number of years. By 'spontaneous' is meant that they are not fixed in time to a particular occasion and that, however much they draw on practised routines, they remain open to variation and extemporisation in a way that a scripted performance never can. Nor does the distinction I am making here – between improvised and scripted theatre – have any necessary connection with the literacy of the performers. The Greek mimes who had used the prompt scripts discovered at Oxrhynchus, and the Italian actors of the 17th C *Commedia dell' Arte* who were reminded of the plot of their current show by posted summaries, were clearly literate though their performances were improvised; many actors of the wholly-scripted *Corpus Christi* plays were not, and had to learn their parts by rote with the aid of rhyming couplets.
9 Ogilvy, p. 608.
10 Ogilvy, pp. 613–4.
11 *Regularis Concordia*, pp.xxiv, 49–50.
12 For these statements, see Baldry, p. 68; Nicoll, p. 83; Marshall, p. 378.
13 The writer is Thomas de Chabham, Sub-Dean of Salisbury from 1213. See below, pp. 69–70.
14 Axton, p.19. Cf. Shakespeare's use of the ass's head in *A Midsummer Night's Dream*.
15 Juvenal, tr. Green, p. 93.
16 Axton, pp.162–3.
17 Kolve, pp. 33 ff.

Chapter 3: The Anglo-Saxon Tradition

1 Ogilvy, p.607.
2 For differing interpretations, cf. Galpin, pp.1–14, and Sachs, pp. 261–3.
3 Alexander, pp. 51–2.
4 Alexander, p.13.
5 Chadwick, p. 87.
6 Whitelock, pp. 91, 107.
7 Alexander, p. 38.
8 Alexander, pp. 40–1.
9 William of Malmesbury, *Gesta Regum*, I, pp. 207, 181.
10 Alexander, p. 42.
11 Bruce-Mitford, pp. 44–6.
12 William of Malmesbury, *Gesta Pontificum*, V, p. 336; for Alfred's *Handboc*, see Keynes and Lapidge, pp. 99 and 268, n. 208.
13 Keynes and Lapidge, pp. 75, 91.
14 Boethius, pp. 294–7; King Alfred, pp.116–8.
15 Waddell, p. 57.
16 Lang, p. 70.
17 Chambers, I, p. 44, n.1.
18 Bullock-Davies, *Register*, p.117.

Chapter 4: Norman Jongleurs and Buffoons

1   Court fools are nearly always listed in contemporary records with the royal minstrels, which is why I include them in my survey; they are usually found to have musical or other minstrel skills.
2   Hayward, pp.14–5.
3   Wace, *Roman de Rou*, ll.3657–88. Text: II, pp.176–8; Welsford, p.114, where the name is given as Golet.
4   Gaimar, I (text), p.10; II (trans.), pp. 6, 223.
5   Gaimar, ll.5271–92; I (text), pp. 223–4; II (trans.), p.167.
6   Henry of Huntingdon: Text, pp. 202–3; Trans., p. 211.
7   *Carmen de Hastingae Proelio*, ll.389–408, pp. 26–7.
8   *Carmen de Hastingae Proelio*, pp. 81–2.
9   Wace, trans., pp.189–90.
10 William of Malmesbury, *Gesta Regum*, p. 415.
11 *The Song of Roland*, tr. Harrison, p.122 (*laisse* 175).
12 I have no proof, of course, that the *cantilena Rollandi* of William of Malmesbury is to be identified with a prototype of *The Song of Roland* containing the passage I have quoted. See Douglas, *The Song of Roland*, pp.99–114, for a contrary suggestion. On the separate question of Taillefer's claim to historicity, Professor Douglas, in another place (Douglas, *William the Conqueror*, p.169, n.5), has this to say: 'It is a good story and might even be true, though it has the elements of myth.'
13 *Domesday Book*, 15, p.162a.
14 See Appendix A for a inventory (as complete as I have been able to make it) of royal harpers and fools from William I to Elizabeth.
15 *Domesday Book*, 4, 1.25.
16 William of Malmesbury, *Gesta Regum*, II, p.504; Barlow, pp.99–100. I am much indebted in my treatment of Rufus' reign to Professor Barlow's biography of the king, and have drawn on his translations of this and other passages in William of Malmesbury and Orderic Vitalis.
17 Barlow, p. 99.
18 Orderic Vitalis, IV, pp.186–9; Barlow, p.104.
19 *Book of the Foundation*, pp. 2–3. The quotation is from an English version c. 1400 of a Latin text originally composed c. 1180, which is contained in the same ms.
20 See pp. 69–70 below.
21 Orderic Vitalis, III, p. 217. Orderic's editor, Marjorie Chibnall, lists 3 references to *mimi*, 2 refs to *joculatores* (one a stylistic variation for *mimus*, applied to the same person) and 3 refs to *histriones*. The choice of terms appears to be indiscriminate; sometimes surprisingly so. Thus, in a crusading episode in which a Persian woman called Fatima is seeking to put heart into some Christian captives: 'Remember the ten-year siege of Troy, call to mind the marvellous deeds of the heroic lords which your *histriones* chant every day' (VI. p.121).
22 Orderic Vitalis, III, pp. 318–21.
23 Barlow, p. 81.
24 Barlow, pp. 396–7.
25 Barlow, p.xi, citing his earlier book, *The Feudal Kingdom of England*.
26 Willaim of Malmesbury, II, pp.649–51. I am indebted to Laurence Wright for his translation of this and other passages; see Wright, 'The Role of Musicians', p. 98.

27 Bullock-Davies, *Register*, p. 218; *Book of Fees*, I, p.151 (Nottingham and Derby).
28 The final, obscure line of the *Song* reads, *Ci faut la geste ke Turoldus declinet* – composed, recited or merely copied out? See *Song of Roland*, tr. Sayers, p. 42; for possible meanings of AOI, *Song of Roland*, tr. Harrison, pp.18–9.
29 For Rahere, see DNB; for the Song School, Harrison, pp.12–3.
30 The quotations are from *Dives et Pauper* c.1407, probably by a Franciscan friar, cited by Kolve, p.133.

Chapter 5: Minstrels in the Age of Chivalry

1 Gerald of Wales, p.108. *Gesta Stephani*, p.17, confirms that only Richard was killed. For *alternatim*, see Page, p.137; I have used Dr Page's translation of the sentence in quotes.
2 Duby, pp. 31–2, 62–5.
3 Chrétien de Troyes, p.1 (from *Eric et Enide*).
4 See Baltzer, *passim*.
5 Barron,p. 29.
6 Baltzer, p. 66.
7 Text and trans. from Baltzer, p. 66.
8 Extracted from trans. in Baltzer, p. 66.
9 Text and trans. from Baltzer, pp. 67–8. I have substituted some translated words by terms from the original text (in italics) where these are of technical interest to us.
10 *Charters of Mowbray*, for Bartholomew, charters 200, 202; for Luke, p.lxiv; for Warin, charter 308.
11 Text and trans. in Baltzer, p.68; but for trans. used here and my interpretation of it, I am again indebted to Laurence Wright, 'The Role of Musicians', pp.100–1.
12 L. Wright, as above, p.101.
13 Chrétien de Troyes, p. 28 (*Eric et Enide*).
14 See n.10 above; also, for Bartholomew's 'quitclaim', *Early Yorkshire Charters*, IX, p. 246.
15 Trans. from L. Wright, 'The Role of Musicians', pp. 98–9.
16 *Dialogus de Scaccario*, pp. 86–7
17 *Rotuli de Dominabus*, p. 72; Bullock-Davies,*MM*, pp. 46–7 and n. 36.
18 Warren, pp. 207–8.
19 Quoted from Warren, p. 210.
20 *Rotuli de Dominabus*, p. 62 and n. 3.
21 See, for example, *Book of Fees*, I, pp.136, 386; II, pp.1174, 1218–9. Also Bullock-Davies, *Register*, p.174, where, in the report of an Inquisition of 1331, Roland is named as 'Roland le Fartere' and his land is reported to have been alienated.
22 *Dialogus de Scaccario* (in 'Establishment of the Royal Household'), p.135.
23 CPR, *Richard II*, 1377–81, p.176; *Pipe Rolls*, 28, 25 Henry II (1178–79), p. 73.
24 Welsford, p.115 (citing *Pipe Roll*, 27 Henry II, Roll 8, m. 1 d.). For later refs to Roger and his holding, *Pipe Rolls*, 37, 33 Henry II (1186–87), p.31; 38, 34 Henry II (1187–88), p.120; *Calendar of Pipe Rolls for Bucks and Beds, Richard I* (1189–99), pp. 36, 94.
25 Round, pp. 298–303.

26 For these, see Round, above, and CPR, *Richard II*, 1377–81, p.176, which lists two later charters.
27 But see Chambers, I, pp.142 ff. for evidence of surviving folk festivals in which fools are associated with the hunting and killing of 'sacrificial' animals.
28 Map, p.11: *Nichil in his letum nisi letiferum.*
29 Poole, p. 333.
30 Bullock-Davies, *Register*, p. 70.
31 For these and for the information that follows concerning Blondel, Broughton, pp. 70–1, 126–8.
32 Broughton, p.128 (citing Leo Weise).
33 *Bedfordshire Records*, II, pp. 267–8; Landon, pp. 22, 155.
34 Text: *Rotuli Normanniae*, pp. 20–1; trans: Welsford, p.115.
35 Bullock-Davies, *Register*, p. 214.
36 *Rotuli de Liberate*, p. 92; Bullock-Davies, *Register*, pp. 3, 171.
37 *Rotuli de Liberate*, pp. 230, 242, 244, 246; Bullock-Davies, *Register*, p. 214.
38 *Rotuli de Liberate*, pp. 148, 248, 253.
39 *Close Rolls of Henry III*, 1231–34, p. 57; CLR, *Henry III*, 1240–45, p. 3.
40 CLR, *Henry III*, 1240–45, pp.136, 219; *Close Rolls of Henry III*, 1237–42, p. 443; CLR, *Henry III*, 1245–51, p.125.
41 *Rotuli de Liberate*, p.153.
42 See photographs in L. Wright, The Role of Musicians', Plate XXXII.
43 For report and photographs, see 'The Independent' of 18 September, 1987.
44 Percy, I, pp. 362–3, 410–1; but see also REED: *Chester*, pp. 461–6, 487–9.

Chapter 6: The King's Minstrels

Henry III

1 Harvey, pp. 91–4.
2 Harvey, p.95.
3 *Close Rolls of Henry III*, 1237–42, pp. 83, 192; CLR *Henry III*, 1226–40, p. 438.
4 *Close Rolls*, 1242–47, p.145; CLR, 1240–45, p. 278.
5 *Close Rolls*, 1247–51, pp.18–56.
6 CLR, 1245–51, p.159.
7 Harvey, p.101; *Close Rolls*, 1242–47, p. 270; CLR, 1240–45, p. 225; 1245–51, p. 363; *Close Rolls*, 1247–51, pp. 483, 496; CLR, 1251–60, p. 321; for Master Michael's verses, Devon, pp.xii–xiii; *Close Rolls*, 1261–64, p. 55.
8 Strickland, I, pp. 357–8.
9 Harvey, p. 97.
10 Harvey, p.102.
11 *Close Rolls*, 1264–68, p.195.
12 *Close Rolls*, 1253–54, p. 256; 1256–59, p. 83; Stamp, p.310; *Close Rolls*, 1253–54, p. 249; 1247–51, p. 468.
13 *Close Rolls*, 1259–61, p. 321.
14 CPR, *Henry III*, 1225–32, p. 359.
15 *Close Rolls*, 1237–42, p. 523.
16 CPR, 1232–47, membrane 7 (March 16).
17 CLR, 1245–51, p. 80; *Close Rolls*, 1242–47, p. 459.
18 *Close Rolls*, 1247–51, p. 362; CLR, 1251–60. pp. 24, 70.
19 Bullock-Davies, *Register*, p.162.
20 *Close Rolls*, 1259–61, p. 454.
21 *Close Rolls*, 1259–61, p. 238.

Edward I

22 BL Add. MSS 7965, f. 52r.
23 Wodderspoon, pp. 244–8.
24 *Manners and Household Expenses*, pp.lxix–lxx.
25 Bullock-Davies, *MM*, p.138.
26 Dr Bullock-Davies informs me that the word derives from L. *Saltare*, meaning, in classical times, to 'dance with gesture'; but in medieval usage – through its affinity with *salire*, to 'leap or vault' – was applied to acrobats.
27 Bullock-Davies, *MM*, p. 57.
28 Bullock-Davies, *MM*, pp. 55–60, 137–8.
29 Bullock-Davies, *MM*, pp.16–17.
30 Chambers, II, p. 239.
31 *Record of Bluemantle Pursuivant*, p. 384.
32 Denholm-Young, 'Song of Carlaverock', pp. 254–7.
33 CCR, *Edward I*, 1296–1302, p. 81; Bullock-Davies, *Register*, pp.123–5.
34 Bullock-Davies, *Register*, p.122.
35 Bullock-Davies, *MM*, pp. 77–9.
36 Prestwich, pp. 42–7.
37 Gough, II, p.146.
38 Bullock-Davies, *MM*, p. 79.
39 Bullock-Davies, *MM*, p.130.
40 Bullock-Davies, *MM*, pp.105–6.
41 CCR, 1288–96, p.497; 1296–1302, p. 75.
42 Bullock-Davies, *Register* p.135.
43 CFR, *Edward I*, 1272–1307, p. 371. The king continues to benefit from Thomas's minority till 1303.
44 Denholm-Young, *History and Heraldry*, pp. 52–3.
45 Nicoll, p.152.
46 Robert (Mannying) of Brunne, p.158, ll.4745–8.
47 Knowles, p. 281; Chambers, I, p. 91.
48 Webb, I, pp.147–9, 154.
49 Bullock-Davies, *MM*, pp. 95–7.
50 Bullock-Davies, *MM*, pp.156–8.
51 Wilkins, pp. 3–4.
52 Bullock-Davies, *MM*, pp. 91–2.
53 Bullock-Davies, *MM*, pp.112–3.
54 Bullock-Davies, *MM*, pp. 84–5.
55 Bullock-Davies, *MM*, p.170.
56 Bullock-Davies, *MM*, pp.113–5.
57 Bullock-Davies, *MM*, pp.104–5.
58 Bullock-Davies, *Register*, pp. 39–40.
59 Bullock-Davies, *MM*, p. 52.
60 Cutts, p. 300 n.
61 Bullock-Davies, *MM*, p. 51.
62 Galpin, p.179.
63 Galpin, p.112.
64 *William Gregory's Chronicle*, pp. 220–1.
65 Bullock-Davies, *MM*, p. 73.
66 Bullock-Davies, *MM*, pp.128–30.
67 Bullock-Davies, *MM*, pp.136–7.
68 *Records of the Wardrobe*, p. 232.
69 CCR, 1288–96, p. 253; CCW, 1244–1326, pp. 47, 56.
70 Bullock-Davies, *Register*, p. 205.

71 Welsford, pp. 203 ff.
72 Chambers, I, p. 387.
73 Chambers, II, Appendix E, pp. 240–2.
74 Bullock-Davies, *Register*, p. 34.
75 Bullock-Davies, *MM*, pp. 44–50.
76 Bullock-Davies, *MM*, pp.126–8, 146–8.
77 REED, *York*, I, 68–70; II, pp. 746–8.
78 I quote from the modern translation by Terence Tiller, cited under Langland, p.153. Goodridge in his prose version for the Penguin Classics has Haukyn claiming to be merely a 'baker', which loses the point. Editors and translators generally have been hard-pressed in trying to explain this passage in allegorical terms!
79 'A number of people produce at will such musical sounds from their behind (without any stink) that they seem to be singing from that region' – *City of God*, Book XIV, Chapter 24, p. 588, tr. Henry Bettenson, Penguin Classics, 1972.
80 Wickham, *Moral Interludes*, p. 203.

Edward II

81 *Life of Edward II*, p.ix.
82 Higden, cited by Johnstone, 'Eccentricites', p. 265.
83 Johnstone, *Edward of Carnavon*, p.130.
84 *Life of Edward II*, p. 59.
85 Tout, *Place of Edward II*, p.158.
86 *King Edward II's Household Ordinances*, p. 46.
87 Stow, p. 414; Chappell, p.19.
88 Johnstone, *Edward of Carnavon*, p. 85 and n. 9.
89 CDS, II, 1272–1307, p. 369.
90 Bullock-Davies, *Register*, p.167; CCW, 1244–1326, p. 570. See also CPR, *Henry VI*, 1436–41, p.90, where Robert is described as an 'idiot'.
91 CDS, II, p.369.
92 Bullock-Davies, *MM*, pp.142–4, 118–9.
93 Johnstone, *Edward of Carnavon*, pp. 64–5 and n.
94 Bullock-Davies, *Register*, p.155.
95 Bullock-Davies, *MM*, p.143.
96 Bullock-Davies, *MM*, p. 67.
97 Bullock-Davies, *MM*, p. 66–7.
98 *Wardrobe Accounts of Edward II*, pp. 27–8.
99 Coulton, p. 561.

Chapter 7: Sir Orfeo

1 Denholm-Young, 'Song of Carlaverock', p. 255.
2 *Roll of Carlaverock*, p. 30.
3 Denholm-Young, *History and Heraldry*, p. 57.
4 Robert (Mannying) of Brunne, p.158, ll.4753–6, 4765–8.
5 1 *Kings*, 16, vv.16, 23. I quote from Mgr Knox's translation of the Vulgate text familiar to Mannying and his contemporaries.
6 *Close Rolls of Henry III*, 1251–53, p. 330.
7 Bullock-Davies, *Register*, p.114.

8   Rastall, p. 31.
9   et faciunt solacium hominibus uel et egritudinibus suis uel in angustiis suis...
      See Rubel, p. 233.
10 See, for example, Barron, p. 85.
11 Warton, I, p. 89.
12 Barron, pp. 75–6.
13 Cutts, p. 290, citing Warton.
14 Warton, I, p. 89; II, p.106.
15 Bullock-Davies, *MM*, pp. 21–2.
16 *Life of Edward II*, p. 59; for Edward III, see next chapter; *Household of Edward IV*,
      pp.131–2; *Ordinances and Regulations*, p. 98.
17 Bullock-Davies, *MM*, pp.11–2.
18 Chambers, II, Appendix E, pp. 240–3; for Bartholomew Wright (not listed by
      Chambers), see *Account Rolls of Durham Abbey*, I, p.129.
19 *Household of Earl of Northumberland*, p.339.
20 CCR, *Edward II*, 1313–8, p. 306.
21 REED: *York*, I, p.70; II, p. 748.
22 REED: *York*, as above.
23 Bullock-Davies, *MM*, pp.145–6.
24 Bullock-Davies, *Register*, pp.11–3.
25 CCR, *Richard II*, 1389–92, p.458; CPR, *Richard II*, 1391–6, p.13.
26 Cutts, p.289, citing Warton. Chambers, I, p.56, n.6, gives the original Latin.
27 Warton, II, p.106.
28 'We redeth oft and findeth y-write' (*Lay Le Freine*); 'This Naciens, of whom y
      write' (*Arthour and Merlin*); 'In thys boke shalle ye fynde wrytte' (*Partonope of
      Blois*); 'Ilke man was of divers cuntré, In book y-wreten we finde' (*Athelston*)
      etc.
29 For William's seal, see frontispiece to Bullock-Davies, *MM*; John Harding's is
      reproduced in *New Grove*, under 'Wait'.
30 See, for example, *Close Rolls of Henry III*, 1242–47, p. 351, where William le
      Harpur acts as attorney for Geoffrey le Harpur against Thomas le Mareschal
      in a dispute over land.
31 Baugh, p. 5.
32 Bullock-Davies, *Register*, pp.125–8, 129–31, 56, 31, 134–5.
33 Quoted by Mathew, p.30, citing *Eustache Deschamps* (ed. G. Raynaud, 1891),
      vol.7, pp. 266–93.
34 Froissart, p. 408.
35 Barron, p. 54.
36 *Life and Campaigns of Black Prince*, p. 85.
37 *Hous of Fame*, ll. 1209–13.
38 *The Knightes Tale*, ll. 1339–40, 1345–8.
39 Tolkien, p.123.
40 *Household Book of Dame Alice de Bryene*, pp. 25–8.

Chapter 8: Minstrels and the Hundred Years' War

1   Froissart, pp.115–8.
2   Sachs, pp. 280–1; *Register of Black Prince*, I, p. 30.
3   *Life and Campaigns of Black Prince*, pp. 31, 81.
4   Geiringer, p. 58.
5   Froissart, pp. 346–7.

172

6   *Life and Campaigns of Black Prince*, p. 79.
7   *Ordinances and Regulations* pp. 3–9.
8   CCR, *Edward III*, 1341–43, pp. 82–3. I have also made use here and in what follows of Rastall, pp.15–21. For Giles' place, see CPR, *Edward III*, 1343–45, p. 221.
9   Nicolas, 'Observations', p.138; CPR, 1358–61, p.446; CPR, 1361–64, pp. 437–8; *Issue Roll of T de Brantingham*, pp. 55, 297.
10 *Register of Black Prince*, IV, pp. 72–3.
11 Bullock-Davies, *Register*, p. 67; CCR, 1374–77, p. 63.
12 Wright, L., 'Medieval gittern', pp. 23–33.
13 CPR, 1338–40, p. 26; 1343–45, p. 300; 1348–50, p.266; 1358–61, p. 448; *Issue Roll of T de Brantingham*, pp. 54, 297.
14 Barber, pp. 22, 30, 37.
15 *Register of Black Prince*, IV, p. 67; Wagner, p. 28.
16 *Register*, IV, pp. 72–3, 101, 157, 161, 163–4, 245, 283, 304, 326, 388, 402.
17 *Register*, IV, pp. 71–3; for the 'ketilhat', p. 245.
18 *Register*, I, p. 30; Geiringer, pp. 83–4.
19 *Register*, IV, p. 402.
20 *Register*, IV, p. 251. A 'Jakelin the minstrel' makes an odd appearance at Caversham in 1380 as an innocent receiver of stolen goods. He had bought a load of timber from the tenant of Caversham Manor who, it later transpired, was not entitled to dispose of it as the whole estate belonged to the king. This might well be a glimpse of our Jakelyn Piper in retirement. See CIM, IV, 1377–88, p. 59.
21 *Register*, II, pp. 208–9, 210–1; CPR, *Richard II*, 1385–89, p. 413.
22 Nicolas, 'Observations', pp. 41–3, 122–3.
23 *John of Gaunt's Register* (B), no. 25.
24 Nicolas, 'Observations', p.109.
25 Froissart, p.168.
26 CPR, 1350–54, p.155.
27 Rastall, pp.15, 18; Wagner, p. 27; Devon, p.171.
28 For the heralds' journeys abroad, see, for example, Devon, p.169 (9 March); for Hanekin as Marshal, Rastall, p.16.
29 Geiringer, pp. 63–4, 67–9.
30 *New Grove*, XII, p. 350, 'Minstrel Schools'.
31 Olson, p.603, citing Strutt, p.164; Rastall, p.17.
32 Bullock-Davies, *Register*, p. 71.
33 *Foedera*, VII, p. 555.
34 CPR, *Richard II*, 1396–99, p.104.
35 *John of Gaunt's Register* (A), II, nos 859–62, 912, 1416, 1660; for Hankyn, see also (B), nos 73, 327 (p.113), 790, 1003; for John Buckingham's marriage, CCR, *Richard II*, 1385–89, p. 81; for John Gibson, (B), no. 556 (p.179); for John Tyas, (A), nos 1238, 1515; for John Cliff, (B), nos 605, 643 (p. 209).
36 *Expeditions to Prussia*, pp.132–3, 137, 141–2; for John Aleyn, p. 269.
37 Jacob, p. 3.
38 Wylie, III, p. 325; IV, pp.170, 180.
39 *Chronicque de la Traison et Mort*, pp.171–2; Tout, IV, p. 53; for Claus, CPR, 1396–99, p. 558.
40 *Foedera*, VIII, pp. 78–9; CPR, 1396–99, pp. 524–5, 538.
41 Devon, p. 274.

42 CPR, *Henry IV*, 1399–01, p. 511; 1401–05, p.167; CCR 1399–02, p. 469; CPR, 1405–08, pp.11, 55.

43 CPR, 1405–08, p. 353; 1408–13, pp. 62, 205, 418. The William Byngeley involved in piracy (pp.353 and 62 above) is not specifically described in those entries as the king's minstrel or servant so we cannot be quite sure that this was, in fact, the cause of the minstrel's fall from favour.

44 Devon, p. 318.

45 CPR, 1399–01, p.141; 1405–08, p. 462.

46 *Foedera*, IX, p. 255; Nicolas, *Agincourt*, p. 389; Rastall, pp. 28–9; for John Cliff's pardon, CCR, *Henry V*, 1413–19, p.172.

47 *Foedera*, IX, p. 260, gives a total of eighteen for the king's minstrels in June, 1415, but not all of these necessarily accompanied him to France. Bradstrete, Chaterton and the two Wildes may have replaced those who died at Harfleur or elsewhere; we know that they became involved at some point because they are included among those who were later to receive the king's legacy; see note 49 below. The names of the unspecified members of the original party were William Baldewyn, John Michel, William Langton, Thomas Hardiberd, and Thomas, Walter and William Haliday.

48 Devon, p. 423.

49 CPR, *Henry VI*, 1422–29, p.102.

50 *Household of Edward IV*, pp.126–7.

51 Devon, pp. 363, 367.

52 Waurin, II, pp. 312–3.

53 Waurin, II, pp. 370–1, 374; Hutchison, pp.158, 190–1.

54 Devon, pp. 361–2; CPR, 1416–22, p. 272.

55 Harrison, pp. 220–25; Bukofzer, pp. 76–9; *New Grove*, XIII, pp. 526–7.

56 Wilkins, p.128.

57 Harrison, p. 224.

58 Wilkins, p. 87.

59 Bent, pp.1–3. The abbreviation 'cn' which appears as part of the inscription on which this indentification is based, stands, I suggest, for *cantor*, not *canonicus*.

60 *Foedera*, IX, p. 335. It dates from April, 1416.

Chapter 9: Minstrels of the Towns

1 CCR, *Edward II*, 1313–18, p. 306; but this does not include the punishments for offenders. The fuller translation quoted here is in Chappell, pp.17–8.

2 CPR, *Edward II*, 1324–7, p. 69.

3 CPR, *Edward III*, 1350–4, p.155.

4 CPR, *Henry VI*, 1446–52, p. 262.

5 CPR, *Henry VI*, 1446–52, p. 502.

6 CPR, *Henry VI*, 1436–41, p.101.

7 Percy, I, pp. 362–3, 410–1; REED: *Chester*, pp. 461–3, 486–9.

8 REED: *Chester*, pp.17–8, 501–2.

9 REED: *Chester*, pp. 463–6.

10 Text: *John of Gaunt's Register* (B), no.1076, p. 341. Trans: Wilkins, p.140, citing R. Plot, *The Natural History of Staffordshire*, Oxford, 1686.

11 I am indebted to an unpublished thesis by M. A. Price for this and the following information about Tutbury; Price, pp.113–42.

12 Price, pp.132–3, citing Blount, pp. 553–5.

13 Bullock-Davies, *MM*, pp. 50–1.

14 *Records of the City of Norwich*, I, p. 4.
15 REED: *Coventry*, p. 8.
16 Bacon, p. 350.
17 Wilkins, p.141.
18 REED: *Coventry*, p.xxi.
19 Mander, p.97; REED: *Coventry*, p.12.
20 Bacon, p.130; REED: *Newcastle*, p. 83.
21 REED: *Chester*, pp.164–5.
22 REED: *Coventry*, pp.xxi, 67,70 *et passim*.
23 REED: *Chester*, p. 43.
24 REED: *Coventry*, pp. 483–4.
25 Warton, II, pp.105–6; I, pp. 90–1.
26 REED: *Coventry*, p. 45.
27 REED: *York*, I, pp. 65–77.
28 Westlake, pp.173, 237.
29 REED: *Coventry*, pp.19, 28, 44.
30 REED: *Chester*, pp. 48–9.
31 REED: *Chester*, p.117.
32 REED: *Chester*, p. 60.
33 REED: *Coventry*, pp. 28, 547, 552.
34 REED: *Coventry*, pp.137, 565.
35 Westlake, pp. 62–3.
36 Salter, pp. 77–8, citing Simeon in *Christ Among the Doctors* (see Text below).
37 REED: *Chester*, p. 244.
38 REED: *Chester*, pp. 65–7.
39 REED: *Coventry*, pp. 220–1.
40 Cawley, p. 203.

Chapter 10: On the Road

1   CPR, *Edward III*, 1367–70, p.131.
2   CPR, *Edward III*, 1358–61, p.15.
3   Bullock-Davies, *MM*, pp.165–7.
4   Devon, p.27; CPR, *Edward III*, 1350–54, p.113.
5   CCW, 1244–1326, p. 203; CCR, *Edward II*, 1323–27, p.185.
6   Bullock-Davies, *Register*, pp.2, 173.
7   CPR, *Edward II*, 1317–21, p.120.
8   Bullock-Davies, *Register*, p. 68.
9   Bullock-Davies, *Register*, pp.107, 160, 118, 191.
10 Bullock-Davies, *Register*, p. 3.
11 Bullock-Davies, *Register*, p. 218.
12 Bullock-Davies, *Register*, pp. 213, 5, 121, 38, 163.
13 *Manners and Household Expenses*, pp. 217, 228.
14 *Manners and Household Expenses*, pp. 258–9.
15 *Manners and Household Expenses*, pp. 263, 268–9, 273, 275–6, 279.
16 For these and following entries, *Excerpta Historica*, pp. 85–132.

Chapter 11: Parting of the Ways, the Final Phase

1 Wolffe, p. 65.
2 CPR, *Henry VI*, 1446–52, pp. 505, 512.
3 CPR, *Henry VI*, 1452–61, p. 278; *Foedera*, XI, p. 375.
4 *Ordinances and Regulations*, 'Household of King Henry VI', p.18.
5 *Great Chronicle*, p. 215.
6 *Household of Edward IV*, pp.131–2.
7 *Coronation of Elizabeth Wydeville*, p. 68.
8 CPR, *Edward IV*, 1467–77, pp. 42, 44.
9 *Wardrobe Account (of Richard III)*, *1483*, pp. 53–4.
10 CPR, *Edward IV*, 1467–77, p.153; *Feodera*, XI, pp. 642–4.
11 CCR, *Edward IV*, 1461–68, p. 339; CPR, *Edward IV*, 1461–67, p. 221.
12 Wolffe, p. 7.
13 *Feodera*, X, p. 387; Wolffe, p. 37.
14 Chambers, II, p.184.
15 Kahrl, pp.101–2; Axton, p.199.
16 REED: *York*, I, pp. 65 (*lusores*), 69 (*ludentes*).
17 Warton, I, p. 91n.
18 Chambers, II, Appendix E vii, p. 256.
19 Devon, p. 516; Chambers, II, p.187.
20 Bradbrook, p. 97.
21 Rastall, pp. 33–4, 37.
22 *Privy Purse Expenses of Henry VIII*, p. 258; *Letters and Papers*, XIII, Part 2, p. 528. For Heywood's later history, see Thomas Warton, *History of English Poetry*, London, 1781 edn, III, pp. 87–96; Chambers, II, p. 203.
23 *Records of the City of Norwich*, II, p.186.
24 *Letters and Papers*, XX, Part 2, p. 497.
25 *Great Chronicle*, p. 208.
26 Doran, pp.123–30. But see also DNB.
27 *Wardrobe Account of Henry VIII*, pp. 249, 252.
28 Armin, pp. 45–6.
29 Rastall, p. 37; Lafontaine, p. 3.
30 *Letters and Papers*, XIII, Part 2, pp. 525–6.
31 *Privy Purse Expenses of Henry VIII*; for individual references, see Index to this. For Wolsey's gift of his fool, see Cavendish, p.104 and note, p. 234. For fool's name, Heywood (who must have known him well) refers to him in Epigram 44 of the *First Hundred* as both Patch and Sexton. Both names recur in the *Privy Purse Expenses*.
32 Chambers, *Elizabethan Theatre*, II, p. 31 and n.3.
33 For Welders (or Wilders) and the two Guilliams, see *Letters and Papers*, XIII, Part 2, pp. 525–6, 539; XIV, Part 2, p. 304; XVI, p. 55 (no.34), p. 98 (no.35), pp.179, 181, 701; XVII, pp. 476, 483. For later references to the Guilliams, Lafontaine pp. 8–9, 12–3, 16–7 (Guillermo Dovett).
34 See note 32 above.

List of Books

Account Rolls of the Abbey of Durham, Extracts from, Surtees Society, 3 vols, Durham, 1898

ADLER, MICHAEL, *Jews of Medieval England,* Jewish Historical Society, London, 1939

ALEXANDER, MICHAEL, *The Earliest English Poems,* Penguin Classics, 2nd edn, 1977

ALFRED, KING, *King Alfred's Version of the Consolations of Boethius,* tr. W. J. Sedgefield, Oxford, 1940

ARMIN, ROBERT, *A Nest of Ninnies,* London, 1608; reprinted for Shakespeare Society, London, 1842

AXTON, RICHARD, *European Drama of the Early Middle Ages,* London, 1974

BACON, NATHANIEL, *The Annalls of Ipswiche,* 1654; ed. W. H. Richardson, Ipswich, 1884

BALDRY, H. C., *The Greek Tragic Theatre,* London, 1971

BALTZER, REBECCA A., 'Music in the Life and Times of Eleanor of Aquitaine' in *Eleanor of Aquitaine: Patron and Politician,* ed. W. W. Kibler, Austin and London, 1976

BARBER, RICHARD, *Edward, Prince of Wales and Aquitaine: A Biography of the Black Prince,* London, 1978

BARLOW, FRANK, *William Rufus,* London, 1983

BARRON, W.R.J., *English Medieval Romance,* London, 1987

BAUGH, ALBERT C., 'The Middle English Romance: Some Questions of Creation, Presentation, and Preservation' in *Speculum,* XLII, 1967, pp.1–31

BEARE, W., *The Roman Stage,* London, 3rd edn, 1964

(BEDFORD RECORDS) *Publications of the Bedfordshire Record Society,* II, Aspley Guise, 1914

BENT, MARGARET, *Dunstaple,* Oxford Studies of Composers, 17, Oxford, 1981

BLOUNT, T.(ed), *Fragmenta Antiquitatis,* re-edited Beckwith, London, 1815

BOETHIUS, *The Consolation of Philosophy,* tr. 'I. T.' (1609); revised H. F. Stewart, London and Cambridge, Mass., 1962

The Book of Fees, commonly called Testa de Nevill, ed H.C.Maxwell Lyte, 2 vols, London, 1920–23

The Book of the Foundation of St Bartholomew's Church in London, ed. Sir Norman Moore, London, 1923

BRADBROOK, M. C., *The Rise of the Common Player,* London, 1962

BROUGHTON, BRADFORD B., *The Legends of King Richard Coeur de Lion,* The Hague, 1966

BRUCE-MITFORD, RUPERT, *The Sutton Hoo Ship Burial: A Handbook,* British Museum Publications, 3rd edn, 1979

BUKOFZER, MANFRED F., 'The Music of the Old Hall Manuscript in *Studies in Medieval and Renaissance Music*, New York, 1950

BULLOCK-DAVIES, CONSTANCE, (MM) *Menestrellorum Mulititudo: Minstrels at a Royal Feast*, Cardiff, 1978

—— (Register) *Register of Royal and Baronial Domestic Minstrels, 1272–1327*, Woodbridge, 1986

(CCW) *Calendar of Chancery Warrants*, HMSO

(CCR) *Calendar of Close Rolls*, HMSO

(CDS) *Calendar of Documents Relating to Scotland*, ed. J. Bain, vol. II,1272–1307, Edinburgh, 1884

(CFR) *Calendar of Fine Rolls*, HMSO

(CIM) *Calendar of Inquisitions Miscellaneous (Chancery)*, HMSO

(CLR) *Calendar of Liberate Rolls*, HMSO

(CPR) *Calendar of Patent Rolls*, HMSO

A Calendar of the Pipe Rolls of the Reign of Richard I for Buckinghamshire and Bedfordshire, 1189–99, ed. G. H. Fowler and M. W. Hughes, Publications of the Bedfordshire Record Society, VII, 1923

The Carmen de Hastingae Proelio of Guy Bishop of Amiens, ed.C. Morton and H. Muntz, Oxford, 1972

CAVENDISH, GEORGE, *The Life and Death of Cardinal Wolsey*, ed. R. S. Sylvester, Early English Text Society, Oxford, 1959

CAWLEY, A. C., (ed.) *Everyman and Medieval Miracle Plays*, London, 2nd edn, 1974

CHADWICK, NORAH K., *Celtic Britian*, London, 1963

CHAMBERS, SIR EDMUND K., *The Elizabethan Stage*, 4 vols, Oxford, 1923

—— *The Mediaeval Stage*, 2 vols, Oxford, 1903

—— (References to Chambers relate to *Mediaeval Stage*, unless otherwise stated.)

CHAPPELL, WILLIAM, *Old English Popular Music*, ed. H. Ellis Wooldridge, vol I, London, 1893

Charters of the Honour of Mowbray, 1107–1191, ed. D. E. Greenway, British Academy Records of Social and Economic History, New Series I, London, 1972

CHRETIEN DE TROYES, *Arthurian Romances*, tr. W. W. Comfort, Everyman's Library, 1914, paperback edn, 1984

Chronicque de la Traison et Mort de Richart Deux Roy Dengleterre, ed. B. Williams, Rolls Series, London, 1846

Close Rolls of the Reign of Henry III, HMSO

The Coronation of Elizabeth Wydeville, ed. G. Smith, London, 1935

COULTON, G. C., *Medieval Panorama*, Cambridge, 1938

CUTTS, EDWARD L., *Scenes and Characters of the Middle Ages*, London, 1926

DENHOLM-YOUNG, N., *History and Heraldry, 1254–1310*, Oxford, 1965

—— 'The Song of Carlaverock and the Parliamentary Roll of Arms as found in Cott. Calig. A XVIII in the British Museum' in *Proceedings of the British Academy, 1961*, London, 1962

DEVON, FREDERICK, (ed.) *Issues of the Exchequer* (Pell Records), London,1837

Dialogus de Scaccario: The Course of the Exchequer, ed. Charles Johnson, London, 1950

(DNB) *Dictionary of National Biography*

Domesday Book, ed. John Morris, 35 vols, Chichester, 1982

DORAN, Dr, *The History of Court Fools*, London, 1858

DOUCE, FRANCIS, *Illustrations of Shakespeare and of Ancient Manners*, London, 'new edition', 1839

DOUGLAS, DAVID C., 'The Song of Roland and the Norman Conquest of England' in *French Studies*, XIV, 1960

—— *William the Conqueror*, London, 1964

DUBY, GEORGES, *William Marshal, The Flower of Chivalry*, tr. R. Howard, London, 1986

EADMER, *Historia Novorum in Anglia: History of Recent Events in England*, tr. G. Bosanquet, London, 1964

Early Yorkshire Charters, vol. IX, ed. C. T. Clay, Yorkshire Archaeological Society, Extra Series VII, 1952

Excerpta Historica or Illustrations of English History, London, 1833

Expeditions to Prussia and the Holy Land made by Henry Earl of Derby, 1390–93, ed. L. Toulmin Smith, Camden Society, London, 1894

Foedera, Conventiones, Literae etc., ed. Thomas Rymer, 17 vols, London, 1704–17

FORD, BORIS, (ed.) *Pelican Guide to English Literature, 1: The Age of Chaucer*, Hardmondsworth, 1954

FROISSART, JEAN, *Chronicles*, ed. G. Brereton, Harmondsworth, 1978

GAIMAR, MAISTRE GEFFREI, *Lestorie Des Engles*, ed. T. Duffus Hardy and C. T. Martin, 2 vols, Rolls Series, London, 1888–9

GALPIN, FRANCIS W., *Old Instruments of Music, Their History and Character*, 4th edn, revised Thurston Dart, London, 1965

GEIRINGER, KARL, *Instruments in the History of Western Music*, London, 3rd edn, 1978

GERALD OF WALES, *The Journey through Wales and The Description of Wales*, tr. L. Thorpe, Hardmondsworth, 1978

Gesta Stephani, ed. K. R. Potter, Oxford, 1976

GOTTFRIED VON STRASSBURG, *Tristan*, tr. A. T. Hatto, Harmondsworth, revised edn, 1967

GOUGH, HENRY, *Itinerary of King Edward the First*, Paisley, 1900

The Great Chronicle of London, ed. A. H. Thomas and I. D. Thornley, London, 1938

HARRISON, FRANK Ll., *Music in Medieval Britain*, London, 1958

HARVEY, JOHN, *The Plantagenets*, London, revised edn, 1975

HAYWARD, SIR JOHN, *The Lives of the III Normans, Kings of England*, London, 1613

HENRY OF HUNTINGDON, (Text) *Historia Anglorum*, ed. T. Arnold, Rolls Series, London, 1879

—— (Translation) *The Chronicle of Henry of Huntingdon*, ed. T. Forester, London, 1853

The Household Book of Dame Alice de Bryene, tr. M. K. Dale, ed. V. R. Redstone, Suffolk Institute of Archaeology and Natural History, Ipswich, 1931

The Household Book of Queen Isabella of England, 1311–12, ed. F. D.Blackley and G Hermansen, Edmonton, Alberta, 1971

The Household of Edward IV: The Black Book and the Ordinance of 1478, ed. A. R. Myers, Manchester, 1959

Household of Henry Algernon Percy, the Fifth Earl of Northumberland, at his Castles of Wresill and Lekinfield in Yorkshire, Regulations and Establishment of, ed. Bishop Thomas Percy, London, 2nd edn, 1827

HUTCHISON, HAROLD F., *Henry V*, London, 1967

Issue Roll of Thomas de Brantingham, Bishop of Exeter, in the 44th year of King Edward III (1370), ed. F. Devon, London, 1835

JACOB, E. F., *The Fifteenth Century, 1399–1485*, Oxford, 1961

John of Gaunt's Register, (A) *1372–76*, ed. S. Armitage-Smith, 2 vols, Camden 3rd Series, XX and XXI, London, 1911. (B) *1379–83*, ed. E. C. Lodge and R. Somerville, 2 vols, Camden 3rd Series, LVI and LVII, London, 1937

JOHN OF SALISBURY, *Policraticus*, tr. J. Dickinson as *The Statesman's Book of John of Salisbury* (Books 4, 5, 6 and selections from Books 7 and 8), New York, 1927

—— Tr. J. B. Pike as *Frivolities of Courtiers and Footprints of Philosophers* (Books 1, 2, 3 and selections from Books 7 and 8), London, 1938

JOHNSTONE, HILDA, 'The Eccentricities of Edward II' in *English Historical Review*, XLVIII (1933), pp.264–7

—— *Edward of Carnavon, 1284–1307*, Manchester, 1946

JUSSERAND, J. J., *English Wayfaring Life in the Middle Ages*, tr. L. Toulmin Smith, London, 8th edn, 1891

JUVENAL, *The Sixteen Satires*, tr. P. Green, Harmondsworth, 1967

KAHRL, STANLEY J., *Traditions of Medieval English Drama*, London, 1974

KEYNES, SIMON, and LAPIDGE, MICHAEL, (eds) *Alfred the Great: Asser's 'Life of King Alfred' and other contemporary sources*, Harmondsworth, 1983

King Edward II's Household and Wardrobe Ordinances, 1323, ed. F. J. Furnivall, Life-Records of Chaucer, II, Chaucer Society, London, 1876

KNOWLES, DAVID, *The Evolution of Medieval Thought*, London, 1962

KOLVE, V. A., *The Play Called Corpus Christi*, London, 1966

LAFONTAINE, HENRY CART DE, *The King's Music: A Transcript of Records Relating to Music and Musicians, 1460–1700*, London, 1909; reprinted New York, 1973

LANDON, LIONEL, *The Itinerary of King Richard I*, Pipe Roll Society, New Series XIII, 1935

LANG, PAUL HENRY, *Music in Western Civilization*, New York, 1941

LANGLAND, WILLIAM, *The Vision of Piers Plowman*, tr. T. Tiller, London, 1981

Letters and Papers, Foreign and Domestic, of the reign of Henry VIII, 1509–47, ed. Brewer, Gairdner and Brodie, 21 vols, London, 1862–1910

The Life and Campaigns of the Black Prince, from contemporary letters, diaries and chronicles, including Chandos Herald's 'Life of the Black Prince', ed. and tr. Richard Barber, London, 1979

The Life of Edward the Second by the So-called Monk of Malmesbury, tr. and ed. N. Denholm-Young, London, 1957

LOADES, DAVID, *The Tudor Court*, London, 1986

MANDER, R. P., 'The Norwich City Waits' in *East Anglian Magazine*, vol. 9, no.2 (October, 1949) pp.96–101

Manners and Household Expenses of England, Roxburgh Club, London, 1841

MAP, WALTER, *De Nugis Curialium: Courtiers' Trifles*, tr. and ed. M. R. James, Oxford Medieval Texts, 1983

MARSHALL, M. H., 'Theatre in the Middle Ages: Evidence from Dictionaries and Glosses' in *Symposium*, IV (1950), pp.1–39, 366–89

MATHEW, GERVASE, *The Court of Richard II*, London, 1968

MILES, ROSALIND, *Ben Jonson*, London, 1986

New Grove Dictionary of Music and Musicians, ed. Stanley Sadie, 20 vols, London, 1980

NICOLAS, SIR NICHOLAS HARRIS, *History of the Battle of Agincourt*, London, 2nd edn, 1832

———— 'Observations on the Institution of the Most Noble Order of the Garter' in *Archaeologia*, XXXI (1846), pp.1–163

NICOLL, ALLARDYCE, *Masks, Mimes and Miracles: Studies in the Popular Theatre*, London, 1931

OGILVY, J. D. A., *'Mimi, Scurrae, Histriones*: Entertainers of the Early Middle Ages' in *Speculum*, XXXVIII, 1973

OLSON, CLAIR C., 'The Minstrels at the Court of Edward III' in *Publications of the Modern Language Association of America*, LVI, 3 (September, 1941), pp. 601–12

ORDERIC VITALIS, *The Ecclesiastical History*, ed. and tr. M. Chibnall, 6 vols, Oxford, 1969–81

Ordinances and Regulations for the Government of the Royal Household from King Edward III to King William and Queen Mary, A Collection of, Society of Antiquaries, London, 1790

PAGE, CHRISTOPHER, *Voices and Instruments of the Middle Ages: Instrumental practice and songs in France 1100–1300*, London, 1987

PERCY, BISHOP THOMAS, *Reliques of Ancient English Poetry*, ed. H. B. Wheatley, 3 vols, London, 1889

Pipe Rolls: The Great Roll of the Pipe, Pipe Roll Society

POOLE, A. L., *From Domesday Book to Magna Carta, 1087–1216*, Oxford, 2nd edn, 1955

PRESTWICH, MICHAEL, *The Three Edwards: War and State in England 1272–1377*, London, 1980

PRICE, M. A., *The Status and Function of Minstrels in England Between 1350 and 1400*, MA thesis, University of Birmingham, 1964

Privy Purse Expenses of Elizabeth of York: Wardrobe Accounts of Edward IV, ed. N. Harris Nicolas, London, 1830

The Privy Purse Expenses of King Henry the Eighth (November 1529 to December 1532), ed. N. Harris Nicolas, London, 1827

RASTALL, RICHARD, 'The Minstrels of the English Royal Households' in *Royal Musical Association Research Chronicle*, IV (1967), pp.1–41

The Record of Bluemantle Pursuivant, 1471–2 in C. L. Kingsford, *English Historical Literature in the Fifteenth Century*, Oxford, 1913

The Records of the City of Norwich, ed. W. Hudson and J. C. Tingey, 2 vols, Norwich, 1906–10

(REED) *Records of Early English Drama: Chester*, ed. L. M. Clopper, Manchester, 1979; *Coventry*, ed. R. W. Ingram, Manchester, 1981; *Newcastle upon Tyne*, ed. J. J. Anderson, Manchester, 1982; *York*, ed. A. F. Johnston and M. Rogerson, 2 vols, Manchester, 1979

Records of the Wardrobe and Household 1286–1289, ed. B. F and C. R. Byerly, London, 1986

Register of Edward, The Black Prince, 4 vols, HMSO, 1930–33

Regularis Concordia: The Monastic Agreement, tr. Dom Thomas Symons, London, 1953

ROBERT (MANNYING) OF BRUNNE, *Handlyng Synne*, ed. F. J. Furnivall, Part 1, Early English Text Society, London, 1901

The Roll of Arms of the Princes, Barons, and Knights Who Attended King Edward I to the Siege of Caerlaverock, in 1300, ed. Thomas Wright, London, 1864

Rotuli de Dominabus et Pueris et Puellis de XII Comitatibus (1185), ed. J. H. Round, Pipe Roll Society, 1913

Rotuli de Liberate ac de Misis Praestitis, Regnante Johanne, ed. T. Duffus Hardy, London, 1844

Rotuli Normanniae in Turri Londinensi Asservati, Johanne et Henrico Quinto Angliae Regibus, vol. I (1200–05), ed. T.Duffus Hardy, London, 1835

ROUND, J. H., *The King's Serjeants and Officers of State with their Coronation Services,* London, 1911

RUBEL, HELEN F., 'Chabham's *Penitential* and its Influence in the Thirteenth Century' in *Publications of the Modern Language Association of America,* XL (1925), pp.225–39

SACHS, CURT, *The History of Musical Instruments,* London, 1942; reprinted 1977

SALTER, F. M., *Mediaeval Drama in Chester,* Toronto, 1955

The Song of Roland, (A) tr. Robert Harrison, New American Library, New York and London, 1970. (B) tr. Dorothy L. Sayers, Harmondsworth, 1957

STAMP, A. E., 'Some Notes on the Court and Chancery of Henry III' in *Historical Essays in Honour of James Tait,* ed. J. G. Edwards, V. H. Galbraith and E. F. Jacob, Manchester, 1933

STOW, JOHN, *Survey of London,* Everyman's Library, London, 1912

STRICKLAND, AGNES, *Lives of the Queens of England,* 8 vols, London, 1852; reprinted Bath, 1972

STRUTT, JOSEPH, *The Sports and Pastimes of the People of England* (1801), ed. J. C. Cox, London, 1903, reprinted Bath, 1969

TOLKIEN, J. R. R., (tr.) *Sir Gawain and the Green Knight, Pearl and Sir Orfeo,* ed. C. Tolkien, paperback edn, London, 1979

TOUT, T. F., *Chapters in the Administrative History of Mediaeval England,* 6 vols, Manchester, 1920–33.

———— *The Place of the Reign of Edward II in English History,* Manchester, 1936

WACE, MASTER, (Text) *Roman de Rou et des Ducs de Normandie,* ed. H. Andresen, 2 vols, Heilbron, 1879

———— (Translation) *Master Wace: His Chronicle of the Norman Conquest from the Roman de Rou,* tr. E. Taylor, London, 1837

WADDELL, HELEN, *The Wandering Scholars,* paperback edn, Harmondsworth, 1954

WAGNER, ANTHONY RICHARD, *Heralds and Heraldry in the Middle Ages,* Oxford, 1956

Wardrobe Account of Henry VIII (1535–6) in *Archaeologia,* IX, London, 1789

Wardrobe Account (of Richard III), 1483 in *The Antiquarian Repertory,* I, London, 1807

Wardrobe Accounts of the Tenth, Eleventh and Fourteenth Years of Edward II, A Brief Summary of, ed. T. Stapleton, Society of Antiquaries, London, 1835

WARREN, W. L., *Henry II,* London, 1973

WARTON, THOMAS,*The History of English Poetry,* 3 vols, London, 1774–81

WAURIN, JOHN DE,(A collection of) *Chronicles and Ancient Histories of Great Britain, Now Called England,* tr. Sir William Hardy and E. L. C. P. Hardy, 3 vols, Rolls Series, London, 1864–91

WEBB, JOHN, (ed.) *A Roll of the Household Expenses of Richard De Swinfield, Bishop of Hereford, During Part of the Years 1289 and 1290*, 2 vols, Camden Society, London, 1854–5

WELSFORD, ENID, *The Fool: His Social and Literary History*, London, 1935

WESTLAKE, H. F., *The Parish Gilds of Mediaeval England*, London, 1919

WHITELOCK, DOROTHY, *The Beginnings of English Society*, Harmondsworth, 2nd edn, revised 1974

WICKHAM, GLYNNE, *Early English Stages 1300–1600*, 2 vols, London, 1963

——— (ed.) *English Moral Interludes*, London, 1976

——— *The Medieval Theatre*, London, paperback edn, 1980

WILKINS, NIGEL, *Music in the Age of Chaucer*, Chaucer Studies, 1, Woodbridge and New Jersey, 1979.

William Gregory's Chronicle of London in *The Historical Collections of a Citizen of London in the Fifteenth Century*, ed. J. Gairdner, Camden Society, 1876

WILLIAM OF MALMESBURY, *Gesta Pontificum*, ed. N. E. S. A. Hamilton, Rolls Series, 5 vols, London, 1870.

——— *Gesta Regum Anglorum* and *Historia Novella*, ed. T. Duffus Hardy, 2 vols, London, 1840

WODDERSPOON, JOHN, *Memorials of the Ancient Town of Ipswich*, Ipswich and London, 1850

WOLFFE, BERTRAM, *Henry VI*, London, 1981

WRIGHT, LAURENCE, 'The Medieval Gittern and Citole: A case of mistaken identity' in *Galpin Society Journal*, 30 (1977)

——— 'Misconceptions Concerning the Troubadours, Trouvères and Minstrels' in *Music and Letters*, 48 (1967)

——— 'The Role of Musicians at Court in Twelfth-Century Britain' in *Art and Patronage in the English Romanesque*, Occasional Paper (New Series) VIII, 1986, pp. 97–106

WYLIE, JAMES HAMILTON, *History of England under Henry the Fourth*, 4 vols, London, 1884–98

Index of Named Minstrels

Where surnames are merely descriptive (Ralph Harpour, John Piper etc.), or preceded by 'of' (*de*) or 'the' (*le*), minstrels are indexed under Christian names; these are usually translated from the Latin or French, but second names given in their original form. Indications of speciality (if any), status, and reign in which each minstrel chiefly worked are added for purposes of indentification only.

ADAM DE CLITHEROE, harper to E1, 95

ADAM DE LA HALE (ADAM LE BOSSU), visiting French minstrel, composer and playwright, E1, 72

ADAM WITH THE BELLS, visitor to York, H6, 136

ADELINDA, *joculatrix* to Earl Roger, W1, 35

ADENET LE ROY, visiting French minstrel and composer, E1, 72

ALAN THE TRUMPETER, E1, 135

ALBRYGHT, RICHARD, minstrel of Hadenham, H6, 120

ALEMAN, German minstrel to H3, 58

ALEXANDER DE WINDSOR, wait to E1, 75

ALEXANDER LE HARPUR, J, 52

ALEYN, JOHN, piper to Henry of Bolinbroke, possibly composer, 111, 116

ALGOOD, WILLIAM, piper to Henry of Bolinbroke, 111

ALKIN, minstrel at Watford, E1, 137

ARMIN, ROBERT, stage-fool, Eliz.I, 151–3

ARNOLDE, player of recorders, H7, 141

ARTHUR, lutanist to H8, 154

ASKEW, ROBERT, Newcastle wait, Eliz.I, 126

A WODDE, JOHN (see HEYWOOD, JOHN)

BALDEWYN, WILLIAM, minstrel to H5, 114

BARBER, ROBERT, trumpeter to E3, 103

BARBOR (or BARBERUS), bagpiper to E3, 110

BARNBROKE, WILLIAM, minstrel of Coventry, H6, 131

BARRY HARPOUR, at Durham Abbey, E4, 94

BARTHOLOMEW, gigue-player to Roger de Mowbray, H2, 45–6

BAUDET, taborer to E1/2, 76–8

BERDIC, *joculator* to W1, 35

BERNARD LE FOL, French fool, E2, 86

BERNARDO, harper to E6, 161

BETTS, JOHN, Ipswich wait, Eliz.I, 125–6

BLAKALL, THOMAS, fool to H7, 140

BLAKBOWRN, WILLIAM, minstrel of Coventry, H8, 131

BLONDEL, probably-mythical minstrel to R1, 1–2, 50–1

BLONDEL DE NEELE, French troubadour, 50

BLYNDE CUNNYINGHAM, rewarded by H7, 141

BOLENGER, JOHN, sackbut-player to H8, 154

BOWMAN, THOMAS, minstrel to H8, 154

BRADSTRETE, WILLIAM, trumpeter to H5/6, 113, 143

BREWER, BARTRAM, chamber--minstrel to H7, 153

BROTHIR, JOHN, trumpeter to Henry of Bolinbroke, 111

BROWN, JOHN, piper to H5, 113-4

BROWNE, ROBERT, player and tumbler, Eliz.I, 148

BUCKINGHAM, JOHN, clarioner to John of Gaunt, 108, 111

BUNTANCE, JOHN, chamber--minstrel to H7, 153

BYNGELEY, WILLIAM, piper to H4, 111-3

CAEDMON, 7C poet and harper, 20

CALEYE, COPINUS, minstrel to E2, 135

CALLY, PETER, minstrel of Chester, Eliz.I, 130

CALTHORN, THOMAS, minstrel to E4, 145

CAUMZ, JOHN, 'King of our minstrels', R2, 110

CHATERTON, THOMAS, trumpeter to H5/6, 113, 143

CHEUPAYN, WILLIAM, see ROBERT

CLARIN, minstrel to Geoffrey de Lusignan, H3, 58

CLAUS NAKERER, minstrel to H4, 112

CLAY, LAMBYN (or LAMBERT), taborer to E1/2, 76-8

CLEY (or CLAYS) LE TABORER, possibly identical to LAMBYN, above, E3, 77

CLIFF, MASTER JOHN, nakerer to John of Gaunt, 111

CLIFF, JOHN (II), minstrel to H5, 113-4

CLIFF, JOHN (III), chamber-minstrel to H6, 119, 143-5

CLIFF, WILLIAM, minstrel to E4, 145

CLOUGH, ROBERT, harper to E2, 97

COKARD, JOHN, taborer to Black Prince, 106

COLLE, magician in Chaucer, 14

CONCIUS PIPER, minstrel to Bartholomew de Burgherssh, E3, 135

COOK, minstrel of Coventry, E4, 130

CORFF, WILLIAM, harper to H5, 160

COUNTZ, piper to Black Prince, 106

CRAKYLL, ROBERT, trumpeter to Henry of Bolinbroke, 111

CRISTEAN, WILLIAM 'dumb' minstrel to E4, 145-6

CRUDWORTH, ROBERT, alias ROBERT HARPER, minstrel of Coventry, H6, 131

DAVEROUNS, ROBERT, violist to Prince of Tarentum, E2, 86

DAVID LE HARPOUR, minstrel pretending to be of king's household, E2, 119

DEGO, Spanish fool, H7, 140

DEPE, JOHN, trumpeter to E1, 74

DICK, fool to H7, 140

DODMORE, WILLIAM, blind harper to R2, 95, 97-8, 110, 112-3

DRAKE, MASTER JOHN, waferer to E1/2, 80

DRUET, LE ROY, King-herald and fiddler to E1, 65, 73

DUNSTAPLE, JOHN, singer and composer to Duke of Bedford, H6, 116

DUREME, (?) minstrel to Bishop Bek, E1, 71

ELLERTON, MATHEW, Coventry wait, H6, 125

ENGLISH, JOHN, leader of players to H7, 147

EUSTACE DE REYNS, first 'minstrel' (so-named) to H3, 59

EVANS, TIMOTHY, rebec-player to H8, 154

EYNESHAM, WILLIAM, minstrel to E4, 145

FORTUNATUS DE LUCA (SIR), minstrel-knight to H3, 59

FRYSH, HANKYN, piper to (?) Black Prince, 106, and John of Gaunt, 111

GARSIE, JOHN, trumpeter to E2 as Prince of Wales, 85

GARSINGTON, ELIAS, harper to E2, 97

GEFFREY, RICHARD, piper to H5, 113

GELRE, King of Arms to Count of Holland, poet and artist, R2, 65–6

GEOFFREY DE WINDSOR, wait to E1, 75

GIBSON, JOHN, minstrel to John of Gaunt, 111

GILDESBURGH, NICHOLAS, trumpeter to H6, 143

GILES, luter and chamber-minstrel to H7, 153

GILES TRUMPOUR, minstrel to E3, 103

GLASGERION, Breton bard mentioned by Chaucer, 98

GODESCALE PIPER, minstrel to E3, 104

GODFREY, waferer to H2, 47

GODYERE, WILLIAM, trumpeter to H6, 143

GOLES, (?) fool to W1 as duke of Normandy, 29–30

GOUGH, HANS, piper to John of Gaunt, 111

GRENE, HENRY, Leicester Herald to John of Gaunt, later 'King of Heralds' to H4 (see also LE ROY HENRY), 111–2, 116

GRENE, THOMAS, minstrel to E4, 145

GREY, LE ROY, King-herald to E1, 67

'GRISCOTE',(?) character in minstrel-interlude, E1, 81–2

GUILLIAM DUFAYT, chamber-minstrel to H8, 154–5

GUILLIAM DE TROSSHIS (or TROSSHES), chamber-minstrel to H8, 154–5

GYLET OF IPSWICH, fiddler, H3, 61

HALIDAY, THOMAS, minstrel to H5/6, 143

HALIDAY, WALTER, minstrel to H5/6, 'Marshal' to E4, 119, 143–5

HALIDAY, WILLIAM, minstrel to H5, 114

HAMMOND LESTIOUR, estive-player to E1, 73

HANEKIN FITZ LIBEKYN, piper to E3, 104, 109

HANS, minstrel to Black Prince, 106

HARDIBERD, THOMAS, minstrel to H5, 174, n.47

HARDING, Newcastle wait, H6, 129

HARDING, JOHN, wait to E2/3, 96, 104

HARDING, WILLIAM, wait to E3, 104

HARPER, THOMAS, valet and (?) harper to H6, 89

HAUKYN, fictional waferer of *Piers Plowman*, 80–1

HENRY, MASTER, harper to Sir Edmund Mortimer, E1, 70

HENRY CITHARISTA, harper to H2, 49

HENRY DE BLIDA, harper to E1, 68

HENRY LE HARPER, probably identical to DE BLIDA, above, E1, 68

HERBERT, *joculator*, E3, 90

HERT, WALTER, royal minstrel, E3, 110

HEYWOOD, JOHN, minstrel to H8, buffoon and playwright, 148–9, 153

HIDE, JAMES, harper to H7, 161

HILTON, JOHN, harper to R2, 160

HITARDUS, *joculator* to Edmund Ironside, 28

HOBY, WILLIAM, minstrel of Ware, H6, 120

HORE, WILLIAM, minstrel of Hunden, H6, 120

HOWTON, WILLIAM, Coventry wait, H6, 125

HUGH, harper to Abbot of Reading, E1, 70

HUGH DE NAUNTON, harper to E1, 92–93, 97

HULTESCRANE, HENRY, piper to John of Gaunt, 111, 116

JACOMINUS, minstrel-fool to H3, 59–60

JAKELYN, piper to Black Prince, 106–7

ROBERT, alias WILLIAM CHEUPAYN, fool to (?) Q. Philippa of Hainault, E3, 160

ROBERT ('HORNY'), *nebulo* to W2, 36

ROBERT (II, not BUFFARD), fool to E2, 86

ROBERT BUFFARD, fool to E2, possibly identical to ROBERT FATUUS, 85

ROBERT FATUUS, fool to Q. Eleanor of Castile, E1, 85

ROBERT OF DUNWICH, trumpeter, E4, 138

ROBERT PARVUS (LE ROY), King-herald and minstrel to E1, 64

ROBERT LE SOT, messenger, H3, 135

ROBERT LE TABURER, visitor to Durham Abbey, E1, 94

ROGER, blind harper at Durham, E4, 95

ROGER, piper to John of Gaunt, 111

ROGER CITHARISTA, royal harper, J, 52

ROGER FOLLUS, otter-hunter to H2, 48, 53

ROGER TRUMPOR, minstrel to E3, 103

ROLAND LE PETTOUR (FARTERE), *joculator* to H2, 47, 81

ROUNLO, MASTER RICHARD, violist to E1, 72, 77

RYGEWAY, harper at Durham, E1, 94

RYKELL, JOHN, conjuror to H5, 15

SAUTHE (or SANCHE), JAMES, clarioner to John of Gaunt, 111

SCOGAN, buffoon of uncertain date, 150–1

SCOT, fool rewarded by H7, 140

SENDELL, THOMAS, Coventry wait, H6, 125

SEXTON, alias PATCH, fool to H8, 154

SHILLING, companion to Widsith, 23–4

SHURLOCKE, minstrel of Chester, Eliz.I, 130

SIMOND LE MESSAGER, messenger to Q. Eleanor of Castile, E1, 135

SMEATON, MARK, virginals-player and chamber minstrel to H8, 154–5

SMELLTES, piper to John of Gaunt, 111

SNAYTH, CORNUCE, fiddler to H5, 113

SOMERS, WILL, fool to H8, 151–3

SOZ, minstrel to Black Prince, 106

STAKFORD, GILBERT, trumpeter to Black Prince and R2, 107

STURMYN, trumpeter-wait of Norwich, E3, 126

TABOURNER, ANSELM, minstrel to Sir John Chandos, E3, 134–5

TABOURNER, PAUL, minstrel to Sir John Chandos, E3, 134–5

TAILLEFER, warrior-minstrel, W1, 8, 30–5

TARLETON, RICHARD, fool to Eliz.I, 79

THOMAS CITOLER, minstrel to E2/3, 104

THOMAS FIDLER, minstrel of Chester, Eliz.I, 130

THOMAS FOOL, messenger, E3, 135

THOMAS HARPOUR, at Durham Abbey, E4, 94

THOMAS JESTER, fool to H8, 161

THOMAS OF TUNLY, violist at Ipswich, E1, 73

THOMAS WAFRER, waferer to Black Prince, 106

TOM FATUUS, resident at Durham Abbey, E3, possibly identical to TOM LE FOL, 79

TOM LE FOL, fool to E1, 78–9

TRAVAIL, JACK, player-minstrel rewarded by H6, 146

TURGES, JOHN, harper to Q. Margaret of Anjou, H6, 160

TURNEBROCHE, minstrel of Coventry, E4, 130

TUROLDUS, (?) harper-poet, H1, 39

TYAS, JOHN, minstrel to John of Gaunt, (?) 'Old Hall' composer, 111, 116

ULYN, piper to Black Prince, 106–7

VALA, IVO, citoler to E2/3, 104

VAN WELDERS, PHILIP, lutanist and chamber-minstrel to H8, 154–5